ADVANCE PRAISE

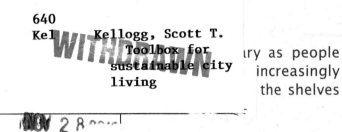

"This important manua̶̶̶̶̶... ̶̶̶̶̶̶ry as people increasingly recogni̶̶̶... ̶̶̶̶ increasingly relocalize. *Toolbox fo̶*̶ ̶̶̶̶̶ the shelves of all city dwellers." D̶̶̶̶ ̶̶̶̶̶̶̶

"These simple, yet pow̶̶̶̶ ̶̶̶̶̶eps can transform your life and your concept of sustainability. Radical sustainability—intimately connected to urban living and urban people doing for themselves—is critically important. This book provides us with relevant tools to change what we do and valuable thoughts to push the conversation forward. If you care about low income urban people and their/our future you are going to read this book." Renée Toll-DuBois, Eagle Eye Institute

"The Rhizome Collective is a force that gets stuff done...it's a surprisingly effective model for connecting people with dreams to the resources they need." *Austin Chronicle*

"They had a really great idea of where they're going with the site. It was so sustainable, and the practices they're using are very innovative. We didn't see them anywhere else." Amber Perry, Environmental Protection Agency (EPA)

"One group distinguishing themselves as a major environmental force is the Rhizome Collective." *The Green Building Program Newsletter*

"This is so cool. I can't wait to get home and try it myself." Anonymous, overheard at one of the R.U.S.T. workshops

TOOLBOX FOR
SUSTAINABLE CITY LIVING

SCOTT KELLOGG AND STACY PETTIGREW

ILLUSTRATIONS BY JUAN MARTINEZ

TOOLBOX FOR

SUSTAINABLE CITY LIVING

(A DO-IT-OURSELVES GUIDE)

SOUTH END PRESS CAMBRIDGE, MASSACHUSETTS

Discounted bulk quantities of this book are available for organizing, educational, or fundraising purposes. Please contact South End Press for more information.

Cover design by Benjamin Shaykin
Cover illustration by Juan Martinez and Beth Ferguson
Interior design by Alexander Dwinell, South End Press collective
Printed in Canada by union labor on recycled paper

Library of Congress Cataloging-in-Publication Data

Kellogg, Scott T.
  Toolbox for sustainable city living : a do-it-ourselves guide / Scott Kellogg and Stacy Pettigrew ; illustrations by Juan Martinez.
      p. cm.
  "Most of the systems described are ones that we have built and experimented with over the past eight years at the Rhizome Collective [formed in 2000] in Austin, Texas"--Introd.
  Includes bibliographical references and index.
  ISBN 978-0-89608-780-4 (pbk. : alk. paper)
  1. Sustainable living--Handbooks, manuals, etc. 2. Organic living--Handbooks, manuals, etc. 3. Conservation of natural resources--Handbooks, manuals, etc. 4. Self-reliant living--Handbooks, manuals, etc. 5. Urban ecology--Handbooks, manuals, etc. I. Pettigrew, Stacy. II. Title. III. Title: Sustainable city living : a do-it-ourselves guide.
  GF78.K45 2008
  640--dc22   2008011738

12   11   10   09   2 3 4 5 6 7 8 9

South End Press
read.write.revolt.
7 Brookline Street #1
Cambridge, MA 02139
www.southendpress.org

CONTENTS

ACKNOWLEDGEMENTS

We would like to thank our parents—Bill and Karen Pettigrew and Norm and Cindy Kellogg—whose numerous hours of babysitting made this book possible; Juan Martinez, Beth Ferguson, and David Bailey, John Dolley Jr. for their drawings and woodcuts; Starhawk and Lisa Fithian for their photographs; Leah Penniman, Javid Afzali, Richard Littel, and Lauren Ross for their comments; Aunt Barbara for typing Stacy's first stories; our grandparents; and everyone involved with the Rhizome Collective and the Albany Free School Community.

This book is dedicated to Eleanor Elodea Kellogg.

INTRODUCTION

In the coming decades, humanity will be faced with an enormous challenge—to survive the implosion of a society that has overextended its natural limitations in every capacity. The converging crises of climate change, energy depletion, and environmental degradation seriously threaten our speciesí survival. Despite the growing awareness of the severity of these threats, the mechanisms that drive them are well in motion and are terribly difficult to stop.

The future is unknown. Climate models and oil consumption projections can be analyzed, but precise details of what and when changes will occur cannot be completely predicted. What is certain, however, is that if our current trajectory remains unchanged devastating collapse is unavoidable. A massive social transformation is needed. Driven by the current economic modelís need for perpetual growth, todayís society is marked by unrelenting consumption and an increasing disparity between rich and poor. This path has no future. In order to survive, we must become a culture that consumes drastically fewer resources and is strongly rooted in the principles of sustainability, egalitarianism, and cooperation.

Accomplishing this transition will be no easy task. To be successful a diversity of tactics will need to be employed on every level of society. The largest and most important changes will take place on a grassroots level. While people acting on the grassroots are not individually responsible for the looming crises, the scale and depth of the changes necessary must be based and emerge from the grassroots. One critical component of this transition is the design of ecologically sustainable, community-based infrastructure. It is this component that this book addresses. This manual is a toolbox of skills, technologies, tactics, and information to give people access to, and control over, lifeís necessities: food, water, energy, and waste management.

WHAT IS SUSTAINABLE?

When first coined, the word *sustainability* captured a very powerful concept. Its many definitions essentially boil down to the idea of living in such a way that the resources available today will continue to be available for an indefinite number of future generations. Sadly, the term has been almost completely co-opted by corporations, governments, and international financial institutions.

For example, a mainstream sustainable development program might propose installing a series of solar panels in a rural village. But solar panels only have about a 25-year life span, provided they are not damaged sooner, and after this period the panels are useless. Typically these projects don't consider whether or not the village will have the technical expertise, access to tools or manufacturing, or money necessary to repair or replace the panels. Without these resources the village finds itself in a position of dependency. When the panels fail they must wait for someone to donate another set. These types of projects maintain a colonial trajectory.

Sustainable development has joined the lexicon of the International Monetary Fund (IMF), the World Bank, and the United Nations and is often used in their public relations campaigns as a euphemism for neoliberal economic development. The only *sustainability* created by a program which forces people to abandon their traditional means of sustenance in favor of exclusively raising a single cash crop for export is the ability of wealthier nations to *sustain* their monopolies of power.

The ideologies of *natural capitalism* and *green consumerism* dilute the concept of sustainability even further. The mainstream sustainability movement puts the emphasis on green consumerism—the idea that environmental devastation can be avoided simply through changes in consumer spending habits. This has led to businesses from large retail stores to the petroleum industry attempting to sell themselves and their products as being *green*. As the genuine sustainability of many of these products is dubious, the use of *green*, *sustainable*, and *environmentally friendly* as marketing terms has only further devalued the concept of sustainability.

Green consumerism encourages consumption of a different variety. It does nothing to challenge the patterns of over-consumption and excess that have created the environmental crisis. Green consumerism only reinforces the destructive capitalist paradigm while giving people a dangerously false sense that real change is being made. Capitalism, natural or not, requires infinite expansion and consumption of material resources. In a world that is fragile and finite, such a system is inherently unsustainable. Any "sustainable" solution that fails to take this into account will not address the fundamental cause of planetary and human degradation.

Radical sustainability, on another hand, is distinct from what mainstream "sustainability" has come to mean. Radical sustainability means rebuilding and reorganizing homes, neighborhoods, and communities in order to create a world that is both sustainable and equitable. It is fundamentally an approach to enable people who do not have political power to gain control over basic resources.

So instead of installing solar panels a radical sustainable development project might use locally harvested wood to construct a windmill that powers alternators made from scrap cars and other salvaged materials that are locally plentiful. The windmill's design would be simple enough to be easily repaired, giving it a lifespan considerably longer than solar panels. Equally important, the design could be replicable, giving neighboring villages independence from charity.

RADICAL SUSTAINABILITY

Radical sustainability is the philosophy that underlies this book.

We use the word *radical* (derived from the Latin word *radix*, meaning root) to stress that we need to address issues at their fundamental root cause, not just the symptomatic manifestations. Radical sustainability confronts the underlying reasons our current path is not sustainable and works to create genuinely sustainable alternatives.

A radically sustainable viewpoint recognizes the inseparability of ecological and social issues and the necessity of ensuring the solution to one problem does not create or worsen another. For this reason it develops autonomous energy infrastructures and it opposes US imperialism around the world and gentrification in inner cities of the United States. It simultaneously supports indigenous movements, women's rights, and police accountability campaigns and works to create healthy soil. These issues—and many others—are as critical to our future as preserving the world's remaining wilderness, fighting global warming, and creating global sustainable food production.

AUTONOMOUS DEVELOPMENT

Central to radical sustainability is the concept of autonomous development. This form of development designs systems that give control over basic resources to the people using them, increasing community self-reliance and aiding resistance to resource monopolies. Design criteria include:

affordability
use of salvaged and/or locally abundant materials
simplicity
user serviceability
ease of replication
decentralization

Primarily, the systems must be able to be used and built by people without capital or monetary wealth. Many of the tools and technologies proclaimed as "sustainable" such as solar panels and hybrid vehicles are extremely expensive, making them inaccessible to the average person. Such technologies often function as novelties for the wealthy or as a salve for guilty consciences.

Use of salvaged and/or locally abundant materials helps minimize expense and keeps production local. In a society that produces as much excess as ours does, there is an abundant supply of trash that can be re-used for constructing many of the systems described in this book. Recycling these materials reduces the demand for virgin supplies and slows consumption overall.

Simple and user serviceable designs ensure that the systems can be built and maintained with skills and knowledge found within the community making use of the system. This avoids a reliance on foreign experts and ensures the long-term functioning of the project.

All of these criteria lead to systems being replicable. Replicable systems are capable of being transferred and adapted to other communities and locations without significant redesign, and therefore have the potential to be implemented on a broad level. Though designs may need to change dramatically from one community to the next based on particular resources or local climate, a commitment to openly sharing technologies and experiences will lead to a greater rate of success.

Lastly, autonomous development systems are decentralized. The decentralization of critical resources is the best defense against resource monopolization. When the means of production and distribution of food, energy, and water are simple, affordable, and replicable, it is very difficult for any single entity to gain complete control over them. The most egalitarian method of resource management is to have multiple, redundant sources that are held in common by the people using them, thus ensuring continuing supply, democratic control, and overall quality.

AUTONOMOUS COMMUNITIES

Along with the development of autonomous design, radical sustainability promotes the development of **autonomous communities**—that is, egalitarian communities that value equality, justice, and mutualism. Not only do these communities work together to provide members with the essential needs of food, water, energy, and waste management, they also develop their own horizontal political structures, transportation systems, media, health care, education, and so forth. Autonomous communities can exist everywhere—

from rural to urban, north to south. Autonomous communities are especially adapted to creating and maintaining a sustainable world.

SUSTAINABLE CITY LIVING

Cities are highly paradoxical places. On one hand they are vital cultural and economic centers, and on the other they are resource vacuums, supporting extraordinarily high population densities at the expense of the surrounding region. Currently, over 50 percent of the global population lives in cities. As this percentage is increasing and the rate of environmental degradation is quickening, it is critical to sustainably meet the needs of the world's urban populations.

A radically sustainable response is to empower urban residents to make their cities capable of providing sufficient food, water, energy, and waste management within their local region. Having access to these resources on a decentralized, local level will promote a community mindset of self-sufficiency and encourage further independence from the destructive and dangerously unstable dominant systems that cities currently rely on for providing their needs.

Permaculture, a multi-disciplinary practice used to design long lasting human communities, is a valuable tool. Its essential goal is to create intensively cultivated spaces capable of providing for as many human needs as possible in as small of an area as possible. By doing so, humans can be self-reliant and lessen their impact on their surrounding environments in a way that doesn't rely on outsourced energy and resources.

Because they are already so intensely cultivated, cities are an ideal location for permaculture designs. Cities have plenty of existing infrastructure that can be utilized: food can be grown in former parking lots, rain collected off rooftops, wastewater recycled in scavenged bathtubs, and power generated from wind turbines mounted on buildings.

THE TRANSITION

Humanity has entered an era of decreasing energy resources. Modern agriculture is highly dependent on cheap energy not only for growing food, but distributing it. Will cities still be capable of supporting their populations when big trucks

How To Use This Book

This book is designed as a toolbox of skills and information for the reader: introducing systems, technologies, and ideas important for autonomous development in urban areas. The book is divided into the chapters Food, Water, Waste, Energy, and Bioremediation. Chapters are divided into sections, each detailing the various aspects of autonomous design relevant to the chapter's theme. Most of the systems described are ones that we have built and experimented with over the past eight years at the Rhizome Collective in Austin, Texas. Some sections contain detailed step-by-step descriptions of how to build a system with accompanying diagrams, while other systems are more briefly explained in order to inspire, share information, and indicate paths for further research. While some of the systems described in the book are highly innovative and have little written about them elsewhere, most of them can be studied in further depth. A resources section at the end of the book provides lists of further readings and websites related to each section. The reader is encouraged to use it. Words and phrases in bold are defined in the glossary at the end of the book.

are no longer delivering food? What will happen when it becomes too costly to heat buildings? Will basic sanitation collapse as water becomes scarcer and more expensive to pump? What will happen to society?

It is critical to plan ahead and start building radically sustainable infrastructure capable of supporting future urban populations while the resources to do so are still available. Instead of waiting for governments, corporations, or city planners to start being responsible, radical sustainability is about people taking initiative today. Transformation from the ground up is our greatest hope for the future.

THE HISTORY OF THE RHIZOME COLLECTIVE

The Rhizome Collective was formed in 2000 out of the momentum created by the then nascent global justice movement. Inspired by the catchphrase "another world is possible," we and the Rhizome's other founding members came together with the shared intention of making that vision a reality. Rhizome was planned to provide secure space for activist and social justice groups, while simultaneously serving as a demonstration of urban sustainability.

The project began with the purchase of an old warehouse in Austin's industrial corridor. We set about the task of converting the derelict structure into a center for community organizing in which the Rhizome Collective would make its home. Many months were spent making badly needed repairs to the building and jumping through the many bureaucratic hoops that stood in the way. Once basic fixes were made, we began experimenting with, constructing, and demonstrating sustainable, autonomous, urban projects. An asphalt wasteland was transformed into a vibrant space housing a constructed wetlands, a bicycle wind turbine, rainwater collection tanks, gardens, fish ponds, solar ovens, fruit trees, and chickens. We built these systems in order to demonstrate the possibility of implementing these permaculture tools and technologies as well as to serve the building's live-in caretakers. In 2004, the Rhizome Collective received a $200,000 grant from the EPA to cleanup a 9.8-acre brownfield that we were donated and plan to turn into an ecological justice education park.

Developing the internal structure of the Rhizome has been one of the biggest challenges. By deciding to use consensus for its decision making process, the collective hoped to be horizontal and egalitarian in its structure. While it has gone through many transitions, the Rhizome Collective eventually evolved into a spokescouncil. Persons appointed as representatives by the various spokes of the Rhizome meet regularly to report on their respective group's activities, review proposals, and plan the collective's direction.

The many organizations based in the warehouse have worked to bring about cultural transformation on many levels. They include Bikes Across Borders, The Inside Books Project, The Austin Independent Media Center, Food Not Bombs, Art and Revolution, and KPWR—People's Will Radio. In keeping with the metaphor of the rhizome, an underground root-like network linking individual plants, these groups operate autonomously, yet share common resources and pledge mutual support to each other.

All of these elements combined are a manifestation of our philosophy of dual power anarchism: to be working for social change within today's society while at the same time building functional alternatives to oppressive dominant institutions.

A Note on Failure

Failure is a great teacher. Mistakes expose weaknesses and lead to better designs. Those fortunate enough not to be living at a subsistence level today have the luxury of making mistakes. Because the glut of surplus created by capitalism's wastes provides us with a safety net, a small scale crop failure or fish die-off is not likely to be catastrophic. In the future, that surplus safety net may be unavailable, leaving less freedom to experiment. Now is the time to make errors and learn from them.

In the process of creating and living with the sustainable systems described in this book, we have learned from many mistakes. It is certain that over the course of time, more design flaws will be discovered. We encourage readers to share the successes and failures they experience in implementing these systems so that we may all collectively benefit.

FOOD

Global food production is perilously dependent upon massive petroleum inputs. The processes of mechanical tilling, planting, harvesting, irrigation, fertilization, pest control, processing, and distribution all require vast amounts of fossil fuels. As fuel prices begin to increase and the truer cost of industrial farming surfaces, food will become more expensive and inevitably decrease as it becomes more difficult for large industrial farms to continue to operate. This could result in food shortages around the world. In order to avert widespread starvation, humanity will be challenged to rapidly reverse decades of poor agricultural practices and relocalize food production. As transportation costs increase, it will be critical to bring food production back into the vicinity of cities, or into cities themselves, where the majority of the world's population lives.

In today's world, urban communities rarely have access to affordable nutritious foods. This does not have to be the case. Community autonomy is based on **food security**, and cities have the potential to become centers of food production.

Not only can existing community gardens and urban farms be greatly expanded, but within most cities there are numerous other spaces that could be used to produce food. Vacant lots can be transformed into thriving gardens. Roadways and parking lots dedicated exclusively to cars can be closed to vehicular traffic, depaved, and reclaimed for food production. Potential gardening spots also exist overhead: window boxes and rooftops (with sufficient reinforcement) have the potential to produce significant quantities of food. Many urban homes have a small plot of dirt in their backyards that hopefully receives some sun. Shady areas can be used for raising microlivestock or growing mushrooms. Manicured parks and golf courses are begging to be made into edible food forests. By developing these many unused spaces, communities can ensure their food security.

In addition to being localized, the development of a food production system that is organically based, diverse in the variety of foods it grows, and centered around local economies needs to be encouraged. Such a system is a logical response to large agri-businesses' increasing domination of agriculture, which has resulted in genetically modified monocultures that poison the environment, pose health risks, and are susceptible to disease and failure.

Building healthy soil, the foundation of all land-based food production, is a long and laborious process. It is also something everyone can do. It is essential that this work begin today, while surplus energy and organic matter are available. Each day, enormous quantities of organic matter are dumped into landfills. Instead of being reused, food waste, wood chips, manure, and grass clippings rot in landfills and produce methane, a potent greenhouse gas. This organic material is exactly what needs to be diverted from waste streams and properly composted to create good soil. It is also equally important to take advantage of the remnants of petroleum energy to transport this material to the sites of future food production. Once energy shortages are apparent, it will be far more difficult to do this work. The waste streams of surplus organic matter that exist today will dry up.

This chapter contains very little about techniques for straightforward vegetable gardening. This in no way diminishes its importance. Actual gardening techniques (planting, cultivating, harvesting, seed saving, eating) are well covered in many other worthwhile books. Some of those specifically discuss urban gardening, and the lessons of others can be easily applied to urban areas. Rather than duplicate existing material, this book focuses on the creation of environments in which such growing is possible and this chapter explores less-common methods of food production. As with all the tactics in this manual, the reader is encouraged to build connections between the skills discussed here and skills already possessed, while creating autonomous sustainable infrastructures in which to apply them.

By using intensive gardening methods to best utilize available space and focusing on producing the foods most suitable for the local climate, a significant portion of a community's vegetables could be grown within city limits. It is also good to focus on those vegetables that are least suited for import; that is, those that consume the most processing and transportation energy when grown far away. Bioshelters and cold frames can extend a community's growing season well into winter months.

Major obstacles to urban gardening are gaining access to space and poor soil quality. These issues are addressed in the chapter on bioremediation (page 179) and the discussion of access to land (page 206).

This chapter focuses on methods of food production appropriate to urban areas that are not as thoroughly documented as gardening: aquaculture, edible aquatic plants and animals that can be raised in homemade ponds, and microlivestock, small birds and mammals that can easily fit into an urban environment. It also looks at how yards and parks could be turned into food forests, systems of fruit and nut trees grown among perennial vegetables and how mushrooms can be grown on logs in confined, shady spaces. Finally it addresses cultivating insects, never in short supply in cities, as food. This chapter also discusses extending growing seasons by using bioshelters and removing asphalt to increase usable urban land.

Strategies to combat global warming have placed emphasis on reducing carbon emissions from electricity production and transportation, as these create a large percentage of global greenhouse-gas emissions. Attention should be given to the carbon emissions resulting from food production as well. Worldwide, 13.5 percent of all greenhouse-gas emissions result from agriculture.[1]

MICROLIVESTOCK

For millennia, humans have been domesticating other animals. Used for their meat, milk, eggs, skins, feathers, manure, labor, and companionship, animals have played a pivotal role in the development of human cultures. Domesticated animals have allowed humans to prosper in environments that might have otherwise been uninhabitable. Cows, sheep, and goats are able to digest cellulose-rich grasses and woody plants, converting nutrients inaccessible to humans into meat and milk. Animals store nutrients into the cold months, allowing humans to continue eating after plants have ceased to grow.

Because large animals require large amounts of space to graze, it is impractical and difficult to sustainably raise them in urban environments. In a confined space, they will severely compact the soil and eliminate all vegetation, requiring large quantities of supplemental feed. They will quickly foul their space and be more prone to illness.

In a quirk of ecological history, the majority of large domesticable animals were found only on the Eurasian continent. Centuries of close contact gave Europeans enhanced resistance to many diseases that originated from domesticated animals, including smallpox. The immune systems of populations, like Native American peoples, that did not widely domesticate large animals were not conditioned to animal viruses and therefore more susceptible to them. When Europeans carrying animal diseases came into contact with non-resistant populations, the consequences were devastating. Native American mortality rates approached 96 percent.[2]

Large animals are also very inefficient at converting protein from feed to body mass. Ten pounds of feed are required for a cow to put on one pound of weight, a 10:1 ratio. In comparison, the protein conversion ratio for chickens is 5:1, and it is less than 2:1 for fish.

In an urban setting, it makes far better sense to raise **microlivestock**, domesticated small animals that consume relatively little and have minimal impact on the land. Examples of microlivestock include chickens, turkeys, ducks, and other fowl, as well as small mammals such as rabbits and guinea pigs. These animals are all efficient protein converters, require little space, are lightweight and don't compact soil, and produce few offensive odors when properly attended. For these reasons, microlivestock are appropriate for cities.

CHICKENS

Chickens can be found in cities throughout the world. Kept either in small coops or allowed to freely roam the streets, they are at home in urban environments. Bred from a Southeast Asian wild jungle bird, chickens were among the first animals to be domesticated. Valuable for more than just meat and eggs, chickens control insects and build and fertilize soil.

Chickens are constantly moving around, scratching at the soil in search of insects and seeds. This action has the combined effect of aerating the upper layer of soil and breaking down leafy material into dirt. Simultaneously, their nitrogen-rich droppings fertilize the soil. Voracious predators, chickens will hunt everything from grasshoppers to lizards to cockroaches to ticks.

MANAGING CHICKENS

There are several ways to manage a chicken system in an urban setting. Options range from keeping birds cooped at all times to allowing them partial to full access to a yard or open area (**free**

range). Available space and time, along with neighbor relations, will determine what is realistic.

COOPS

Many chicken owners build coops for their chickens. Some use coops as a nighttime shelter, when predators are more active. Others may keep their birds inside all day. A coop can also provide shelter from rain and winter in cold climates and may be required by law in some places. A coop with an open door can also serve as a nesting area for free-range birds. Coops can be built out of a variety of materials and can be beautiful additions to a city landscape.

While some predators found in the country (coyotes, hawks, and snakes) are not as common in cities, raccoons, opossums, skunks, cats, rats, dogs, and hungry humans can cause their own share of problems. A coop must be well built to provide effective protection. If a predator manages to get in, a coop becomes a deathtrap—the birds are unable to escape. An opossum or raccoon will kill every bird it can catch, often only eating their heads or gullets.

Firmly nailing thick-gauge metal **hardware cloth** to the frame will keep most predators out of a coop. Despite its name, thin chicken wire can be easily chewed through or ripped out. Because many predators are able to burrow under a coop, the bottom of the hardware cloth should be partially buried and lined with bricks or rocks. The design should include a human-size door. Smaller openings can be made for chickens.

Coops must be cleaned regularly. The frequency of cleaning depends on the bird density, but foul odor is a surefire indicator that it's time for a cleaning. Letting the birds range freely will reduce the time between coop cleanings. Fresh bedding must also be provided as needed. Straw and sawdust make great bedding materials. Rich in manure, fouled bedding is a great compost ingredient.

Albany Free School Chicken Coop—collectively managed by neighbors in the inner city of Albany, NY

The chicken coop at the Rhizome Collective

The Chicken Tractor

Chickens can be used to prepare an area for gardening by making use of a **chicken tractor**. A chicken tractor is a cage without a bottom that can be moved around a yard. Chickens are placed in the cage and allowed to graze. In the area covered by the tractor, the chickens will:

• eat all the weeds,

• remove any insect pests,

• till up the soil by scratching at it, and

• fertilize the soil with their droppings.

After the chickens have done a satisfactory job of conditioning the soil the tractor can be moved to a new spot. The prepared area is ready for planting.

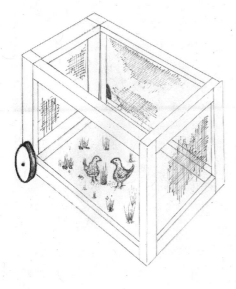

COOP & YARD SIZE

US organic standards require a mere 1.5 square feet of indoor space per bird. In a survey conducted by the Northeast Organic Farming Association, small commercial organic producers actually gave their birds an average of almost 5 square feet of indoor space each. Outdoor yard access was also provided.[3] A lower density of chickens means less maintenance, fewer smells, and healthier, happier birds.

FREE RANGE

In an ideal situation, chickens have access to an open area. A chicken can provide for many of its own nutritional needs by foraging for insects, weeds, and seeds. Free-range chickens are also less prone to confinement stress and many of the diseases that may be brought on by prolonged enclosure. And according to a recent study, their eggs are more nutritious.[4]

Free-range birds can either be kept in a coop at night or allowed to roost in the open. Night cooping of free-range birds requires the daily ritual of opening up the coop in the morning and closing it at night, which for some can become tiresome.

A chicken's natural roosting instinct can also be utilized. Chickens can be encouraged to fly up into the branches of trees or roosting platforms at sundown. Nailing sheet metal flashing around a tree's trunk and main branches, and those of any touching trees, will protect sleeping birds. Predators like raccoons and opossums are unable to scale the sheer surface of the metal and are foiled from attacking. If no trees are available, a roosting platform consisting of branches suspended between metal poles can be built.

Actively growing gardens need to be fenced off from free-range chickens. Chickens will devour most vegetables and leafy greens, and their constant scratching will damage the roots of plants. An 8- to 10-foot fence should be sufficient to deter all but the most determined chickens. Alternatively, chicken wings can be clipped.

This process involves trimming the tips of the wing feathers, which prevents them from truly flying. Clipping wings does not cause the bird pain as there are no nerves in feathers. Keep in mind that chickens with clipped wings will not be able to fly directly into trees to roost or escape from predators. However, they will be able to hop-flutter up a series of roosting platforms to a final roost. Make sure the steps are not attached to each other so a predator can't climb up.

Some free-range systems are designed so that chickens are allowed to graze a section of yard, eating its weeds. Before the chickens have devegetated the area completely, they can be "corralled" into a different area with movable fences, giving the first area an opportunity to regrow. (See The Chicken Tractor, page 7.)

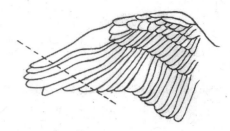

Clipping the wings of free-range chickens can help keep them away from the garden

A: Logs suspended horizontally make good roosting platforms.

B: Shorter roosting platforms can be built to allow chickens to hop-fly up to taller ones.

C: Predators are unable to scale up the sheer metal posts.

Sheet metal flashing protects sleeping birds from predators

CHICKENS AS SPACE HEATERS

In cold climates, chickens can be kept inside bioshelters or greenhouses in the winter to take advantage of the heat given off by their bodies. A small group of chickens can help to moderate the temperature inside a bioshelter and will benefit from the warmth themselves. Chickens also give off carbon dioxide, which helps certain plants to grow faster. (See Bioshelters, page 50.)

FEEDING CHICKENS

Chickens are omnivorous, eating both plants and animals. Their favorite foods include seeds, cockroaches, lizards, worms, grasshoppers, maggots, oats, maggoty oats, and watermelon. Much of a chicken's diet can be obtained from kitchen scraps or from dumpstered foods. Discarded produce that humans would not consider eating due to mushiness or partial mold is fine for chickens. Nutritious weedy plants that chickens love, like clover, amaranth, or elderberries, can be planted in the chicken yard to supplement their diet.

Insects can be raised for chicken consumption as well. A sheet of plywood or cardboard that is kept moist provides a fine breeding ground for bugs. When it is overturned, chickens will rapidly gobble up whatever was living beneath it. (See Insect Cultivation, page 55.) Vermicompost system worms (see page 118) and spent barley hulls from beer breweries make great chicken feed as well.

Some people choose to supplement their chickens' diets with commercial feed to increase their egg production during the winter or purely for convenience. Chicken feed is available at feed stores, which can be sometimes found not too far outside of smaller cities. It can also be shipped.

BREED SELECTION

Most chickens resemble their wild ancestors as much as poodles do wolves. Production breeds like white leghorns have been bred down to be docile egg-layers with few intact survival impulses. (White leghorns have a reputation for drowning in rain storms.) In selecting breeds, older heirloom varieties are best, as they've had fewer of their instincts bred out of them. Intelligence and self-reliance are desirable traits. The Aracauna, originally from South America, is a hardy, independent, beautiful bird that lays green and blue eggs. The Rhode Island Red is also a robust, cold-tolerant breed. Bantam chickens, not a breed in themselves, are diminutive versions of any particular breed. Being smaller, they consume less and have an even lighter impact on land than regular chickens.

EGGS

At 4 to 6 months old, female chickens (hens or pullets) are mature and will start laying eggs. If there is a rooster around, the eggs will be fertilized and can develop into chicks. Hens will lay eggs without a rooster—the difference is the unfertilized eggs will never hatch even though the hens may try to sit on them.

The amount of eggs chickens lay varies with the season and their age. In their prime (aged 6 months to 2 years) and in the summer months, chickens may average an egg every one to two days. As a chicken ages, and as the days become colder and darker, egg production declines. How often chickens lay is also proportional to the amount of protein in their diet—the more protein they eat, the more eggs they lay.

Eggs should be collected regularly and eaten fresh. Eggs that sit around too long will become rotten and can attract rats and snakes. Providing hens with straw-lined boxes or similarly protected cozy areas will encourage them to predictably lay in the same spot. Even with such spaces provided, free-range hens may choose other spots for laying, such as inside old tires or beneath logs, requiring a daily egg hunt.

Occasionally a chicken will develop the habit of eating her eggs. This can be easily discouraged by placing a few ceramic or wooden

A few chickens in the yard

Chicken, chicks, and egg

eggs in the layer boxes. A few pecks at the hard fake egg will make egg eating seem like a bad idea to the offending chicken. It is also helpful to gather fresh eggs daily.

Broodiness is the genetic trait that makes a hen sit on a nest of eggs, causing the eggs to hatch. Commercial breeders have deselected broodiness in egg-laying hens because a chicken will stop laying eggs once she starts brooding. However, to have a colony of successfully reproducing chickens, broody hens are required. A broody hen is more likely to be found among older breeds of chickens. It would be quite rare to find this characteristic among production breeds.

In order for a chicken to go broody, a critical mass of eggs needs to be laid in a pile—usually around 8 to 12 eggs. Once a chicken starts sitting on the pile, she will only get off the nest once a day until they hatch. She will become viciously defensive of the eggs and attack anything that comes near. A chicken is just as likely to sit on infertile eggs and has no way to know if the eggs she's sitting on were laid by her or not. To prevent hens from going broody, be sure to collect the eggs regularly.

RAISING CHICKS

Raising chicks is the cheapest way to get chickens. Chicks can be bought from feed stores and day-old chicks can be delivered by mail from hatcheries. Starting with chicks ensures healthy birds—many adult chickens for sale are diseased. Chicks should be kept in a box or small crate and kept warm, dry, and away from cold drafts. An electric heating pad in the bottom of the box should provide enough heat. Covering the box with a blanket reduces heat loss. The temperature should be kept at 95 degrees Fahrenheit the first week of their life, and can be lowered five degrees each week after. Chicks need water and special chick starter feed. They can also be fed crumbled hard boiled eggs for added protein. If they are going to be free-range birds, slowly introduce the chicks to the outside as they mature. Keep them in the crate at night, safe away from critters, until they begin roosting around two months of age. Raising chicks is a learned skill: don't despair if some are lost.

LEGALITY

Most cities have regulations regarding chickens, ranging from complete prohibition to restrictions on the number of birds to detailing the distance they must be kept away from neighbor's properties. Depending on how strict local authorities are, and how often neighbors complain, it may be possible to get away with bending the laws.

It is part of the local culture of some neighborhoods to have chickens ranging about the streets. Unfortunately, this is not the case in most places. Skeptical neighbors can often be won over by offers of fresh eggs. Keeping smells and noise to a minimum is critical for maintaining positive neighbor relations. Chickens can be kept under the radar in a backyard, or even in a basement, especially if there are only hens and no rooster. Roosters are very loud animals, and some people are horribly annoyed by them. Contrary to popular misconception, roosters don't crow just in the morning. They cock-a-doodle all day and night. This can be a serious problem for light sleepers. Hens will still lay eggs without a rooster, they just won't hatch chicks.

OTHER BIRDS

Turkeys: Colonizers brought turkeys, which are native to the Americas, back to Europe, domesticated them, and then brought them back across the Atlantic. The modern commercial Thanksgiving turkey is a pathetic creature. Heavily inbred and selected for weight gain, these disease-prone turkeys can barely support the weight of their own bodies. Older turkey breeds, such as Narragansett, Blue Slate, Black Spanish, Bourbon Red, and

Beware of the Rooster

Roosters are potentially dangerous animals. Their feet have bony spurs that can grow up to an inch long. Roosters are capable of jumping into the air and striking out with their spurs at eye level. This can create a particularly hazardous situation if children are present. Overly aggressive roosters should not be allowed to reproduce so their traits are not passed on. Too many roosters and not enough hens will lead to violent conflicts between the roosters and harassment of the hens. At least eight hens are needed for each rooster.

Mr. Friend, the turkey

Muscovy ducklings

Royal Palm, have more of their survival instincts intact. Even though they are closer to wild turkeys, these breeds are still difficult to rear. They have high mortality rates and lay few eggs. While not impossible, it is difficult to raise chickens and turkeys in the same quarters, as baby turkeys are particularly susceptible to chicken diseases, such as black head disease. Despite these drawbacks, turkeys perform the same beneficial functions as chickens and are very entertaining to have around.

Muscovy ducks: Muscovy ducks are technically not ducks, but a type of water fowl native to Central America. (All other domestic duck breeds have been bred from the mallard.) Originally domesticated by the Maya, these claw-footed birds would enjoy a pond or place to swim, but do not require one. Their vocalizations are a pleasant, quiet hissing, making them neighbor-friendly. Highly prolific breeders, they lay eggs that are comparable to those of chickens in size, nutritional value, and quantity. Females will often perch in trees at night, but the males are too cumbersome to get off the ground.

Guinea hens: Native to Africa, guinea hens are loud birds—their constant high volume KA-PECK! KA-PECK! really hits a nerve with some people. However, among domestic birds they are the supreme insect hunters and are known for removing ticks from yards.

Pheasants: The ancestor of the chicken, pheasants are beautiful wild birds raised for show and for sport. They will likely fly away once they reach adulthood.

Other microlivestock fowl: Domestic ducks (Indian Runner, mallards), geese, and peafowl all can be integrated into a sustainable urban landscape. Ducks are renown for their ability to purge a garden of slugs while causing minimal harm to vegetables. Peafowl (peacocks and peahens) are beautiful birds whose shrill cries are loud but enchanting.

MAMMALS

Rabbits: Well known for their prolific breeding, rabbits are typically raised for meat in small cages that can be kept outdoors. They can be fed a vegetable-based diet of food scraps. Vegetarians can benefit from raising rabbits as well. "Rabbit tea," a fertilizer made from rabbit droppings, is prized by gardeners.

Guinea pigs: Small cute rodents typically raised in the United States as pets, guinea pigs are a dietary staple in Andean South America, where they are known as cuy. Their needs are similar to those of rabbits.

TREE CROPS AND EDIBLE FORESTS

The limited supply of horizontal space in cities demands that vertical space be maximized. Because fruit and nut trees produce food in an overhead canopy, they fit well into a metropolitan landscape. Food-producing trees also contribute to air quality and provide shade and windbreaks.

ANNUAL AND PERENNIAL CROPS

In the ecological sciences there is a concept called succession. Succession is the natural process where open fields slowly fill in with weeds and brushy plants and eventually transform into forests.

Annual crops are those that grow from new seed every growing season. Most vegetables we eat are annuals. To grow annuals, the soil must be tilled and the garden plot must be frequently weeded to allow the crops the chance to grow without competition. Keeping a field open resets the processes of succession. Since a natural progression is being worked against, growing vegetable crops is a fairly labor-intensive method of food production.

Since 1900, 93 percent of American food diversity has been lost. The Slow Food movement is a global network of local groups striving to bring back food diversity in a sustainable and socially just way. Horrified by the loss of variety caused by mass-produced food, the group has created the "Ark of Taste," a listing of endangered products. Through different programs, they encourage people to support producers of these food products and to be producers themselves. Numerous old microlivestock breeds are on the US list, including: the "Old Type" Rhode Island Red chicken, Plymouth Rock chicken, the American Buff goose, American rabbit, Bourbon Red turkey, and Narragansett turkey.[5]

A peach blossom

It is safer to grow food trees in soil that may be polluted than it is to grow vegetables. Contaminants are much less likely to pass from soil to roots to trunk to branches and accumulate in fruit bodies than they are to make it into vegetable crops. Little comfort should be taken in this knowledge, however. It is always best to avoid growing food in contaminated soil and to test when in question. (See Bioremediation, page 179.)

Fruit and nut trees are examples of **perennial crops**, meaning they continue to produce food without requiring replanting. Getting perennial crops started requires an initial high investment of energy, but once they have become established, they produce food year after year with relatively minimal energy input on the grower's part. (Most species of food trees require several years of growth before they produce nuts or fruits.)

Food trees can be planted with perennial vegetables to produce simulated ecosystems, or "food forests," that mimic the natural processes of succession. A food forest does not need to be tilled annually and needs considerably less weeding than a vegetable garden.

PLANTING TREES

Trees are ideally planted when the cold has caused them to become dormant (after their leaves have dropped off and before new buds have opened) but when the ground is not frozen. Planting trees while they are dormant minimizes the shock of being transplanted. Depending on climate, this window of time will vary.

To plant a tree, dig a hole at least twice as wide and just as deep as the root mass of the tree. Loosen the soil on the edges of the hole with a pitchfork to help the tree to send out its roots. Place the tree in the hole, and back fill around it with topsoil and some finished compost. Water newly planted trees for the first few years while they are establishing their roots. Gradually reduce watering as the root network develops. For its first summer, give a tree regular weekly soakings that are the equivalent of 1 to 2 inches of rain.

An area's average minimum winter temperature determines what types of trees can be grown. The United States Department of Agriculture (USDA) has created a hardiness map of North America, divided into zones, which is a useful guide for determining what varieties of plants are appropriate in what areas. Similar maps exist for other regions of the world. Cold-hardy varieties of many trees have been developed and can be obtained from local nurseries. With the exception of the paw paw, most fruit and nut trees need full sun.

Trees are either self-pollinating or need a partner tree or trees to produce fruit. When deciding what type of fruit tree to plant, make sure to research if it is a self-pollinating species or if more than one tree will be required. Space constraints may permit only self-pollinating trees.

OTHER PERENNIAL FOOD CROPS

There are a number of perennial edible plants that grow as vines and can be trellised. Trellis structures can be affixed onto the sides of buildings, and are a fabulous way to make use of vertical space. These "green walls" can shade the sides of buildings in the summer and act as a wind barrier in the winter. Trellisable perennial plants include: kiwi fruit, hardy kiwi fruit, passion fruit, and grapes. (Annuals like pole beans, squash, cucumbers, and peas also trellis nicely.)

Berries are another delicious perennial. Blackberries and raspberries grow in thorny brambles. They typically fill in clearings in the wild and do well on the edges of clearings. They can also be pruned to climb trellises. Blueberries come in high bush and low bush varieties and prefer colder climates and acidic soil.

In drier, hotter climates, cacti grow prolifically and can be incorporated into urban space. It is common to see cacti fences in some regions. Nopales' pads are edible (be careful: the spineless varieties still have little spines!) and the fruit of prickly pear cacti is made into jam and wine.

Some communities have built edible parks filled with food-producing plants, such as the Bountiful City Project in Asheville, NC. Fruit trees can also be planted along sidewalks, allowing people to gather fresh foods as they go about their way. Both are good ways to establish community food security.

Fruit and Nut Tree Options

almonds	mulberries
apples	oaks
apricots	olives
black walnuts	paw paws
cherries	peaches
chestnuts	pears
figs	pecans
hickories	persimmons
jujubes	plums
kumquats	pomegranates
loquats	

A cactus fence on trash day

MUSHROOM LOG CULTIVATION

A major obstacle to growing food in cities is the shortage of space that receives adequate sunlight. Many times buildings and trees shade an area to the point where it's impossible to grow vegetables. However, edible and medicinal mushrooms (fungi) can be grown on logs in areas that receive marginal sunlight. They do not require contact with soil, and can be grown indoors, on fire escapes, rooftops, or hung by ropes from the sides of buildings. Fungi only need to be protected from wind and intense sun and to be kept moist through occasional watering. Properly cared for, mushroom logs can provide many years of nutritious food to urban dwellers.

Log culture is a method of growing mushrooms that mimics the natural process of fungi growing on dead trees. Holes are drilled into logs and **plug spawn** are inserted, inoculating the log. Plug spawn are small wooden dowels colonized with fungi that are purchased from specialty suppliers.

Following inoculation, the fungi colonize the entire log, using its mass as nutrients. Mushrooms will begin to grow on the sides of the logs within six months to two years, depending on the size of the log, the vitality of the strain of fungi, and climate conditions. Additional **flushes**, or crops of mushrooms, will continue to grow and may continue for several years following the initial fruiting. The amount of flushes a log can produce depends on the type of wood and the size of the log.

LOGS

The best types of logs to use are dense **hardwoods**, such as oak, maple, beech, elm, ash, or alder. Softwoods, or coniferous trees like pine, hemlock, and spruce, are less desirable. Aromatic tree species such as cedar are not recommended, as the antifungal properties that make them ideal for outdoor construction also make them poor choices for mushroom cultivation.

The woody cellulose inside the log is food for the fungi. The fungi will keep growing as long as food is available. The denser the wood type is, the longer it will take for fungi to colonize the log, and more flushes of mushrooms will be produced. When the nutrients inside the log have been used up, the fungi cease to produce mushrooms. At this point, the log will be thoroughly decomposed into a pulpy mush that can be composted.

It is possible to find freshly cut logs inside of cities. Many tree mulching businesses, arborists, or city parks departments will have piles of logs waiting to be mulched that they are often happy to give away for free. Hopefully, whoever cut the logs can identify the type of tree. Guessing the tree species by looking only at the bark on the log is difficult.

Logs should have been cut at least two to three weeks prior to and no longer than three months before they are inoculated. Trees produce anti-fungal compounds that dissipate two to three weeks after being cut down. After three months, it is likely that another

The following edible and medicinal species of fungi can be grown on log cultures:

Edible/Medicinal
Oyster
Shiitake
Maitake, or Hen of the Woods
Chicken of the Woods
Lion's Mane

Medicinal
Reishi
Turkey Tail
Chaga (grows only on birch trees)

Some of these are valued for being gourmet or medicinal and can be sold at a premium, creating the possibility for an urban microindustry.

type of fungi will have already begun colonizing the log and will compete with the plug spawn. Never use logs that show obvious signs of previous colonization, such as fruiting mushrooms or excessive mold growth.

The ideal diameter for a mushroom log is 6 to 10 inches. Larger ones will take many years to colonize. Space availability is the determining factor in choosing the length of the log: anything from 1 to 6 feet is acceptable.

PLUGGING THE LOG

Approximately fifty plugs will cover a 3-foot log with a 6-inch diameter. Drill holes with diameters equal to the diameter of the plug into the log to a depth equal to the length of the plug. The holes should be placed in a diamond pattern, spaced 3 to 6 inches apart. Hammer the plugs into the holes. Paint over the plugs and the two ends of the log with melted beeswax or cheese wax to prevent contaminants from getting in. Any holes or deep gashes in the bark should also be covered with wax.

Plugged logs can be stacked in crisscrossing patterns called **ricks** that allow easy access to fruiting mushrooms. Inoculated logs should be kept out of contact with soil, as they will rot quickly and be taken over by competing organisms. Reishi and maitake mushrooms should be planted vertically in a pot full of sand or gravel.

Ideally, the bark of the log should always be moist. Natural humidity may be sufficient to maintain adequate moisture levels in climates with regular rainfall. In dry climates, or during droughts, supplemental watering is necessary. Always use collected rainwater or dechlorinated water.

After a log has been inoculated for six months to two years a mushroom fruiting can be stimulated by soaking the log in water for a 24-hour period. This tricks the fungi into thinking that a heavy rain has occurred and that it's an optimal time for attempting to reproduce by producing mushrooms that cast out spores. Leave at least a few weeks between attempts at forced mushrooming.

AQUACULTURE

Aquaculture is the practice of cultivating aquatic plants, algae, and animals for the purpose of creating food, fuel, fiber, and fertilizer. The small scale ecological systems that are a key component of sustainable cities must require minimal energy inputs, be organically managed, and recycle their own wastes. Aquaculture can produce high yields of edible products in small spaces, making it an ideal method of urban food production. Urban aquaculture designs can be as elaborate as a recirculating system in a greenhouse or as simple as a kiddie pool with some plants and goldfish.

THE CASE FOR AQUACULTURE

For thousands of years, humans have lived near water and practiced some form of aquaculture, whether harvesting plants, collecting crawfish and clams, or fishing. Today, over one billion people rely on fish as their main source of protein.[6] Sadly, in recent years it has become difficult to impossible for people to survive directly off oceans, lakes, rivers, and swamps.

The sea is becoming inaccessible to all but the wealthiest people. Coastal gentrification occurs when property near or on the coast increases in value to the point where people making their living off the sea can no longer afford to live there. Centuries-old seafaring cultures are being lost as people are forced inland to make room for upscale housing developments, tourist hotels, and water-consuming industries such as power plants.

In traditional societies, an imperative for conservation and the technological limitations of the pole and the net kept the fish harvest in balance with oceanic resources, rarely depleting them. Today, giant ships towing dragnets vacuum the oceans. Due to an increasing global demand for fish as food, the stocks of many fish species have been severely depleted and oceanic ecosystems have been severely disrupted. "Peak fish," the point at which world fisheries reached their climax and have since gone into decline, was passed in the late 1980s. A large four-year study financed by the National Science Foundation analyzed the damage wrought on oceanic ecosystems by global warming, pollution, and overfishing. They concluded that if the loss of marine biodiversity continues at its current rate, all fish and seafood species populations will collapse by 2048.[7]

Waterways have greatly suffered from the expansion of industry and human settlements. The dumping of industrial wastes, toxic storm-water runoff, fuel spills, and the discharge of untreated sewage have left many aquatic organisms unfit to eat. Pollutants like **PCBs** (polychlorinated biphenyls), pesticides, and mercury easily accumulate in the aquatic food chain. Certain fish are at high risk for such toxic bioaccumulation, limiting the number of them any person should eat in a lifetime. Health warnings have been issued advising the public, especially pregnant women and children, to avoid eating many species of fish altogether.[8] It is also risky to harvest many wild edible aquatic plants, as they too can accumulate toxins found in their environment. (For methods of treating contaminated water, see Wastewater Recycling, page 94 and Floating Islands, page 84.)

Another dangerous modern innovation is industrial fish farming, in which fish are stocked at obscenely high densities, often resulting in disease. Little different from factory farms, these environmentally damaging operations require massive chemical, energy, and pharmaceutical inputs. Industrial-scale aquaculture operations also contribute to environmental degradation. Many mangrove swamps have been destroyed in coastal regions to make room for offshore shrimp farms. The removal of mangrove swamps contributed to the destructive power of the 2004 Asian tsunami, as the missing swamps would have dissipated its energy.

It is important to distinguish between large-scale, commercial aquaculture programs and small-scale, ecologically based ones. Small-scale systems have low stocking densities, process their own wastes, and don't result in the degradation of natural habitat. Growing aquatic foodstuffs in good quality water assures that they're not polluted. To some degree, small-scale aquaculture systems can replace the access to natural fisheries lost due to degradation and displacement.

AQUACULTURE SCIENCE

Aquatic environments are among the most biologically productive ecosystems in nature. An ecosystem's photosynthetic productivity can be measured by its **net primary production** (NPP), or the amount of new plant or algae matter created within a certain area over a year. **Estuaries**, swamps, and marshes have NPP ratings equal to that of rainforests.[9] A thriving swamp produces more plant life per acre than the most fertile farms. Granted, not everything that naturally grows in a swamp is edible or palatable, but there are many delicious edible water plants that can be cultivated in constructed aquatic environments, providing many calories of food.

Plants aren't the only food that can come from water. The huge amounts of algae produced in an aquatic system support entire food chains, including edible fish, crustaceans (crawfish, lobsters, shrimp), and mollusks (mussels, clams, oysters).

There are several reasons why so much grows in water so fast:

• Life requires water. Land plants and animals spend much of their time and energy seeking out water or waiting for water to come to them. A wetland plant is immersed in water, so when its sun, nutrient, and temperature requirements are met, it can grow prolifically. Many aquatic plants are floating.

Instead of building extensive root and stem structures, their energy is focused on growth and division.

• Aquatic animals live in a virtually zero-gravity environment. Unlike a land animal that constantly expends energy moving against gravity, a fish merely floats and can move rapidly with just a flick of its tail. This is one reason why, within the range of animals grown for food, fish are among the most efficient converters of protein to body weight.

• Growing food in water makes excellent use of three-dimensional space: food-producing potential is maximized by growing things at the surface, bottom, and mid-level depths of a pond. For example, edible plants can float on the surface of a pond, while edible tubers grow in the mud at its bottom. Fish occupy the vertical space in between surface and bottom. As urban horizontal space is limited, taking advantage of vertical space is essential.

For all these reasons, small-scale aquaculture systems are ideal for the urban environment. Outdoor systems also have the added feature of being wildlife attractors. After only a few months, a pond will attract birds, dragonflies, bees, frogs, snakes, snails, and fish. Some of these critters will come on their own, others will arrive as eggs stuck to the legs of pond-hopping birds.

DIFFERENT AQUACULTURE SYSTEMS

The focus in this chapter is on freshwater systems. While saltwater aquaculture is possible, it is much more complicated, and there are few examples of it working on a practical level for inland autonomous communities.

Two different types of aquaculture systems are described below: the passive pond and the intensive recirculating system. Passive systems are cheaper, easier to make, and more appropriate for beginners. Intensive systems require a significant investment of time and money and a reasonable understanding of aquatic ecosystems.

PASSIVE POND SYSTEMS

The simplest aquaculture setups needing the least maintenance are called passive systems. They are referred to as "passive" because they do not use extensive mechanical filtration and aeration, relying instead on the development of resilient, stable ecosystems. Best for plant aquaculture and lower density fish raising, passive systems are basically small ponds made out of some sort of waterproof container. They are relatively worry-free and can be placed in a backyard, on a rooftop, or in a greenhouse.

PASSIVE POND CONTAINERS

The easiest way to make a passive pond is to fill an impermeable container with water. Kiddie pools, plugged up bathtubs, old washtubs, and plastic-lined, food-grade 55-gallon barrels cut in half all have pond potential. Choose materials that won't rust or break down in the sun too quickly. Make sure no residual amounts of hazardous materials are present. Using only materials labeled "food grade" is the best way to ensure this. Avoid galvanized metal: the zinc in the metal leaches into the water and is toxic to fish, although a fish-safe epoxy sealant can be used to coat the inside of galvanized metal containers to make them suitable.

The container can be dug into the ground or left on the surface. Ponds in cold climates must be put underground to prevent them from freezing solid and killing all the fish. Ponds are very heavy—a gallon of water alone weighs 8 pounds. If not directly supported by the ground, any structure that they are placed on needs to be well reinforced.

A stock tank pond with half barrel cells orbiting

THE CARPET SANDWICH

It is difficult to make a pond by just digging a hole in the ground. Most soils do not have a high enough clay content to adequately retain water. One cheap option for making an in-ground pond without using an existing container is the carpet sandwich. Carpet sandwiches, a time-tested permaculture mainstay, use old carpets and plastic sheeting to make a simple pond.

Supplies needed:

Old carpet pieces
Construction plastic or other
  impermeable membrane
Shovel
Rocks

How to:

1. Dig a hole and line it with overlapping pieces of old carpet. The carpet should extend 1 foot beyond the edge of the hole.
2. Place the construction plastic over the carpet. The plastic must be one continuous sheet without any holes.
3. Add a second layer of carpet over the plastic.
4. Put a ring of rocks around the outside of the pond, holding down the layers of plastic and carpet.

A small leak can easily drain a pond and destroy the system. The carpet protects the impermeable membrane from rocks, dog claws, pitchforks, and other sources of accidental puncture. Unless organic, carpets require a period of "weathering" before use. Carpets often are made with toxic synthetic glues and may have been sprayed with flea poisons and other chemicals. It is a good idea to only use carpets that have been sitting outside in the rain for a good six months or have been comparably washed.

While construction plastic can be bought cheaply, it is not the most durable material. Swimming pool businesses will often give away old pool liners, which are much thicker. More expensive pond liners made of EPDM rubber or butyl rubber can also be purchased.

POND DESIGN CONSIDERATIONS

A good pond has wavy edges and/or rocks that protrude above the surface in order to create islands, or **edge**. Edge creates **ecotones**, transitional habitats that many species can use. For example, frogs like to sit on rocks near pond banks where they can lay their eggs in shallow waters. Ponds with steep sides and no islands are unfriendly habitats. Ponds needn't be much deeper than 30 inches, as most biological functions occur within this zone.

To make a more friendly habitat, create "ledges." Ledges provide surfaces to place plants on at varying depths, as different species prefer to grow either fully or partially immersed in water. Ledges can be made by sculpting them into the dirt, in the case of a carpet sandwich, or by stacking rocks in the pond at different heights.

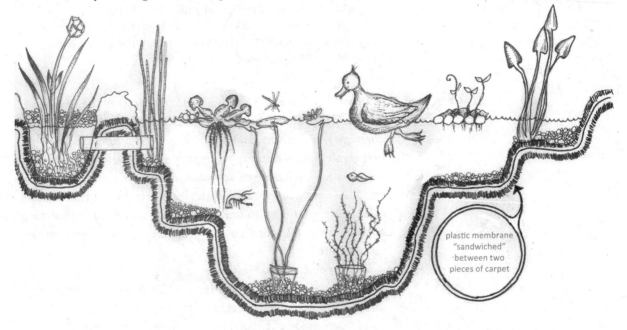

plastic membrane "sandwiched" between two pieces of carpet

A carpet sandwich pond showing edge ecotones

Always consider children when designing a pond. While educational and fun, ponds can be dangerous. Like pools, ponds should be fenced to prevent tragedy. Include at least one side with a gradual slope so people and animals can get out if they accidentally fall in.

GETTING STARTED

Once the pond has been constructed or installed, it is time to start setting it up. Begin by layering the bottom of the pond with a few inches of clean gravel. The gravel creates a medium for plants to root in and a habitat in which bottom organisms can grow. Fill the pond with water and allow it to sit for a few days, letting the chlorine volatilize. After a few days, mix in a few handfuls of good soil and compost to seed the pond with nutrients and beneficial microorganisms. Inoculating the pond with organisms from an established, healthy pond will also give it a microbiological kick start. An easy way to do this is to suck up water and muck from a nearby pond with a turkey baster and inject it into the new one. Select a few different types of rocks and put them in the pond. In a new pond it is important to have mineral diversity to give organisms the essential minerals they need for growth. It is now time to add plants and snails. (See Aquatic Animals, page 38, and Plant Aquaculture, page 40.) Plants can either be kept in gravel-filled pots for easy removal or planted directly into the gravel.

It is possible to incorporate fish into a small pond. Small fish, like minnows or goldfish, are easiest to raise, as a pond's ecosystem can effectively process their wastes. Large volumes of water are needed to raise large fish (longer than 4 inches) in a passive system. While many factors influence a passive pond's fish stocking capacity, a safe guideline is at least 100 gallons of water per large fish. Fish 1 to 2 inches in length, like minnows, can be safely stocked at one to two fish per 10 gallons. Greater stocking densities require a system that incorporates aeration and filtration.

MOSQUITOES AND PONDS

The stagnant water found in many outdoor and indoor ponds provides ideal breeding habitat for mosquitoes. It only takes a few days for thousands of eggs to be laid, develop into larvae, and hatch into mosquitoes. Not only are mosquitoes capable of carrying and transmitting disease, they make our lives miserable when their numbers explode. Any pond system must have some way of controlling mosquito populations.

Minnows are the easiest, least toxic way of controlling mosquitoes. Small populations of minnows eat mosquito larvae and require no additional feeding or aeration. Gambusia minnows (*Gambusia affinis*), a species of guppy, are aggressive mosquito hunters. Although native to a large part of North America, gambusia easily out-compete other fish species. Before introducing gambusia, it is important to make sure the pond is located within their native range. In colder climates, minnow species such as the fathead (*Pimephales promelas*) are more appropriate. They can be obtained from bait shops.

INTENSIVE RECIRCULATING SYSTEMS

Like land animals, fish and other aquatic organisms produce waste products, and in water like on land, a key to maintaining life is proper treatment of that waste. In a pond, lake, or river, these wastes are processed by a community of plants and microbes that share the fish's environment. When waste accumulates faster than it is broken down, it can lead to fish becoming sick or dying. It's all a matter of balance.

When fish breathe they take oxygen out of the water. Over time the oxygen will re-enter the water from the atmosphere and through the photosynthesis of plants. Again, if oxygen is used up faster than it is replaced, the fish will die. For these reasons, small ponds are limited in the number of fish that can be raised in them—ponds can only process so much waste and the water can only store so much oxygen and be recharged so quickly.

In order to increase the number of fish that can be raised in a small body of water (such as a pond or barrel), the natural functions of plants and microbes need to be augmented by mechanical processes: filtration and aeration. Filtration reduces harmful compounds made by fish. It does this by forcing water across materials that provide habitat for the microbes that convert fish wastes into plant nutrients. Aeration involves using mechanical processes to increase the rate of oxygen absorption by the water. A pond that employs extensive filtration and aeration is called an intensive recirculating aquaculture system.

In a natural pond, oxygen diffuses into water from the atmosphere and through plants. In an intensive system, the rate of oxygen diffusion must be enhanced by mechanically aerating the water. The most common way is with an air pump. Air pumps can be easily bought at pet stores. They are sized by the volume of water

A pond constructed from an old hot tub

they can aerate. The water can also be aerated by pumping it over a waterfall.

The only way to accurately determine if there is enough oxygen in an aquaculture system is to use a dissolved oxygen meter, an expensive and sometimes unreliable tool. Short of this, it is better to err on the side of over-oxygenating. Fish should appear vigorous and excited to eat. Lethargy could be an indicator of insufficient oxygen.

A recirculating system can hold many more fish than a passive system. They work well in urban environments where space is limited and the need for food is large. Their major drawback is that they require electrical energy inputs to drive the pumps that keep the fish alive. If power is lost or if a pump breaks and the system is not restored, the fish will die very quickly. As a result, recirculating systems require daily inspection and a good deal of maintenance.

Recirculating aquaculture systems can be set up in backyards, on reinforced roofs, and in greenhouses or bioshelters—basically anywhere with the full sun that the plants that purify and oxygenate the water need. Remember that water weighs 8 pounds per gallon, so even a small system will be extremely heavy.

DESIGN FOR A RELATIVELY SIMPLE RECIRCULATING SYSTEM

A recirculating aquaculture system can be built using a series of food-grade 55-gallon barrels that are connected to each other. A pump in the bottom of the last barrel returns water to the first one, creating a circular loop. Each barrel, or cell, is host to a different ecosystem that performs a unique supportive function for the organisms living in the entire system.

There are many variations of this design. It can be scaled up or down as space allows. The following system can fit in a space that is roughly 10 feet by 4 feet.

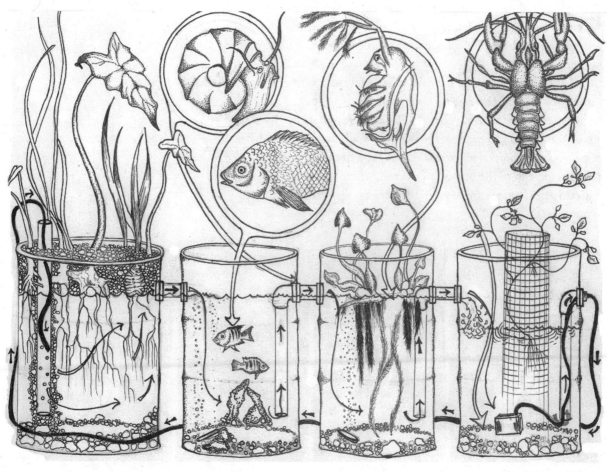

cell one   cell two   cell three   cell four

Illustration of recirculating system

Cell 1: This cell is the biofilter. Completely filled with gravel and **emergent plants**, like cattail, bulrush, and taro, it gives the recirculated water a final polish before it goes on to the fish. The surface area of the gravel and the roots of the plants provide habitat for water-purifying microorganisms that assist in denitrification. (See Stocking Densities and Denitrification, page 36.) These microorganisms arrive on the roots of plants or from an inoculation from another pond.

Cell 2: Cell two contains the fish. It has a few inches of gravel at its bottom, and perhaps some large rocks or rooted plants to provide shelter for the fish. (They will be less stressed if they have some hiding spots.) In order to break down dead matter, snails are an essential component of this cell. A tube from the aeration pump should run to the bottom of the cell, where it is attached to an **airstone**. Airstones are oxygen diffusers that are attached to air pumps.

Variation of intensive recirculating system

Intensive systems

Cells 3 and 4: Cells three and four are water purifiers. Their job is to begin processing the wastes produced by the fish in cell two. These cells have several inches of gravel at the bottom, and have **submergent** plants, like milfoil and hornwort, rooted in them. When fish wastes suspended in the water come into contact with these plants, they bounce off of them and sink to the bottom of the barrel, where they form a layer of sedimentary ooze that provides habitat to a number of small organisms. Fast-growing plants such as duckweed, azolla, and water hyacinth float at the top of these barrels where they act as scrubbers, removing excess nutrients from the water. These plants should be harvested regularly and fed to humans, fish, or microlivestock; composted; or made into methane. (See Biogas, page 153.)

Thick layers of green algae will grow on the sides of these barrels, which will also help to remove excess nutrients from the water. Snails should also be placed in these cells. They will assist in removing dead algae. Cells three and four should have airstones in them as well, which can be powered from the same pump.

Zooplankton can also be found in these cells. These tiny buglike aquatic creatures typically arrive on the roots of plants. They can be scooped up in mesh nets and fed back to the fish in cell two.

Crawfish can be put into either cell three and/or four. They will feed off dead plant material and fish wastes.

Cell four can contain an aquaponics component. (See Aquaponics, page 37.)

A water-circulating pump should be put at the bottom of cell four. Run a hose from it back to a pipe that runs to the bottom of cell one. This will ensure that the water remains in circulation. A pump capable of delivering 100 gallons per hour should be sufficient for most systems.

PLUMBING

The plumbing should be arranged in each of the cells so that water is discharged into the top of the barrel and is taken out from the bottom. This top to bottom water flow ensures that a complete exchange of water occurs in each cell. Cell one could go bottom to top (as it does in the drawing) as long as the intake and outlet are opposite. For cell one, the important thing is that the water crosses the whole tank—top to bottom or bottom to top. The other cells should be plumbed top to bottom to treat possible ammonia build-up. Use bulkheads to make seals on the sides of the barrels. (See Barrels, Bungholes, and Bulkheads, page 80.) Standard 2-inch, schedule 40 PVC (polyvinyl chloride) pipes and fittings work well to direct the flow of water and can be threaded into the bulkheads.

STOCKING DENSITIES AND DENITRIFICATION

The number of fish that can be put in a recirculating aquaculture system depends on its age and stability, the number of plants relative to its fish population, and the amount of food that is added. One fish per gallon of water in the second cell is a very high stocking density. Ten gallons for each fish is a more reasonable starting point. Basically, the higher the stocking density, the greater the amount of energy needed to keep the system alive.

Fish produce ammonia as a waste product. When too much ammonia builds up in the water, it can become deadly to a fish population. In a natural system, ammonia is removed through the biological processes of different types of bacteria. The bacteria first convert the ammonia to nitrite, then to nitrate, and finally it is released into the atmosphere as nitrogen gas. This process is called the denitrification cycle.

Denitrifying bacteria need to be given adequate habitat, either on gravel on the bottom of the pond, the roots of plants, or store-bought plastic filtering media. The bacteria also need time to develop in proportion to the amount of ammonia being produced in a system. This can take up to several weeks, so it is important to monitor ammonia levels and fish health after setting up a new aquaculture system. The ammonia test in a simple aquarium test kit

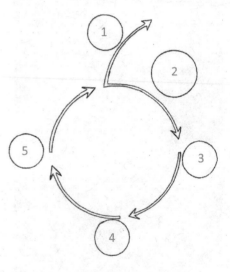

Aquaculture Nitrogen Cycle

1. Nitrogen gas released
2. Nitrate feeds plants and algae which are eaten by fish. Fish produce ammonia as a waste product.
3. Ammonia/Nitrosomas bacteria
4. Nitrite/nitrobacteria
5. Nitrate

should be sufficient for most systems. High ammonia levels irritate fish gills. Fish rubbing their gills on surfaces is an indication of dangerously high ammonia levels. As denitrifying bacteria are developing, ammonia levels can be reduced by frequent water changes. The decay of uneaten fish food will also produce ammonia—don't feed fish more than they can eat!

FISH FOOD

Fish are as varied in their preferences for food as they are in their body types and habitats. The fish species that are most ideal for raising in small-scale aquaculture systems have diets consisting primarily of plant matter, insects, and decomposing material—all considered to be low on the food chain. Sources of this food can include compost scraps, worms from a vermicompost system, spent barley hulls from a beer brewery, trapped cockroaches, or duckweed harvested from an aquaculture pond. It is also possible to purchase high-protein fish food from pet stores.

Hanging a light bulb above a pond will attract insects. Flying in erratic circles, they will frequently crash into the pond and become fish food. Another technique, one that would likely be unpopular with neighbors, is to hang a piece of rotting meat above a pond. Housefly maggots eating the meat will fall into the pond and be devoured.

FISH WASTE AS FERTILIZER

An added benefit of raising fish is that their manure is an excellent fertilizer for gardens. It can be collected from the bottom of ponds with a siphon vacuum and be applied to soils. It is also possible to preserve it in containers for later use by adding one teaspoon of phosphoric acid per gallon of fish manure.

AQUAPONICS

Aquaponics is the practice of growing plants in the nutrient-rich wastewater produced by fish in an aquaculture system, rather than in soil. The plants are floated on rafts with their roots dangling into the nutrient-rich waters. In addition to providing the plants themselves for harvest, this method also uses the plants to purify the water by taking up excess nutrients.

Aquaponics works best with plants that are naturally adapted to living in water, like watercress, duckweed, and water spinach. It is possible to grow some non-aquatic plants, like basil and lettuce, aquaponically, but these plants will eventually suffer from a lack of soil nutrients.

Trellising aquaponic plants like watercress and water spinach can be grown on a cage. This is made by bending plastic chicken fencing material into the shape of a cylinder and standing it vertically in the water with 25 to 50 percent of the cage sticking out of the water. The cylinder shape will allow the roots of the plants to grow into the center of the cylinder, while supporting the plants' stems. (See cell four in Intensive System Illustration, page 33.)

Aquaponics should not be confused with hydroponics, a system that involves growing terrestrial plants using recirculating water that has been synthetically fertilized. Since hydroponics is energy intensive and relies on artificial fertilizers, it has limited application in sustainable autonomous systems.

AQUATIC ANIMALS

With a high rate of protein conversion, omnivorous diet, and good use of three-dimensional space, fish make an ideal choice of animal to raise in concentrated conditions in urban environments.

TILAPIA

Tilapia is the most common species of fish grown in urban aquaculture. Originally from Africa and the Middle East, it is a prolific breeder and is tolerant of crowding and less than pristine water quality. An omnivorous fish, tilapia is relatively easy to feed. It will eat earthworms, duckweed, or vegetable scraps. Tilapia is also a filter feeder, meaning it can eat microalgae suspended in the water, a food niche at the bottom of the food chain exploited by few fish species. All these factors combined make tilapia a good choice for aquaculture.

Tilapia's main drawback is its inability to survive at temperatures below 55 degrees. In cooler climates, this requires that the fish be grown either seasonally, in bioshelters, or with considerable energy inputs for heating water. One option is to grow tilapia in outdoor ponds in the warm months, harvest the fish, and then collect the young to be raised (in a smaller tank) indoors in the winter.

Mixed-sex tilapia, needed to keep the fish population going for multiple generations, are difficult to obtain. Many fish hatcheries only sell all-male populations. Another obstacle to raising tilapia is that it is illegal in some states. Tilapia is considered an invasive fish and should never be released into the wild.

OTHER FISH SPECIES

There are many fish species native or naturalized to the United States that are legal, easy to obtain from private fish hatcheries, and cold hardy that are also suited for small scale aquaculture. Bullheads, catfish, sunfish, and carp meet these characteristics and feed close to the bottom of the food chain. If they are provided with a rocky, covered shelter, bullheads are known to breed in small-scale pond systems. Trout and bass can also be raised, but require high levels of protein and precise water temperatures and conditions.

CLAMS

Part of a family of organisms called bivalves, clams play an important role in aquatic ecosystems. As filter feeders, clams constantly pass water through their bodies, cleaning it at the same time. Fifty percent of freshwater clam species in the United States have gone extinct, largely due to habitat degradation. Raising endangered species in captivity for release into wild waterways could greatly boost their chances for survival. Unfortunately, it is impossible to breed most clams in small aquaculture systems because their reproductive cycles are dependent on river flows and fish to transport their larvae. However, the Asian river clam, *Corbicula fluminea*, has been successfully raised in small aquariums for food and for water purification. It is found in many US waterways. Although it is a non-native species, it doesn't seem to affect native populations of bivalves.

SNAILS

Snails play a critical role as debris consumers in an aquaculture system. Snails can be collected from the sediment or undersides of vegetation in just about any waterway. A couple snails of the same species will quickly multiply.

CRAYFISH

Crayfish are freshwater crustaceans that resemble small lobsters. Found in many parts of the world, crayfish can be raised alongside many fish species in an aquaculture system and are considered a delicacy.

PLANT AQUACULTURE

There are many aquatic plants that can be grown in a small-scale aquaculture system, independently or in combination with animal systems. Aquatic plants grow prolifically and can be used for food, fertilizer, or livestock feed; as a high-nitrogen material in compost; or as fuel in methane digester systems. It is always best to use plants that are native to the climate they will be raised in—take special care with exotics that they do not escape into natural waterways! Plants can be obtained from water garden nurseries, or, in some cases, carefully transplanted from the wild. The following are some useful aquatic plants.

ARROWHEAD (*SAGITTARIA LATIFOLIA*)

Native to North America, this water plant produces an attractive purple flower. Its small, egg-shaped roots were an important food to indigenous Americans. Boil or steam the root to remove an otherwise bitter flavor. Arrowhead spreads rapidly and can be grown in cold or warm climates.

AZOLLA (*AZOLLA FILICULOICIDES*)

Azolla, or fairy moss, is a minute floating fern. Several varieties are native to North America. As its growth conditions, harvesting, and preparation are quite similar to those of duckweed, the two can easily be grown together, forming an interesting mix of floating green edible stuff.

Azolla also has an important agricultural use. Like legumes and clovers, it has a symbiotic relationship with the blue-green algae, or cyanobacteria, living on its roots. The algae's role is to pull nitrogen out of the atmosphere, "fixing" it into a form where it is usable by plants. Azolla can be harvested and tilled into soil as a nitrogen supplement, effectively performing the same function as a nitrogen-fixing cover crop. Low-tech azolla cultivation could reduce global dependence on synthetically produced nitrogen fertilizer, an energy intensive, polluting product used worldwide in conjunction with chemical pesticides.

In Southeast Asia, azolla is commonly grown with rice, ducks, and tilapia in a system called **polyculture**. The different elements in polyculture all benefit each other in an integrated pattern of inputs and yields: the wastes of one become the food of another.

CATTAIL (*TYPHA SPP.*)

A reed plant found commonly across the United States, cattails have brown, fuzzy seed heads that resemble cigars. In addition to being a valued wetlands plant, cattail produces edible tubers and shoots. The root can be dug up, peeled, and eaten like a potato. Propagating cattails is easy. Dig up the **rhizome** of the plant and split it up. Plant the pieces several inches below the soil or gravel, in water or wet ground. Be careful: Cattails' pointy rhizomes can poke through pond liners.

DUCKWEED (*LEMNA SPP.*)

Tiny, floating, and leafy, duckweed is the world's smallest flowering plant. There are several species and it can be found in most parts of North America, though its range is global. Although it is considered to be a nuisance plant by many because of its tendency to cover the entire surface of lakes and ponds, this trait is what gives duckweed the potential to be a major food source for humans and livestock. Duckweed can double its mass daily under optimal conditions. A floating plant with no root or stem, it puts all its energy into division. Duckweed's efficient growth makes it one of the highest yielding crops per acre.[10] It is commonly used in wastewater treatment systems because of its rapid nutrient uptake ability. It is also a good source of nitrogen for compost piles and can be used as a **green manure** for land gardens.

The rapidly growing duckweed is also nutritious, giving it huge potential for world food production. Duckweed has a rich protein structure that is closer to an animal's than a plant's. Harvesting duckweed is quite easy—it can be scooped off the water's surface with a net or strainer; just make sure to leave enough to regrow. If grown in absolutely clean water, duckweed could be eaten raw by humans. However, it is a good idea to steam it before eating in case any pathogens happen to be attached.

Duckweed can be fed to chickens and other fowl. It can also be fed to tilapia and other herbivorous fish. Because it is largely water by weight, it is best to dehydrate duckweed before feeding it to fish to avoid filling their stomachs with water. Duckweed can be grown successfully in a recirculating aquaculture system, using the wastes produced by the fish as a nutrient source.

LOTUS (*NELUMBO SPP.*)

An edible water plant originally from India, lotus is most prized for its beautiful flower. The rhizome and seeds are edible.

RICE

A dietary staple of many cultures, rice can also be grown on a small scale in aquatic food systems. Several varieties are adapted to growth in the United States. Start seeds in moist soil and transfer to water once they have begun growing. Another option is wild rice, a native water grass originally cultivated by indigenous Americans.

TARO (*COLOCASIA ESCULENTA*)

Taro is one of the world's most widely cultivated crops. The edible, nutritious part of the plant is its root, or corm. It can be prepared in a variety of ways similar to a potato. It is important to cook it—it is toxic when eaten raw! Taro is the main ingredient in the Hawaiian dish poi.

WATERCRESS (*RORIPPA NASTURTIUM-AQUATICUM*)

Watercress is a common salad ingredient. Found in many grocery stores, it can be grown by placing a single cutting in water. Watercress performs well in aquaponic designs.

WATER HYACINTH (*EICHHORNIA PANICULATA*)

While not exactly a top choice for edibility, water hyacinth deserves mention for its many other uses. Water hyacinth is frequently used in wastewater applications because of its rapid growth rate and nutrient uptake ability. This same quality makes it a nuisance plant in many parts of the world. Water hyacinth is despised for its tendency to choke out waterways with its tendril-like networks of floating bulbs and leaves. Never let it escape into the wild! People living with it have used it for a livestock feed, a mushroom-growing substrate, a biomass for methane gas production, and fibers for basket weaving.

WATER MIMOSA (*NEPTUNIA OLERACEA*)

Water mimosa is mainly found in tropical Asia, where it is cultivated in still water like rice. Rich in minerals and vitamin C, the young leaves, shoot tips, and young pods are eaten and the roots are used medicinally.

WATER SPINACH (*IPOMOEA AQUATICA*)

This high-iron, leafy plant grows prolifically in warm climates. Originating in China, water spinach is now found in many parts of the world. Special care is needed when cultivating it to ensure it does not escape into natural waterways. It is a highly aggressive plant. Many waterways in Florida have been choked by it, and its sale has been banned in several southern states. Water spinach can be grown either in soil or water and will quickly cover the area of a pond. Although it is difficult to obtain, a small cutting is all that is needed. It is necessary to bring it indoors over winter in northern areas. Water spinach can be harvested and eaten like a salad green.

ALGAE

Vascular photosynthetic organisms are what we traditionally think of as plants—organisms that possess stems, roots, and leaves. Algae are photosynthetic organisms that lack these vascular structures. Algae range from tiny single-celled organisms (microalgae) to giant sea kelp. Some algae live on land (like lichens, which are actually fungi/algae symbionts) but the majority are aquatic.

MICROALGAE

Microalgae are fundamental to aquatic ecosystems. Growing prolifically when given sunlight, nitrates, carbon dioxide, and other nutrients, algae provide food directly or indirectly for other consumers. Without them, many life forms on Earth could not survive. They can be observed in ponds and lakes, turning them a green or green-blue hue in the summer months.

In the simplest sense, aquatic food relationships can be imagined as a pyramid. Abundant microalgae form the base of the pyramid. It takes many microalgae to feed a number of zooplankton, which are on the next level of the pyramid. The zooplankton can support only a few minnows, which are then food for even fewer big fish at the top of the pyramid. As one moves up the pyramid, energy is lost in the form of waste heat and excretions. For this reason, much more energy is required to produce 10 pounds of fish than 10 pounds of algae. It is most efficient to eat as close to the bottom of the pyramid as possible. There are several species of microalgae, including chlorella, aphanizomenon, and spirulina, that are highly nutritious and have supported traditional cultures for centuries.

It is very difficult to culture a pure strain of desirable microalgae in an open pond. Competing algae cells can spread from pond to pond on just about anything—birds, plants, bugs, even the wind. Among the many types of microalgae are some that are toxic to humans (such as microcystis and cylindrospermopsis). Since a jar of algae-rich water contains millions of minute single algae cells, there is no way to separate out the good from the bad without a microscope. Reliable tests to screen for toxic varieties of algae on a large scale are unavailable. While desirable strains of microalgae can be safely cultivated in sterile con-

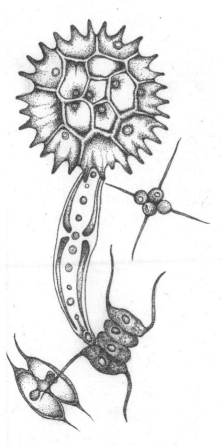

ditions, this option is generally unavailable to the majority of the world's population.

However, toxic varieties do not frequently occur where spirulina grows, because spirulina prefers water with a high pH. Spirulina also has a unique pigment that makes it easy to differentiate from potentially toxic algaes. It is difficult to separate less distinguishable varieties of algae from toxic ones with the unaided eye.

Spirulina, also called blue-green algae or cyanobacteria, is a spiral-shaped single-celled photosynthetic algae. It contains a highly digestible protein structure that has an excellent nutrient profile. A staple of the Aztec diet, spirulina grows in the alkaline lakes of Mexico and Africa. During a spirulina bloom, the thick algae mats on the surface of lakes are easily scooped up with nets or buckets. It is dried and eaten as cakes or powder. Spirulina is also cultivated in massive production facilities and sold as a nutritional supplement.

Unfortunately, spirulina production is very site specific. Difficult to grow outside of its native habitat, it requires sunny, alkaline water with a limited temperature range. To culture spirulina, a high pH environment must be created by adding large amounts of baking soda (sodium bicarbonate) to water. The bicarbonate raises the pH and provides a carbon source to the algae. This should only be done in constructed ponds. Altering the pH of a natural body of water would kill off native species.

OIL FROM ALGAE

Certain species of algae produce very high concentrations of oil in their bodies. Some varieties' masses are 50 percent oil, and in laboratory experiments, some algae strains produced many more times the amount of oil in a given space than the highest oil-producing agricultural crop.[11] These oils could be extracted from the algae and used to power diesel vehicles. Since huge amounts of algae can be grown off sewage, there seems to be a great potential to use waste products to power an algae-based energy infrastructure.

Yet, growing oily algae is not as simple as some would hope. The growth of oils, or lipids, requires considerable time and energy. Less oily algae easily out-compete oily algae. It is difficult to grow oil-producing strains in large numbers outside of sealed environments. Huge environmentally-controlled indoor ponds would be necessary to produce any significant quantity of oil, an unrealistic option for decentralized autonomous communities. The search continues for oily algae that grow in large populations in natural freshwater environments. Because they have fewer competitors in an inland setting, culturing oily marine algae in outdoor saltwater ponds may hold some promise. Other high lipid-content organisms include soldier fly larvae and some species of molds and plants.

DEPAVE THE PLANET (OR AT LEAST THE DRIVEWAY)

In today's cities, an extraordinary amount of space has been allotted for the exclusive use of automobiles. Parking lots and roads occupy some of the best potential gardening space. People looking to build gardens on top of former parking lots or roads are often compelled to remove the asphalt cap. Doing so allows plant roots to go deep and extract minerals from the soil beneath and allows water to infiltrate the ground. If food production is to become localized in cities, it will be necessary to remove the layers of asphalt that cover the soil.

PROBLEMS WITH ASPHALT

Asphalt is an impervious material, which means no water can pass through it. This makes it an ideal material for roads: the earth below it stays dry and is unlikely to wash away and become rutted like dirt or gravel. For similar reasons, it is also widely used in roofing shingles.

Asphalt is derived from petroleum mixed with an aggregate (sand and gravel) as well as numerous toxic solvents. Its manufacture and use releases volatile organic compounds (**VOCs**), including the carcinogenic benzene and toluene.[12] Because of their molecular structure these toxins are persistent, or hard to break down, which means they are able to wreak havoc long after they have been unleashed.

Normally, rainfall seeps into the ground, where it is either taken up by plant roots or recharges groundwater. Water that is not absorbed creates streams that flow into rivers. When rain falls on asphalt, none of it is absorbed. Instead, it all runs off, usually into sewers. As it flows over paved areas, the rainwater picks up a toxic load of gas spills, benzene particles, and other pollutants. The sewers receive enormous influxes of this polluted water in heavy rainstorms and often overflow. Untreated sewage and contaminated rainwater escape into waterways. Aquifers are not recharged and the water cycle is disrupted.

Like concrete buildings, asphalt has high **thermal mass** properties, storing heat from the sun. This heat is released slowly, contributing to the **urban heat island effect**, where cities are as much as 10 degrees warmer than surrounding rural areas.

TEARING IT OUT

Removing asphalt is relatively easy. Most asphalt is only 1 to 2 inches thick and comes off in sizeable sheets rather than small bits. It is extremely satisfying to feel the soil beneath take its first breath in years.

How to:

1. Start from an edge or make a hole with the pickaxe.
2. One person pries up the edge of the asphalt with the pickaxe while the other thrusts the rockbar as far under the asphalt as possible.
3. Lift up a piece of asphalt using the leverage of the rockbar.

Supplies needed:

Rockbar: a 4–6 foot heavy iron rod with one end pointed and the other chisel-shaped
Pickaxe

4. Hold the asphalt up with the pickaxe and thrust the rockbar farther under.
5. Break off the piece and repeat.

WHAT NEXT?

Under the asphalt is a layer of road base. Road base can be limestone, crushed granite, gravel, or even pulverized old asphalt. We recommend that the road base also be removed. This will be difficult because it has been severely compacted from cars driving over it. At the very least, dig out dark spots on the road base surface. The spots are likely to be petroleum spills. Contaminated road base should be landfilled. If not contaminated, road base could be reused in natural building projects, as clean fill, or to mark paths.

The soil underneath is going to require considerable tilling and fluffing before it can be planted in—it has been compacted and cut off from water and air for years. Spreading bacteria-rich compost over this newly exposed ground will speed up its process of rehabilitation. (See Bioremediation, page 179.)

The question of what to do with the old chunks of asphalt is a difficult one. It's not advisable to reuse it because oils may ooze out when it gets hot. While companies exist that recycle old asphalt into driveways, the landfill may in many cases be the only practical option.

ASPHALT ALTERNATIVES

Huge amounts of space and energy are dedicated to making cities accessible to vehicular traffic. The construction of interstates and byways in cities has had devastating effects on communities. Entire neighborhoods have been razed. Others have been literally divided, often along racial and class lines. Many cities built highways parallel to waterfronts, tragically cutting themselves off from the body of water that historically supported the city.

Today, roads are still being built through urban areas to alleviate congestion. As energy prices will inevitably increase in the future and fewer people will drive, this is shortsighted planning. In instances where an area must be made accessible to vehicles, it is vastly preferable to use materials such as crushed stone, granite, gravel, or paver stones (concrete bricks engineered to allow water to pass through them).

CONCRETE

Asphalt should not be confused with concrete, another impervious material commonly used in driveways. From the mining of limestone (its main ingredient) to its dehydration at thousands of degrees for hours on end, concrete production requires enormous energy inputs.

Concrete removal is also considerably more labor intensive than asphalt removal. It can be smashed to bits with a sledge hammer, cut by a masonry blade on a circular saw (a huge, dusty mess), or jackhammered. Concrete's one plus is that it doesn't leach contaminants, so it can be cut into **urbanite** and used in gardens, benches, or foundational structures. Use caution if cutting concrete, as many times it has been poured around metal lattices that could cause the saw to buck or jump, harming the user or the masonry blade.

BIOSHELTERS

Most biological processes drastically slow down or come to a stop when temperatures drop below freezing. Unless they are kept in warm interior environments, many of the systems described in this book will only be operative in warmer seasons. **Bioshelters** keep biological systems active during the winter using only the heat of the sun. They can extend the growing season of plants or even be a year-round growing environment.

While a bioshelter is similar to a greenhouse in terms of construction (see Construction, page 53) and function (an insulated structure that allows sunlight to enter), it also contains objects that passively store heat. Thermal mass is the property of materials that allows them to soak up, retain, and release heat. Rocks, sand, bricks, and water have very high thermal mass. It takes a large amount of heat to increase their temperature. Likewise, as they cool, a comparable amount of heat is given off. The higher the mass, the longer the material stores the heat. Inside a bioshelter, high thermal mass materials are heated by the sun's rays. As the bioshelter cools off, that heat is released, keeping the interior temperature well moderated. In this way, thermal mass performs like a thermal battery: storing heat for times when the sun is obscured. Placing enough thermal mass inside of a bioshelter can help to keep it warm during cold nights and stretches of cloudy days.

Water has excellent thermal mass properties. The Gulf Stream, the oceanic current that transfers heat from the tropics to the temperate regions of the Atlantic, is evidence of this. Without the Gulf Stream's ability to soak up, transport, and release heat, the British Isles and the northeastern United States/southeastern Canada would be vastly colder places.

Water's thermal mass properties can be harnessed by placing containers filled with water inside of a bioshelter. These containers can be 1-gallon milk jugs, 5-gallon buckets, 55-gallon barrels, or whole ponds. Small containers heat up quickly and only hold onto their heat for a day or so. Large containers need many days of sun to bring their temperature up, and slowly release that heat over a similar amount of time. In climates that experience prolonged sunless periods, larger containers make more sense. Water containers painted black will soak up a greater amount of heat. They should be placed along the inside of a bioshelter's north-facing wall.

Containers of water in a bioshelter can double as aquaculture tanks. Aquatic plants and animals will benefit greatly from being

Interior of a bioshelter

inside a heated enclosure during colder periods. Bioshelters can also provide space to house constructed wetlands and rainwater collection systems. A well-designed shelter can prevent rainwater tanks from freezing solid, and can enhance the performance of a constructed wetland during the winter. Chickens will be happy inside a bioshelter during cold times, and their body heat will also help keep the space warm.

Exterior view of a bioshelter

It is even possible to have a compost pile inside of a bioshelter. As composting is a thermal process that can produce temperatures well over 100 degrees, the heat released by a compost pile will aid in keeping a bioshelter warm. This process is called **biothermal heating**. A well-maintained compost pile will also produce carbon dioxide, which is beneficial to plants.

LOCATION

An area that receives abundant sunshine is the ideal location for a bioshelter. In cities, these areas can be difficult to come across. Buildings and trees in neighbor's yards often create shade that may reduce or entirely block the amount of sun falling on a particular area. Because the sun's angle gets lower in the winter, it is important to observe the amount of sun a potential spot receives not only at different times of the day, but seasonally as well. As a bioshelter will function primarily in the winter, it should be sited in a location that gets full sun in the cold months. The presence of some deciduous trees can be a good thing. In the summer they provide some shading that can prevent a bioshelter from overheating, and in the winter, when they lose their leaves, sunlight will come through.

A bioshelter should be built horizontally along an east-west axis. In the Northern Hemisphere it should face the south (and in the Southern Hemisphere face north). This will ensure that it receives the maximum available sunlight.

Ideally, a bioshelter would be attached to the south-facing side of a building where it is protected from cold northern winds. The thermal mass of the building's wall can also be used for heat storage. (Brick and concrete buildings are great for this purpose.) A freestanding shelter should have a well-insulated northern wall.

CONSTRUCTION

A bioshelter is a simple stick-frame structure built with 2"x4"s and lined with some sort of **glazing**. Glazing is a transparent material that allows sunlight through, but blocks wind and insulates against heat loss. Appropriate glazing materials for a small bioshelter include construction plastic, recycled glass windows, or greenhouse plastic. Construction plastic can be bought very cheaply in large rolls and stapled onto a stick frame. Its disadvantage is that after six months of exposure to the sun, it becomes very brittle and eventually disintegrates.

Old windows can be built into the frame of the structure to act as glazing. Old windows should always be tested for lead paint. If lead is present, the windows should be stripped or encapsulated using lead-safe practices before being installed.[13] Double-paned windows are optimal, as the air between the panes acts as an insulator. A drawback of glass windows is that they can be easily broken by falling tree branches or vandals. An advantage of windows is that they can be opened in the summer for ventilation.

Special greenhouse plastics that are UV-resistant, insulated, and shatter-proof can also be purchased from garden shops and nurseries. They are fairly expensive.

To hold heat, bioshelters must be airtight. All cracks need to be sealed with caulk.

It is ideal to use cedar lumber to build the stick frame. Bioshelters produce a lot of internal humidity that causes condensation on the surface of wood, leading to rot. If cedar is unavailable, be sure to bevel the edges of flat wooden surfaces so that condensation can drain off. The floor of a bioshelter can be earthen with a covering of woodchips or gravel.

The eastern, western, and northern walls of a bioshelter should be opaque and insulated to minimize heat loss. To maximize solar gain, a bioshelter should be twice as long (on its east-west axis) as it is wide (on its north-south axis).

The southern wall should be angled to directly face the sun in the winter. This ensures that the most sunlight passes directly into the bioshelter and the least amount is reflected away. A rough guide for determining the proper angle is to add 20 degrees to the latitude where the shelter is being built. For example, the latitude of Philadelphia, Pennsylvania, is approximately 40 degrees north, so 60 degrees would be a good angle for the south-facing wall of a bioshelter built there.

In extremely cold climates, bioshelters designed for year-round operation may require supplemental heating to prevent freezing during extended sunless periods. If a wood stove is used, be sure adequate space is given between the stove's chimney and glazing materials that may crack, melt, or catch fire if heated. It is also possible to place insulated curtains against the glazing at night to reduce heat loss.

While the purpose of a bioshelter is to collect heat for the living systems inside of it, without the living systems it could be used as a passive solar heat collector for a building. A structure built over a door or window leading into a building would collect heat during the day. At night, opening the window or door would allow the day's heat to enter the building. Such a system could assist with lowering a building's heating expenses.

In the summer, a bioshelter needs to be ventilated so it doesn't overheat and kill everything inside. Walls made with plastic glazing can be rolled up, and doors and windows can be opened for cross ventilation. Remember that heat rises, so opening a window near the top of the shelter will have a superior cooling effect to opening one on the bottom. Even with maximum ventilation, it may be necessary to place a temporary shade cloth over the structure in the summer to prevent overheating.

INSECT CULTURE

Compared to other livestock, insects rank high in overall sustainability. The amount of land and food needed to raise insects is minimal compared to cattle, poultry, or fish. Insects eat close to the bottom of the food chain and are highly efficient protein converters. They are able to feed on garbage, turning it into concentrated nutrients.

Fish and fowl savor insects and will change them into a palatable protein in the form of meat or eggs. Supplementing livestock's diets with insects can reduce the need to buy commercial feed.

INSECT CULTIVATION

Insect cultivation is ideal for the urban environment because insects can be raised in small plastic cages kept indoors and stacked on each other. Put several individuals of the same variety into the same cage and provide table scraps and water. They will rapidly multiply.

Insects can be collected from the wild using nets or traps. Study the lifecycles of different species to ensure they are raised in optimal conditions. Commonly raised species include: mealworms, crickets, grasshoppers, butterflies, beetles, bees, ants, and many others.

SIMPLE INSECT BREEDING METHODS FOR CHICKENS

An easy, low intensity method of breeding insects is to create conditions ideal for their reproduction. Laying sheets of cardboard or pieces of wood on the ground and keeping them wet will create an excellent bug habitat. The sheets should be big enough so they cannot be turned over by chickens. Periodically turning them over with the chickens nearby will provide a bug lunch for the birds.

BARREL BREEDER

Another insect breeding technique is the barrel breeder. This method is used in conjunction with the woodchip bio-filter on a kitchen graywater filtration system. (See Wastewater Recycling page 94)

How-to:

1. Fill a 5-gallon bucket with woodchips and use it as a filter to a constructed wetland. (See Wastewater Recycling.) It will catch the food particles and oils from the kitchen wastewater.
2. Drill numerous ½-inch holes in the bottom of a 55-gallon barrel. Place it so the holes are on the ground.
3. Put 5 gallons of clean woodchips on the bottom of the barrel.
4. When the chips are clogged and foul, empty the bucket into a 55-gallon barrel.
5. Layer 5 gallons of clean woodchips on top of the dirty ones to help the material compost and absorb excess fluids and odor.
6. Continue this process of layering clean and soiled until the barrel is full.
7. Let the full barrel stand for a few months. Insects will enter the barrel from the holes in the bottom and eat the bits of food and grease. The contents will slowly break down into a rich, bug-laden compost.
8. Empty the barrel in front of chickens and they will engorge themselves on the tasty insects.
9. The remaining compost can then be spread in a garden, or used as an inoculant in another compost pile.

Supplies needed:

Woodchip biofilter
55-gallon barrel
½-inch drill bit/ drill
Woodchips

ROACH TRAP

Placed strategically, this simple roach trap will quickly fill with the bodies of dead roaches, creating chicken food and reducing the indoor breeding population.

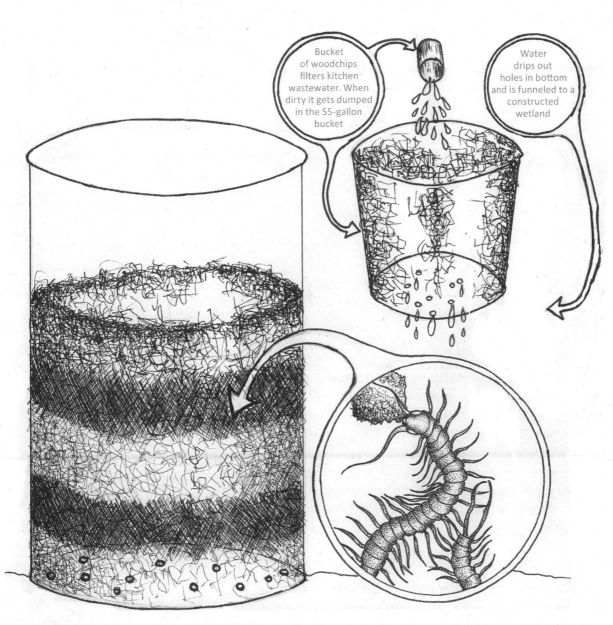

Bucket of woodchips filters kitchen wastewater. When dirty it gets dumped in the 55-gallon bucket

Water drips out holes in bottom and is funneled to a constructed wetland

Barrel breeder: A 55-gallon bucket is filled with alternating layers of clean and dirty wood chips. Holes at the bottom allow bugs (which eat the remaining food) to move in and out of the barrel and for the water to drain.

How-to:

1. Cut off the top quarter of a plastic 2 or 3-liter bottle.
2. Coat the inside of the bottle with cooking oil to prevent trapped roaches from climbing out.
3. Invert the top and place it inside the bottle, with the edges even. Hold into place with binder clips.
4. Pour molasses or soda in the bottom for bait.
5. Place it in a high traffic roach area.
6. Let the dead bodies accumulate—they are also great bait!

Supplies needed:

Plastic 2 or 3-liter bottle
Binder clips
Cooking oil
Molasses or soda

Molasses-coated roaches are a great treat for chickens. They can also be composted.

SIMPLE INSECT BREEDING METHODS FOR FISH OR CHICKENS

MAGGOTRY

Maggots are the larval form of the housefly. Commonly seen on decaying matter, they are often regarded with disgust. However, systems for the deliberate cultivation of maggots, called maggotrys, have been developed in the Global South. Fly eggs hatch on putrefied material in controlled environments. The protein-rich maggots are harvested before they become flies and are fed to livestock. Similarly, a piece of rotting meat can be hung over a pond, attracting flies. Maggots fall into the water below, becoming food for fish in the pond.

BLACK SOLDIER FLY

Less offensive than the housefly maggot is the larvae of the black soldier fly. Unlike a housefly, black soldier flies do not spread disease because they do not come in contact with human feces or food. The soldier fly has no mouth and does not eat. Instead, the adult fly

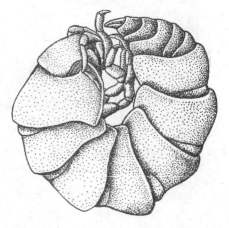

lives off of food stored during the larval stage. The black soldier fly also do not come inside of human dwellings, preferring to remain outdoors.

Soldier fly larvae are cultivated on compost or manure in outdoor containers. The protein rich larvae can be fed to animals. Also rich in oil content, the larvae can be pressed to make oil for fuel. Larvae that manage to escape and turn into flies pose no threat to human health.

ENTOMOPHAGY

Entomo = insect + *phagy* = eating: the practice of eating insects.

Many cultures have some tradition of insect eating. It would not be odd to sample culonas ants in Colombia, scorpions in China, or caterpillars in Congo. Across the globe, insects provide many people with protein, fat, and nutrients. Over 300 million insect species have been identified. Their ubiquity and success in reproduction make them ideal candidates for a future food source in a world of declining resources.

Perhaps westerners can overcome their cultural biases against entomophagy and share in the potential of this underexploited food resource.

CAUTION!!!

As the authors of *Man Eating Bugs* warns, "If you are allergic to shrimp, shellfish, dust or chocolate, never eat an insect. Even the non-allergic, unless in a survival situation, should never eat a raw insect. Certain insects store compounds that make people sick, some are poisonous, others may be carcinogenic. Be as cautious with insects as you would be if you were gathering mushrooms. Know your insects."[14]

It is estimated that each person in the US inadvertently consumes several pounds of insects a year that have been accidentally processed into food.

PUTTING IT ALL TOGETHER

The key to establishing community food security is to have food coming from multiple and diverse sources. Urban farms and gardens can grow a considerable amount of vegetables, while fruit and nut trees in parks can provide a foragable community crop. Fire escapes can be home to mushroom logs and trellising vegetables. Neighborhood microlivestock collectives can be formed, with members sharing the responsibilities and benefits—cleaning the coop, feeding and watering the animals, and collecting the eggs. Interlocking backyards make ideal locations for collective microlivestock operations and expanded bird runs. Local aquaculture specialists can offer fresh, locally grown fish.

Growing food in a city is a wonderful way to build community, support local economies, and be rooted in a place. Considering how far removed most modern city dwellers are from the process of raising food, even the simple act of growing a few vegetables on the fire escape can be a huge step toward self-reliance.

WATER

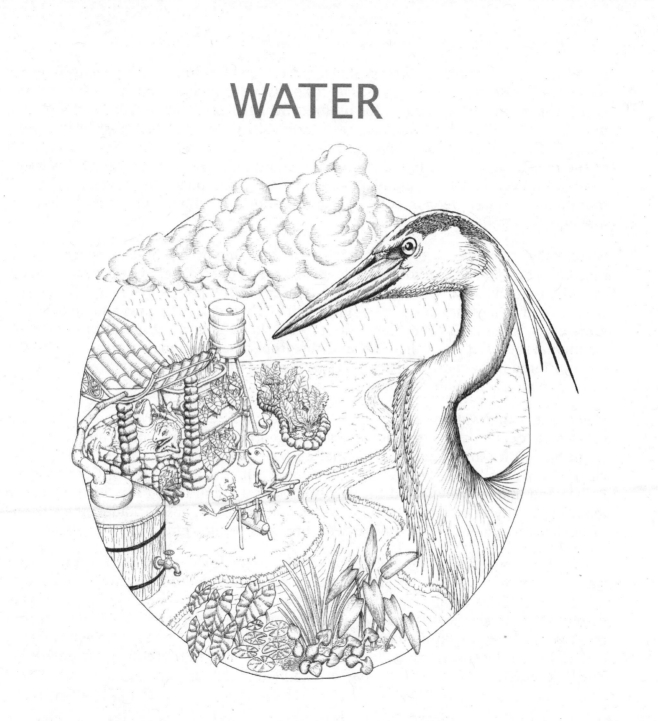

Of all human resources, water is the most critical for survival. Not only is water necessary for drinking, it is also crucial for growing food and sanitation. Sadly, water is frequently abused and taken for granted. While water is abundant on the planet, only 2.5 percent of that water is fresh (non-salt) water. Of that fresh water, 69.5 percent is inaccessible for human use, locked in glaciers and permafrost. Nearly all of the remaining water is found in slowly recharging aquifers from which it is being used at an ever-increasing, non-sustainable rate.[1] Additionally, each year, more and more water sources are being contaminated by agricultural and industrial pollutants, making them unfit for use.

Historically, rights to water have been held in common by human societies, but recently, government and corporate leaders have begun to treat water as a resource to be bought and sold. At the World Water Forum at The Hague in March 2000, water was defined as a commodity. The rights to the public water supplies and distribution systems of localities in the Global South have been sold to corporations. As their traditional sources of water have become the property of foreign corporations, citizens have suffered from enormous increases in the cost of water, while still relying on the same poorly functioning systems for delivery.

Many believe that water is a right belonging to all people that should never be bought or sold or denied or controlled. People's resentment toward corporate control of water has grown into a global resistance to water commodification. In 2000, the US corporation Bechtel purchased the rights to the public water supply of Cochabamba, Bolivia and immediately raised the price of water so high that it was unafforable to many of the city's residents. Through months of protests and blockades, the citizens of Cochabamba managed to drive out Bechtel and regain control of their water.

The reasons to be concerned about our water supply don't stop with the practices of water-hoarding private corporations. Municipal water systems are prone to failure, environmentally damaging, energy intensive, and at times deliver water of questionable quality. Municipalities often draw water from large reservoirs artificially created by ecologically devastating dams.[2] Rivers that once flowed to the ocean are being sucked dry by desert megalopolises, their waters denied to those living downstream. The Colorado River, for instance, was once a beautiful river that supported abundant wetlands and estuaries on its path to Mexico's Sea of Cortez. Today, it has been dammed in order to supply water to desert farms and for the sprawling populations of Las Vegas and Los Angeles. With 95 percent of its waters being retained in the US, Mexico now receives a virtual trickle. The water that arrives in Mexico is heavily polluted with pesticides and fertilizers from American agricultural runoff.[3] People concerned with environmental sustainability and social equality should deeply question the origin of their water.

In cities in particular water is given little regard. Most people presume that fresh water will always be available with a simple turn of the tap. Few are aware of the complexity of the **hydrological cycle** or the enormous amounts of energy needed to bring water to them. In a future of declining energy resources, it is questionable whether our current water delivery systems will be able to continue functioning. Weather patterns that change as a consequence of global warming will cause some previously rainy climates to become drought prone. It will become increasingly difficult to provide water to cities in these dry locations. Furthermore, disasters can cut off water supplies or make them undrinkable for extended periods of time. Autonomous communities would be wise to have redundant sources for a need as basic as water.

This chapter will explore practical techniques that can be used by communities in any country to ensure their water security without being reliant on poorly functioning water utilities. It details how to collect and store rainwater, low-tech methods for purifying water, and innovative technologies to remediate polluted bodies of water. One section describes the safe reuse of old 55-gallon barrels and gives step-by-step instructions for attaching plumbing to them.

RAINWATER COLLECTION

Since ancient times, people all over the world have been catching rainwater. While it is most commonly done today in arid, water-stressed climates, it makes sense to do it in rainier regions as well. Global warming may shift climate patterns, causing periods of drought in places where rain is currently abundant. Rainwater collection is also an achievable alternative for those wishing to reduce their reliance and demand on municipal water systems.

Many of the contaminants present in surface, ground, or tap water are not likely to be found in rainwater. The process of water evaporating, condensing in the atmosphere, and coming down again as rain is known as the **hydrological cycle**. It is a purification process. When water evaporates, environmental contaminants are often left behind. Additionally, rainwater is free of the contaminants added to municipal water during the disinfection process and those that are leached in from old pipes. Rainwater is among the purest water available.

Rainwater collection is performed by funneling rain that lands on rooftops through gutters into containers called **cisterns**. The water is then stored until it is to be used for gardening, drinking, or other household uses. Most neighborhoods have the potential to collect thousands of gallons of water from their rooftops, providing themselves with a free source of clean water and protecting their water security. As more and more communities around the world have their water supplies privatized, rainwater collection will be an important tactic in ensuring that water remains a free resource, common to all.

A backup water source can become crucial during emergencies when clean water is in short supply. Of all human needs, water is among the most important. No one can survive more than a few

Globally, 69 percent of water used is used for agriculture, 21 percent for industry and 10 percent for domestic purposes. In the United States, however, industry uses the largest proportion.[4]

Abundant in cities, impervious covers like roads and concrete sidewalks prevent rain from infiltrating the soil and recharging **groundwater**, forcing it instead into storm sewers that discharge into rivers that lead to the ocean. Collecting rainwater mitigates the negative effects of impervious covers to some extent. When rain is captured and used over time for things like gardening, it is given time to work its way back into the soil where it can recharge local **aquifers**.

days without it. A rainwater system can complement use of city water—it is important to have a redundancy of critical systems.

SETTING UP A SIMPLE RAINWATER COLLECTION SYSTEM

The simplest and most practical use for rainwater in a city is to water gardens. With minimal cost and skill, a bare-bones system can be constructed using a cistern made from a 55-gallon barrel or garbage can that will provide enough clean water to water a vegetable plot.

LOCATING THE ROOF AND DOWNSPOUT

The first step is to find a building from which to collect the rainwater. Ideally, this building is located near the gardening site. The next step is to determine where the water drains off of the roof.

If the roof is sloped, it is likely that a gutter runs along its edge. The gutter catches the water coming off the roof and funnels it into a metal or plastic pipe, or downspout, that runs vertically down the side of the building. The next time it rains, check the selected downspout to make sure water is actually coming from it. Sometimes in houses with multiple downspouts little to no rainwater goes through a given spout. If there is no gutter on a sloped roof, one needs to be installed. (It is a fairly easy process—consult a home-repair guide for instructions.) Old gutters can be salvaged and reused. Gutters can also be homemade by slicing open tubing lengthwise.

Buildings with flat roofs may have a downspout on the outside or the inside of the building. For the purpose of rainwater collection, it is important that the building drain on its exterior. Interior drainage systems are very difficult to tap into without punching holes in the walls.

Bring the barrel (see below) or garbage can next to the downspout. The existing downspout may discharge water directly onto the ground or underground. Regardless, the downspout should be cut to end at least a foot above the barrel.

MAKING A BASIC RAIN BARREL

How to:

1. If using a 55-gallon barrel with a lid, cut the lid off using a jigsaw or a reciprocating saw. (See Barrels, Bungholes, and Bulkheads, page 80.)
2. Stretch the piece of window screen across the open top of the barrel or garbage can. Tie down the screen around the outside of the barrel with the old bicycle inner tube to hold it in place. The screen keeps out leaves, chunks of debris, mosquitoes, and animals like cats and squirrels that could fall in and drown.
3. Place the barrel under the downspout so the water flows into the barrel. If necessary attach a 45 degree elbow to the end of the downspout. When it rains, the water will go through the screen and fill up the barrel. If the barrel fills up, the water will flow over the top.
4. To get the water, remove the screen and scoop it out with a bucket or watering can.

Supplies needed:

A clean, food-grade 55-gallon barrel (see Barrels, Bungholes, and Bulkheads, page 80) or a large plastic garbage can
3 foot x 3 foot window screen
A used bicycle inner tube

Extra precautions should be taken if the barrel is going to be accessible to young children. It can be fenced in, or a closed-top barrel can be used, with water flowing directly through a 2-inch opening.

ADDING A DELIVERY SYSTEM

The simple design above works for a small garden, but some sort of water delivery method is desirable for anything larger. A hose is the easiest way to get water from one place to another. Putting in a hose requires installing a **bulkhead** on the side of the barrel near its

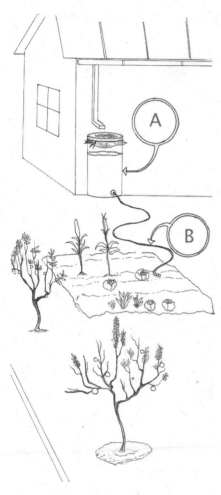

Simple rain barrel: Rain flows off the roof through the gutter and into a barrel (A) with a window screen stretched across the top. From there a hose (B) uses gravity to deliver the water to a nearby garden.

bottom. (See Barrels, Bungholes, and Bulkheads, page 80, for step-by-step instructions.)

If the garden is downhill from the barrel, gravity will move the water, though depending on the slope it may not move fast enough for impatient gardeners and may not be sufficiently pressurized to work with a drip line or soaker hose.

If the water moves too slowly, or not at all, the **head** needs to be increased. Head is the pressure resulting from the height of water. One foot of head is equal to one half PSI, or pounds per square inch. So, if the top of a barrel of water was 6 feet above the end of a hose, the water pressure would be 3 PSI. While not a tremendous amount, 3 PSI is probably enough to slowly water a garden. In comparison, a typical house's water pressure is 40–60 PSI.

To create the maximum amount of head, a rain barrel should be positioned at the highest spot available. If the highest spot is not near a downspout, it is possible to direct water from the spout to the barrel with a flexible pipe like polyethylene tubing or corrugated drain pipe. In some cases, an aqueduct system supported by posts may need to be built.

If no natural rises in elevation are present, a rain barrel can be put on top of a sturdy stack of concrete blocks to increase its head. Tripods that hold a barrel 10 to 15 feet off the ground can be purchased from sporting goods stores. (They are meant to hold deer feed.) Positioning a barrel on a balcony or fire escape will create even more pressure. Water weighs approximately 8 pounds per gallon, so a full 55-gallon barrel weighs about 440 pounds. Make sure that any structure supporting a rain barrel is strong enough.

Another way to use gravity to pressurize water is to pump it to a raised barrel. This technique is most commonly used when water is collected and stored on the ground in a container much larger than a 55-gallon barrel. (See Expanded Water Storage Capacity, page 68.) Water is pumped from the big tank to a smaller barrel that is located on a tripod, tower structure, or reinforced roof.

There are multiple advantages to this method: The barrel can be located higher than the downspout and doesn't need a rigid aqueduct built to it. Instead, a hose can easily run from the pump to the barrel. The pressure of the pre-pumped water in the barrel is stored as potential energy, ready to be used. Rather than running constantly, the pump only needs to be activated to refill the barrel. This is especially handy when using solar- or human-powered pumps, whose energy is not always available. Only as much water as may be needed has to be pumped at a time, so the raised container can be as small as 55 gallons.

EXPANDED WATER STORAGE CAPACITY

It is possible to use rainwater for more than watering a small garden. Rainwater collection can meet the water needs of households or entire urban farms. For these purposes, more than 55 gallons of storage capacity will be needed. The simple rain barrel method described above can be expanded by plumbing together a series of 55-gallon barrels. Laid on their sides, the barrels are connected through their 2-inch openings with standard piping. Barrels can also be stacked in a pyramid formation and strapped together with braided cable or cargo tie-down straps, or put into a "wine rack" structure.

Larger operations may require a larger storage capacity than can be practically provided by barrels. Water storage vessels come in a range of sizes and are made from a variety of materials. They can be purchased or constructed. Size requirements and available funds will determine what style is appropriate.

POLYETHYLENE

Available in sizes ranging from 55 to 5,000 gallons, polyethylene tanks are most commonly used by ranchers for storing water for their livestock. They are also used by a number of businesses for

55-gallon barrels in "wine rack" structure

55-gallon barrels stacked into a pyramid (plumbing not yet installed)

general liquid storage. The tanks are lightweight (can be moved by one or two people), durable, and convenient for storage of large volumes of water. Typically they are cylindrical, although now flat, upright tanks designed to be placed against a wall and take up minimal space are being made specifically for urban environments. They can be bought from feed stores or specialty suppliers and often can be delivered. Polyethylene tanks are not exactly cheap.

The tanks are often black or dark green. Being opaque prevents sunlight from hitting the water and causing algae to bloom, which can cause a bad taste or be harmful. Polyethylene is considerably less toxic than chlorinated plastics, like PVC. It does not produce dioxin if burned.

Like most plastics, polyethylene will degrade when it is exposed to UV light for prolonged periods. It is best to locate the tank in the shade.

FERROCEMENT

Ferrocement tanks are made by applying concrete across a lattice and reinforcing it with iron rods ("ferro" means iron). Built on site, ferrocement tanks are ideal for water collection systems over 5,000 gallons where labor is more abundant than money. As they contain enormous amounts of water pressure, they must be built properly, preferably by someone who has experience in their construction. It is best to experiment with building a small version first before attempting to undertake a large one. Once a ferrocement cistern has been built, it is a permanent fixture on a site. For this reason, it is not recommended for non–property owners.

OTHER SYSTEMS

Galvanized metal and fiberglass cisterns also can be bought. While not as lightweight as a polyethylene tank, they are portable when empty.

In traditional societies, mortared stone cisterns and giant ceramic vessels are used for water storage. Building either requires highly specialized expertise.

Rainwater used only for gardening can also be stored in a pond. Pond water is unsuitable for drinking because it is too difficult to keep out contaminants. (See Aquaculture, page 21, for pond construction information.)

SIZING A CISTERN

The size of a cistern depends on how often it rains and how much water is needed. For instance, if a system is designed for occasionally watering a garden in a climate with frequent rainfall, a 55-gallon barrel may be adequate. Regular rain will likely refill the barrel before it is emptied. The barrel would probably overflow during a heavy rain, but it is not necessary to collect every drop because it rains frequently.

On the other hand, a system that is meant to provide a community in a drought-prone climate with all of its water needs will need a much larger storage capacity. It will have to collect and store all the rain that falls during the wet season to make it through the dry period.

The size of a system that is needed in any climate can be calculated using the raincatch potential formula below, annual rainfall data available through agricultural extensions and weather mapping services, and the amount of water that is needed.

RAINCATCH POTENTIAL

To determine the amount of rain that a roof is capable of catching, first find its surface area. (This is what the roof looks like staring straight down at it. Ignore the pitch or angles of the roof—the same amount of water falls on a roof regardless of how steep it is.) The surface area of a roof is equal to the length times the width.

Calculating Raincatch Potential

1. Surface area = length x width
Ex.: 200 sq. feet = 20 feet x 10 feet

2. Raincatch potential per inch of rain = 0.6 gallons x surface area
Ex.: 120 gallons per inch of rain = 0.6 gallons x 200 sq. feet

3. Annual raincatch potential = raincatch potential per inch of rain x annual rainfall
Ex.: 3,000 gallons = 120 gallons per inch of rainfall x 25 inches

The raincatch potential per inch of rain is 0.6 gallons times the surface area (measured in square feet). For example, if a roof is 10 feet wide and 20 feet long, the surface area is 200 sq. feet. As 200 times 0.6 is 120, for each inch of rain that falls, 120 gallons of water could be collected off that roof. If the average annual rainfall is 25 inches per year, then the average collection would be 3,000 gallons per year, because 25 times 120 equals 3,000.

OTHER CONSIDERATIONS

FOUL FLUSH/ROOF WASHER

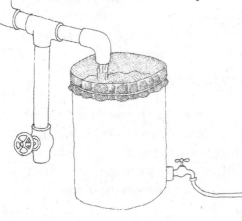

While it is generally safe to collect rainwater in cities, particulate matter in the air could be a concern in highly industrialized areas with lots of smokestacks. Typically, the highest levels of fallout are in the immediate vicinity of the source. In these locations, foul flush systems are important if the water is to be used for drinking. The basic idea is that heavy particulate matter is likely to fall from the sky in the first 20 minutes of rainfall. The foul flush tube is designed to fill up with the water that falls during the first 20 minutes, and then allow clean water to pass over it and go into the cistern. To install a foul flush system, a horizontal run of piping is made from the end of the downspout to the rain barrel. A length of

Codes and Zoning

Some of the biggest obstacles to building an autonomous design in a city are the highly stringent building and zoning codes that regulate development. In most cases, building and zoning codes are well intended. They were originally created to prevent landowners from constructing unsafe, unhealthy, or substandard buildings, and in many cases are the result of previous justice movements. Sadly, these codes were typically only enforced in the wealthy, white parts of towns or used to protect perceived property values and limit autonomous actions. Today's restrictive building codes serve a bureaucratic system that fears liability and supports the construction industry.

It is easy to see the appeal of retreating to less regulated areas of the country like the rural South. However, there is hope of challenging certain codes in cities and the option of ignoring others.

Codes do give guidance as to what is safe or has proven safe in the past. Overloaded electric systems do cause houses to burn down so being code compliant reduces that risk. What is important to remember is that there are other ways to build safe projects. In fact, if it is not safe it is not sustainable. If a rooftop solar collector falls through the roof it's going to be even harder to keep the house warm. Construct projects "to code" even if such codes don't yet exist.

When working with code inspectors remember that this is new technology. Many inspectors are unaware of or skeptical about the need for more sustainable design options in cities. Educating city officials about these concepts is a needed form of activism. Due to the persistence of a few dedicated people, some cities are now accepting ideas like natural construction and biological wastewater treatment.

Unfortunately, codes seldom permit the more innovative aspects of sustainable design. Composting toilets, graywater systems, straw-bale houses, chickens, and urban cohousing may have to be fought for at city hall. This frustrating process can take years.

In some cases, alternative systems are allowable with approval from a professional engineer. Finding a sympathetic engineer willing to approve

vertical tubing is then "teed" into the horizontal pipe (see figure), and has a removable cap or valve placed on its end. This serves as the foul flush tube. Following each rainfall the tube is opened, the dirty water is emptied, and the tube is closed again. The size of the foul flush tube is based on the size of the roof and the average intensity of rainfall in the region. A 4-inch diameter tube that is 4 to 6 feet in length should be sufficient for roofs around 1,000 square feet. Because the intensity of rainfall is highly variable, these dimensions are an approximation.

If rain is only being harvested to water gardens, a foul flush to avoid contaminants is not terribly necessary. The contaminants that would be removed by a foul flusher are insignificant compared to the amounts that end up in a garden whenever it rains.

Foul flush systems also work as roof washers. As it is best to keep organic debris out of a water container, any leafy debris or bird droppings that were on the roof will also wash off in the first twenty minutes of rain.

TYPES OF ROOFING MATERIALS

The best roofing materials to collect water from are slate and ceramic tile. These natural materials do not leach harmful substances. Unfortunately, few buildings are roofed with them, and installing them would be prohibitively expensive for most. Tin roofing is the next best option. It is relatively cheap and easy to install. It may leach some zinc into the water, but this is likely not harmful to humans. Asphalt shingles and flat tar roofs are the least preferable roofing materials, as they leach harmful chemicals into water. A foul flush system is particularly useful with asphalt and tar roofs. During the day, the hot sun brings the toxic tars to the surface of the shingle or roof roll. The first few minutes of rain washes off these chemicals into a foul flush system. The rain that hits the roof after this rinse is not likely to be contaminated as it spends little time in contact with the tar or asphalt surface.

USING RAINWATER IN THE HOME

It is a big jump to go from using rainwater in the garden to using it for washing and drinking. Going "off the water grid" is a challenge, mostly because it requires a very large water storage capacity and way of pressurizing the water. Clever and resourceful people can design a home-use system that relies only on gravity-fed systems similar to those described above, but in most cases the installation of a high-pressure pump and compression tank will be needed. Considerable pressure is needed for activities like showering and clothes washing on multi-storied buildings. This requires a very good knowledge of plumbing systems and should not be undertaken without thorough planning.

DRINKING RAINWATER

Around the world, an estimated 2 to 5 million people die each year from diseases related to dirty water.[5] Rainwater is among the purest types of water available. The primary concern with drinking rainwater is not the quality of the water itself, but what can happen after it is collected.

Pathogenic organisms can find their way into stored water through fecal contamination, either from animals or unwashed human hands. Animals that get into the tank and drown are another source of pathogens. Unlike a pond, a rain tank does not have a fully developed microbial ecosystem. If something dies in it, harmful bacteria will proliferate without competition. The best defense against contamination is to ensure that all openings into the tank are securely screened off. It is also wise to use a foul-flush system and to filter any rainwater before drinking it, and perhaps before using it to wash dishes and shower as well. (See Water Purification, page 75.)

WINTER

Wintertime can pose serious challenges to rainwater collection. In cold climates, an outdoor rain barrel will freeze solid. This

experimental designs can be difficult. It can also be extremely expensive.

Once a precedent has been set in one place, however, the way is paved for replication elsewhere. Only when alternative technologies have been tested and accepted by municipalities will they have any hope of being implemented on a scale large enough to have a significant impact on the environment.

At Rhizome, we wanted to publicly display a composting toilet. We feel it is very important for people to know that human-waste recycling is an option and want to be "out" about it. Our talk about closed-loop cycles meant little while we flushed away our nutrient-rich humanure. Knowing that "fecophobia" runs deep, particularly among public health officials in densely populated areas, we figured that putting an unpermitted composting toilet on display in a high-profile space would be a grand mistake. The health department would likely shut us down before our first 5-gallon poop-bucket could be filled. Instead, we researched the laws on composting toilets.

We were surprised to find that composting toilets were permitted in Austin, provided they met simple National Sanitation Foundation standards. It was only after drafting up detailed plans and submitting them for approval that we learned of the legal obstacle which apparently forbade them. If your building is within 100 feet of an existing sewer line, you must connect all toilets to it. Even though there was no problem with the professionally engineered composting toilet itself, our application was denied because of this seemingly illogical provision. It didn't matter that we already had three working flush toilets and intended the composter to be an auxiliary system. Frustration prevailed.

Then, in 2004, we acquired a 10-acre brownfield, which presented a new opportunity. This unusual piece of urban real estate is more than 100 feet from a sewer line, so the legal obstacle did not apply. We applied a second time for a legally approved composting toilet. After several years of uphill bureaucratic battle against state and city officials, the permit was finally granted! We will now have the chance to demonstrate composting toilets' safety and usefulness, gaining leverage to confront the prohibitive legal obstacles that prevent others from

shouldn't be a problem if the water is only for gardening, as growing generally only happens when temperatures are above freezing, but it creates an obvious problem for other uses.

There are ways to prevent tanks from freezing. A rain barrel can be buried in the ground beneath the frostline, where it should remain mostly liquid. Also, a rain barrel can be put inside a bioshelter or cold frame, which should help moderate the temperatures of both the bioshelter and the rain barrel. (See Bioshelters, page 50.)

If a barrel with a sealed top is kept outside during freezing temperatures, it should be partially drained to keep its frozen contents from expanding and cracking the barrel.

LEGAL ISSUES

Rainwater collection is legal in most places. Some progressive municipalities in dry regions, like Austin, Texas, offer rebates for installing raincatch systems. Other states, however, such as Colorado, New Mexico, and California, have laws that technically forbid rainwater harvesting. These governments believe that whatever rain falls in their states belongs to them and that it is illegal for a citizen to divert it. There is no instance known to the authors, however, where a resident of these states has been prosecuted for collecting rainwater.

The stakes are higher for citizens of nations where water privatization struggles loom. In Cochabamba, Bolivia, people's right to use rain collection systems were actually taken away when the regions water rights were purchased by the US corporation Bechtel.

WATER PURIFICATION

Each year, millions of people around the world die or become sick from drinking water contaminated by pathogens or chemicals. Sadly, many of the deaths and illnesses caused by contaminated water could have been prevented by simple technologies.

People wishing to live "off the water grid" will need to purify their water before drinking. In an emergency, municipal water systems can be cut off or become contaminated. Contaminants may even be present in rain or municipal water in the Global North. As it is important for urban communities to have the ability to purify their drinking water, this section gives a brief overview of drinking water contamination and discusses a few low-tech methods of water purification.

CONTAMINATION

Contaminants that are present in water can be categorized as biological or chemical. Turbidity is often a problem as well.

TURBIDITY

Turbidity is the measure of suspended solids in water. Dirt, loam, sand, clay, algae, leaf mold, and other organic matter all make water turbid. Turbidity can affect water's taste and texture. Suspended particles also serve as hiding places, enabling bacteria and other pathogens to evade purification processes. Turbid water should be filtered before being put through the purification methods described below. This is especially true in the case of ultraviolet (UV) disinfection, as UV rays cannot penetrate through particles. To filter turbid water, pour it though a tightly woven clean cloth, like a T-shirt, sock, or coffee filter, over and over until it appears clean. A sand filter can also be used. (See Slow Sand Filters, page 80.)

CHEMICAL

Whether pesticides from agricultural runoff, metals leaching in from pipes, or intentionally added chemicals, numerous toxic materials often show up in municipal tap water. Because they exist on a molecular, rather than cellular scale, chemical contaminants are much smaller than biological contaminants. They also differ

doing the same. We look forward to the day when we will all be free to not poop in clean water.

═══════════════════════

The amount of work that goes into challenging codes and the relatively low success rate of these challenges is certainly discouraging. A clandestine approach can keep sustainable systems under the radar. Neighbors are a large factor to success. Code enforcers are not likely to ever know about certain things unless someone complains. Planting fruit trees and beautiful gardens on the street can be a great way to win people over. It may also help them overlook the fact that bathtub wastewater makes the gardens so lush. A few hens in the backyard may be ignored if fresh eggs are shared with the people next door.

from biological contaminants in that they are not living organisms. Instead of being simply killed, they must be removed or chemically bound up to be rendered inactive. This makes chemically contaminated water much harder to purify than biologically contaminated water. Removal of chemicals requires commercially manufactured filters or specifically engineered biological systems.

Contamination of collected rainwater can be reduced using foul flush systems.

Lead contamination from pipes is a particular concern in older cities. There are a few precautions that can be taken to minimize exposure. The longer water is in contact with a pipe, the more time it has to absorb lead. Before collecting water for drinking or cooking, open the tap to let water that has been sitting in the pipes run down the drain. Some people let the water run every morning and when returning home from a vacation. Also, lead is more soluble in hot water. Never fill a cooking pot from the hot tap.

Chlorine is added to most municipal water supplies. A powerful disinfectant, it kills most microbiological life it comes into contact with. Soil watered with chlorinated water is also rendered sterile and lifeless. Microbes like bacteria, nematodes, and actinomytes enable plants to use nutrients in the ground. Killing these organisms limits the growth potential of plants.

While the use of chlorine has prevented the spread of many diseases, evidence of its negative health effects is mounting. Chlorine mixes with the organic matter found in all water to form dangerous by-products, including chloroform, a carcinogenic gas.

A container of water can be dechlorinated if it is left sitting uncovered for a 24-hour period, during which time the chlorine will volatilize and escape into the air.

Fluoride is also intentionally added to public drinking water supplies to strengthen teeth. However, the actual health benefits of this industrial by-product from phosphate fertilizer factories are hotly debated, with studies to back up both sides. On behalf of the

Environmental Protection Agency, the National Research Council recently analyzed the research on fluoride. Their report recommended that the EPA lower the acceptable limit of fluoride in water and highlighted numerous areas where possible adverse health effects warranted future studies.[6] The American Dental Association, one of the strongest advocates of fluoridation of public drinking water, recently warned that infant formula should not be made with fluoridated water.[7] The Fluoride Action Network maintains a list of communities that have forgone fluoridation.[8]

Other chemical contaminants that find their way into tap water include pesticides, arsenic, and the fuel additive MTBE (methyl tert-butyl ether).

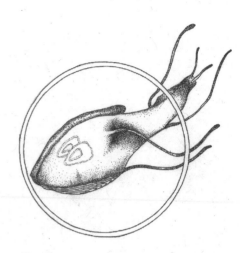

Giardia

BIOLOGICAL

Biological contaminants are living organisms: bacteria, protozoa, and helminthes. While there is argument over whether viruses are actually "alive," they are also included in this category. Major routes of biological contamination of drinking water include human and animal feces and flood waters.

Bacteria are ubiquitous single-celled organisms that coexist with humans. (See Bacterial Remediation, page 184.) However, certain bacteria are human pathogens. Cholera and typhoid are waterborne diseases caused by bacteria, and fecal coliforms are a broad range of bacteria that can colonize water and cause illness. While also single celled, protozoa are typically much larger than bacteria. Amoebas, giardia, and cryptosporidium are all common waterborne protozoa that cause diarrhea, vomiting, and dysentery. Helminthes are worms. Parasitic helminthes that can be transmitted by water include Guinea worms and blood flukes. Viruses are the smallest biological contaminant, consisting of DNA or RNA and a protein coat. Hepatitis and polio are viruses that can be transmitted by dirty water.

The methods discussed below are designed to treat water for biological pathogens.

PURIFICATION METHODS

There are many methods for treating water. Some are cheap and simple, and others are expensive, energy intensive, and rely on toxic chemicals. This section profiles several low-input methods to remove biological pathogens from water that can be built with salvaged materials.

BOILING

Boiling is a quick and easy way to purify water. A vigorous, rolling boil maintained for ten minutes is more than sufficient to destroy the pathogens most typically present in water. It may take longer to kill some viruses and **bacterial endospores**, which is why hospitals sterilize equipment using hot steam at high pressures.[9]

SOLAR ULTRAVIOLET DISINFECTION

Solar disinfection uses ultraviolet light from the sun to purify water. UV light is a type of energy with a wavelength just shorter than blue visible light. Primarily produced by the sun, it can also be made by machines. Solar disinfection is effective at killing biological pathogens, including those that cause cholera, typhoid, giardia, and polio.[10] It will not remove any chemicals.

Solar disinfectors can be made entirely from recycled bottles and require no energy source other than the sun, making them particularly useful in regions where boiling water is hindered by a shortage of cooking fuel. Solar disinfectors are racks that hold glass bottles on a sheet of corrugated metal. Six hours of bright sun will disinfect the water in the bottles. On cloudy days, two consecutive days of exposure may be necessary. The water placed in a solar disinfector must be relatively clear. Cloudy water must be filtered through a cloth or sand filter. While the UV rays are the primary disinfecting agent, heat is also a factor. Water that is kept at 122 degrees Fahrenheit only requires one hour of UV exposure to be free of

Solar disinfector

most pathogens. Painting the metal or the back side of the bottles black will help heat the water.

It is possible to purchase electric UV filters that reliably destroy biological contaminants in drinking water. Water is disinfected as it passes through a chamber lit by a special UV bulb. Electric UV filters operate on the same principles as solar disinfectors, but are fairly expensive, require electricity, and rely on bulbs with a limited lifespan. Their advantage over solar disinfection is the ability to quickly purify water at any time of day.

SLOW SAND FILTERS

Slow sand filters are containers filled with fine sand that filter out particles and pathogens from drinking water. Sand filters operate passively, using gravity for pressure and biological processes to filter out contaminants. The top few inches of a sand filter is a gelatinous **biofilm**, called the schmutzdecke. It provides a habitat for beneficial bacteria, algae, protozoa, fungi, and larger microorganisms. The organisms in the biofilm trap organic materials and harmful organisms.

Large-scale sand filtration systems are employed by some municipalities in the United States for drinking water purification. It is possible to build a low-tech sand filter out of salvaged materials. Slow sand filters must be in nearly constant operation in order to maintain the biofilm, which needs a small, continuous flow of water. This is a disadvantage, of course, if they are intended only for periodic use.

BARRELS, BUNGHOLES, AND BULKHEADS

Metal and plastic barrels are extraordinarily handy when building sustainable systems. They can be used for constructed wetland cells, composting toilets, aquaculture tanks, raincatching systems, and more. While relatively cheap and easy to find in cities, not all barrels are safe to use.

SAFETY ISSUES

Make sure the barrels in a system are considered "food grade," meaning that all they ever stored were food products or non-toxic materials. Never use a barrel from the dump; one found buried, hidden, or abandoned; or one whose previous contents are unknown. Found barrels could have contained anything: gasoline, harmful solvents, or worse. Barrels are often dumped because the toxic materials inside are considered too expensive to dispose of correctly. Both plastic and metal barrels are capable of holding onto residual amounts of the chemicals that were stored in them. Even after repeated washings, the safety of non–food grade containers cannot be guaranteed.

Typically, the original contents of a barrel are printed on its exterior, along with a hazardous materials label describing the hazards of the material inside. Food grade barrels are commonly used to store cooking oils, tomatoes, jalapeños, flavoring extracts, and soda syrups. Other products stored in barrels that can be considered safe include hydrogen peroxide and mineral oil (baby oil).

Never cut into or blow a hole into a barrel with a cutting torch, grinder, or saw without first being certain of its contents. Tiny amounts of combustible materials on the interior can ignite and use the oxygen inside the barrel to explode like a bomb. To be safe, before cutting into a barrel, fill it with water to displace any oxygen.

FINDING BARRELS

Barrel distributors and chemical supply companies are the easiest places to find barrels. Prices vary, but are usually within the $10 to $20 range. Add a few dollars for a resealable lid. Food extract producers, bakeries, and brewing supply stores sometimes give barrels away.

BARREL TYPES

While 55-gallon drums are the most common, barrels can be found in a variety of sizes.

Barrels come in two main materials: plastic and metal. Plastic barrels are lighter weight and less expensive. They also do not rust. If metal barrels are to be used for storing water, they must be lined. Linings consist of a golden or brown thin plastic coating on the barrel's interior. Metal primer can also be used to rustproof the interior of barrels. If the lining is cut or broken, it will rust through over time. Welding the barrel will cause the lining to melt.

Barrel lids are often sealed shut. There are barrels with resealable lids, that come with removable tops with a locking exterior rim. While a resealable barrel usually costs more, it is very useful if access to the interior of the barrel is needed. Accessing the inside of a barrel without a resealable lid requires it to be cut open with a jigsaw or reciprocating saw.

To cut open a barrel, first locate the reinforced, raised rim around the circumference of the top of the barrel. Make sure the cut is made from the top of the barrel, inside of this rim. Cutting outside the rim will ruin the barrel's structural integrity.

BUNGHOLES

The holes on the lid of a barrel are called bungholes. Typically, one of the bungholes has standard 2-inch pipe thread and the other is coarse-threaded. Coarse-threaded bungholes require special adapters to fit a standard size pipe. Bunghole caps are called bungcaps. In the center of each bungcap there is a ¾-inch threaded "female" attachment. A hole can be drilled into this attachment, and a garden faucet or plumbing piece can be screwed into it. This makes it easy to get fluids out of the barrel when it is laid on its side. While special bung wrenches are made, any pair of pliers can be used to open the caps.

Bulkhead (apart and together)

Fine and coarse threaded bungcaps

BULKHEADS

A bulkhead is a threaded, plastic plumbing part that makes a seal against the side of the barrel. It allows plumbing pieces, like a faucet or threaded pipe, to be screwed into the barrel at places other than the bungholes while preventing water from leaking out. A bulkhead is necessary because plumbing that is threaded directly into a barrel without a reliable seal will inevitably leak.

The thread size of the bulkhead will determine what size plumbing can be attached. Threaded plumbing parts, whether they are plastic, galvanized metal, or copper, generally have standard thread sizes that can be made larger or smaller by using adapter pieces commonly found at hardware stores.

Bulkheads are specialty parts that cannot be bought from a standard hardware store. They can be found sometimes at agricultural supply stores or ordered online. A bulkhead typically consists of four parts: a flanged threaded stem, a washer, and two rubber gaskets.

INSTALLING A BULKHEAD ON A BARREL

Supplies needed:

One bulkhead with an interior thread size to match the plumbing part to be attached
A hole saw and drill, or a sharp blade
Desired plumbing

How to:

1. Unscrew the bulkhead, place the threaded stem against the outside of the barrel, and trace around it.
2. Cut out the traced hole with a blade or hole saw. It should be just large enough to slide the threaded stem through, but the stem should not be loose when inserted.
3. Place one of the rubber gaskets on the threaded stem, and push it through the hole so that the wide, flanged end of the stem and the gasket are against the *inside* of the barrel.
4. Slide the second gasket over the stem on the outside of the barrel, and then screw the washer onto the stem. Tighten it down against the gasket and the outside of the barrel. Do not overtighten, as this can cause the gasket to buckle and will make the barrel leak.

5. Screw the desired plumbing (pipe or faucet) into the threaded opening.

FLOATING TRASH ISLANDS

Floating islands occur in nature when part of a lake's bank breaks away from the shore and floats around, sometimes for years. The islands act as the lake's liver, purifying its waters. The roots of plants hold the island together and dangle down into the lake's waters, creating a habitat for bacteria, algae, zooplankton, and other critters. These organisms, as well as the plants themselves, play a role in the uptake of nutrients and degradation of toxins in the water.

Artificial floating islands can be used to clean urban bodies of water. Any polluted canal, river, estuary, lake in a city park, or storm water retention pond would benefit from a floating island.

Storm water runoff has a large negative impact on urban water quality. Before rushing into storm drains, the rain washes across parking lots, roadways, and people's backyards, picking up a load of pollutants and debris. This toxic mixture contains motor oil, gasoline, plastic bottles, floating trash, dog poop, lawn fertilizer, and pesticides. Storm water runoff is difficult to control. Unlike a single heavy polluter, such as a factory, known as a "point source polluter" because its pollution comes from a single "point" which can be treated and regulated, the toxins and debris picked up by storm water runoff originate from multiple sources which are harder to track down. Storm water is referred to as "non–point source pollution." During heavy rains, storm sewers can be overwhelmed and overflow into water bodies. The combined effects of pollution and choking debris threaten the aquatic life in these ecosystems.

Floating trash islands are one strategy to remediate pollution in any body of water affected by storm water runoff. Building one

involves binding together buoyant debris often found along the banks of polluted bodies of water, chiefly capped plastic bottles and Styrofoam chunks. (Which also serves to reuse this trash.) Water plants are then strapped onto the floating media and allowed to develop their root systems. Most water plants do not need to be rooted in soil in order to thrive, and some even do better with their roots freely suspended in water.

BUILDING A FLOATING ISLAND

How to:

1. Roll the plastic fencing into a tube with a diameter of at least a foot. Zip tie it closed along the side and one end, leaving the other end open. The length of the tube will be equal to the circumference of the island. Islands with a diameter of 5 to 10 feet and circumference of roughly 16 to 31 feet work well. (Circumference = diameter x 3.14)
2. Stuff plastic bottles or Styrofoam into the open end of the tube, filling it. Pack them in snugly, while still allowing the tube to be bent. Make sure the bottles are tightly capped, otherwise they could fill with water and cause the island to sink.
3. Bend the tube into a ring and zip tie the ends together, sealing the tube and completing the circle.
4. Stretch plastic fencing across the center of the ring and zip tie it in place.
5. If water plants are in containers, remove them and wash off any gravel. Gently place the plants upright on the fencing in the island's center, touching the inside edge of the bottle-stuffed ring. Work the roots through the holes in the fencing so they will dangle into the water. Zip tie larger roots to the plastic fencing. If possible, try to work the leaves or stems of the plants through the sides of the ring to help to keep them upright. The plants should cover the surface of the island without choking each other out. A combination of plants can be used to encourage diversity. Take care not to introduce an invasive species to an area.

Supplies needed:

Lots of floating plastic bottles or Styrofoam
A roll of plastic construction fencing
Zip ties
Water plants. Irises, bulrush, pickerel rush, arrowhead, duckweed, and watercress are good choices, but just about any water plant will work.
Anchor and rope; or mooring

6. Choose a location. Ideally, the island should be put in full sun.

7. Choose an anchoring system. The island must be secured so that it doesn't float away or drift into a shady area. It can either be anchored to the bottom or placed on a mooring that keeps it in the same location. An anchor can be as simple as a rope tied to a gallon jug filled with concrete. A mooring can be constructed from a metal pole stuck through the floating island and mounted on a concrete base sitting at the water's bottom. A kiddie pool or similar shaped container can be used as a mold to make the base. Stand the pole upright in the center of the mold and fill the mold with several inches of concrete. Once the concrete has set, the pole should be locked into the base and the mold can be popped off. The wide bottom of the base will keep the pole from falling over.

8. Once a location and an anchoring system have been chosen, position the island by boat or on foot, wearing waders.

As the island matures, the plants will grow throughout the plastic fencing. Their dead leaves and stalks will add to the island's mass. Eventually, the shade produced by the plants will protect the bottles from degrading in the sun. Soon after it has been launched, giant sheets of algae will begin to form off the bottom of the island, aiding in water purification. If the body of water is healthy enough to support fish, minnows will take shelter in the roots of the island. Water birds may even nest in it.

Floating islands can still be used in ponds that are dry for part of the year. To do so, install a mooring system in a plastic stock tank greater in diameter than the island. When the water level drops, the island slides down the mooring and comes to rest inside the water-filled stock tank. The tank may need to be manually filled depending on the length and intensity of the dry season. As the water in the pond returns, the island rises with the water level. This method provides a reservoir for many types of life in the pond. Fish, frogs, and birds would leave or perish without it.

Solar-powered air pumps can be attached to islands to remediate eutrophied bodies of water. When a body of water has an excess of nutrients, typically from fertilizer run-off or sewage, algae feed off these nutrients and explode in population. After the nutrients are used up, the algae die and are eaten by bacteria. The growing bacteria populations deplete the oxygen in the water, frequently resulting in fish die-offs. This process is known as **eutrophication**. It can be mitigated or reversed by increasing the amount of oxygen in the water. This can be done by mechanically aerating the water with an air pump. The pump is placed on the island. **Airstone** diffusers are connected to the pump with rubber hosing and submerged as deep as possible directly beneath the island.

A floating island's impact on overall water quality depends on the maturity of the island and its size relative to the water. With enough floating islands, it could be possible to restore vitality to an urban aquatic ecosystem.

PUTTING IT ALL TOGETHER

Of all human needs, water is the most essential for life. Frequently taken for granted, in most cities it simply comes out of a faucet and goes down the drain. Rarely is water's complex cycle considered. An awareness and appreciation of this critical resource can be cultivated by localizing the processes of collecting water, purifying it, and returning it to the ground.

Community water security can be developed by collecting the rain that falls off most buildings and storing it for gardening or for emergency purposes. Rainwater collection is a fundamentally important tactic that communities can use to ensure their well-being and survival. It is a low-cost, low-tech method of making sure that water, a historically free resource, remains available to everyone. If purification systems are built now, they will be in place for when they are needed.

Urban water consciousness goes beyond immediate survival needs, however. The hard work of remediating the poisoned waters that flow through our cities needs to begin. The overall health of human and non-human urban life, and surrounding ecosystems, depends upon it.

Floating trash island at Rhizome brownfield

WASTE

Today's cities consume massive amounts of resources and export large volumes of waste. Cities produce a gigantic effluent of trash, wastewater, and sewage, little of which is managed within their borders. This waste is often brought to surrounding rural or wild areas and dumped in landfills, incinerated in hazardous waste facilities, or discharged into waterways. These practices result in a poisoned environment and broad-scale health problems.

"Waste" is a phenomenon unique to modern society. Previously in history, anything discarded was made use of again by someone or something else. As there were no synthetic materials, refuse was either eaten or it decomposed, leaving behind only bones and ceramic shards. Even into the 20th century, people were able to make a living traveling and collecting scraps of string, fabric, and tin for reprocessing.

Over the past 100 years or so, however, cheap and abundant energy has allowed humans to extract and transform enormous amounts of raw materials into manufactured products. The past century's grossly unbalanced cycles of production, consumption, and disposal transformed the word *waste* into a verb, and with that have come huge problems.

The multitudes of bacteria, fungi, and other decomposers cannot process many of the plastics and synthetic materials produced today. Excess amounts of organic wastes have also overwhelmed nature's capacity to absorb them. What formerly were nutrients have become pollutants. This overproduction has resulted in mountains of trash.

Within this waste stream are unutilized resources—waste products. The volumes of water, organic matter, and potentially reusable materials being buried, incinerated, or flushed out to sea could be used to create sustainable infrastructure in cities.

It is the responsibility of a community to deal with its waste products within its boundaries. Energy-intensive municipal waste-treatment systems may no longer be able to function as cheap energy disappears. Other forms of community waste management will be necessary to prevent widespread disease and pestilence.

Part of sustainable waste management is an awareness of and commitment to environmental justice. Since waste processing has been centralized, there has been a tendency to locate noxious treatment centers in low-income neighborhoods or in communities of color. The resulting soil, air, and water pollution is to blame for the disproportionate amounts of environmentally linked diseases like asthma and cancer in these communities. The task of waste treatment needs to be shared equitably among all residents.

This chapter addresses water and solid waste:

Vast quantities of relatively clean water from households flow into sewers where it mixes with the more hazardous by-products of households and industry. Municipalities spend huge sums of money and energy to pump and treat this wastewater. The section on wastewater describes how this water can be diverted from the sewers, cleansed, and reused for garden irrigation.

Food wastes, wood chips, leaves, brush, and manure are commonly combined with trash and landfilled, instead they can be composted into nutrient-rich soil on a community scale. Energy production and livestock feeds are other potential uses for salvaged organic material. The sections on composting and human wastes detail the composting process.

WASTEWATER RECYCLING

WHY REUSE WASTEWATER?

Apart from some dirt, soap, toothpaste, food particles and a few fecal pathogens, the wastewater from cooking and washing is basically clean. With some filtration, this water can be used for irrigation of crops and be allowed to re-enter the water table. Reuse of wastewater can lessen a community's consumption of water and improve its soil's fertility. Diverting wastewater from the sewer system also reduces pollution and saves energy.

Instead of being treated in its relatively clean state, wastewater typically drains into a sewer where it is mixed with sewage, pharmaceuticals, industrial effluents, and whatever chemicals people pour down the drain or flush. This noxious blend is then pumped to a central location and treated using an energy-intensive, and sometimes chemical-intensive, process. The treated water, which varies in quality, is then commonly discharged into waterways, where it has the potential to cause great environmental harm.

Some cities do not have separate storm water and sewer systems. When rains overwhelm the combined system, it can result in raw sewage spilling over into streets and bodies of water, creating serious health and environmental hazards. In places without wastewater treatment systems, wastewater is mixed with raw sewage and commonly discharged, untreated, into oceans, canals, and rivers.

Wastewater recycling combined with a human waste composting system is an environmentally benign alternative to sewers. In contrast to the enormous amounts of energy needed to pump and treat wastewater, ecological sanitation is a low-energy option. As energy prices increase in the future, it may become necessary for communities to process their own wastewater on a home or neighborhood scale.

Water is a precious resource. Ideally, water is made use of several times before it is finally discharged. For instance, water collected off of rooftops can be used to wash clothes. Next it can be filtered and used for watering plants, from there it can go back into the soil to recharge local aquifers. By reusing wastewater for irrigation, a community's overall consumption of water can be greatly reduced. This is particularly important in dry climates, where water conservation is critical.

Discharging filtered wastewater into gardens helps to build soil health. High moisture content in soils promotes the microbial activity that builds new soil and makes nutrients available to plants.

Household reuse of wastewater also promotes awareness about what is put down the drain. People are far less likely to pour paint or bleach down the drain if it leads directly to their vegetable gardens where the consequences are immediately noticeable.

WASTEWATER BASICS

Household wastewater is classified into two categories, depending on the amount of fecal coliforms and organic matter it contains.

> **Graywater:** Water draining from the shower, bathroom sink, washing machine, dishwasher, or kitchen sink.
> **Blackwater:** Water flushed down the toilet.

These definitions can vary based on local codes. In some states, water from the kitchen sink is considered blackwater because of its high organic matter content. Water used for washing baby diapers is also considered blackwater.

Graywater can be reused and purified far more easily than blackwater. While it is possible to purify blackwater for reuse, the process is far more intensive. Autonomous communities are encouraged to avoid creating blackwater in the first place and instead to develop dry fecal composting systems. (See Recycling Human

Wastes, page 121.) The information in this section applies only to filtering graywater.

While graywater is easier to clean than blackwater, in its untreated state it is far from benign. Because it contains high amounts of nutrients, harmful bacteria will rapidly grow in any unfiltered graywater stored in an open container. After 24 hours, the graywater will begin to smell horrible. To avoid odors, graywater should be immediately put into a filtration system following its discharge. One such system is the constructed wetland.

CONSTRUCTED WETLANDS

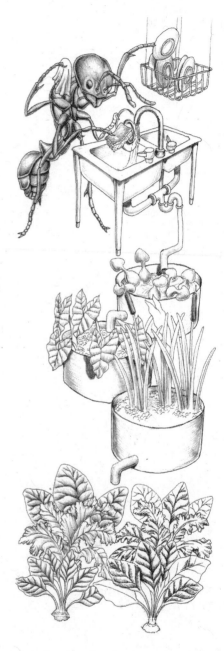

Wetlands are the ecosystems found between aquatic and terrestrial zones, characterized by being saturated with water either all or part of the time. More commonly called swamps, marshes, fens, or bogs, wetlands provide habitat to a number of diverse animal and plant species. Wetlands are nature's purifiers. Often located along the banks of waterways, wetlands filter pollutants that run off the land before they reach open water and cause damage to sensitive ecosystems.

Wetland plants are able to live submerged in water because they have the ability to transport oxygen to their roots. By doing so, they create an ideal habitat for **aerobic bacteria**. This region of high microbiological activity around a plant's roots is called the **rhizosphere**. Water passing through the rhizosphere has its **carbon load**, or the amount of organic matter in it, reduced by the hungry bacteria living there. Just outside of the rhizosphere exists an oxygen-deficient zone filled with **anaerobic bacteria**. In a wetland, the two types of bacteria work in conjunction to clean the water, each capable of breaking down different forms of pollutants. The plants also remove nitrogen and phosphorus, which they use as nutrients, from the water.

Constructed wetlands are a type of wastewater purification system that mimic the function of natural wetlands. Their filtration

Very Basic Plumbing

In a home there are two types of plumbing: water coming in and wastewater going out. Water coming into a home is under pressure and is delivered to its point of use: shower, sink, toilet, and washing machines. Wastewater plumbing carries the water away to the sewer pipes buried beneath the ground in the street. Wastewater drainage pipes rely on gravity to carry the water away and are not under pressure. Drainage pipes have two important features that prevent foul-smelling sewer gas from entering a home. P-traps are the U-shaped curves in pipe that are easily visible under a sink. The constant presence of water in the bottom of the u prevents gas and critters from finding their way up the drain. Drainage pipes are also connected to a main vent pipe that typically vents out onto a roof, allowing methane and other sewer gases to float away.

Cutting into drainage pipes can be a serious undertaking, often involving digging up pipes, removing flooring, or crawling beneath a building. It is a good idea when replumbing, particularly in a rented home, to incorporate three-way valve systems that connect to the

processes can reduce the amounts of nitrogen, phosphates, organic material, and other pollutants found in graywater, making it usable for watering plants or for simply discharging onto soil. Constructed wetlands can be built on a variety of scales: everything from small, home-use designs to large-scale municipal treatment systems. In addition to cleaning water, constructed wetlands are beautiful and can provide shelter for wildlife.

DESIGN BASICS

Constructed wetlands are made by filling containers (called cells) with gravel and wetland plants. Graywater is plumbed from its source and discharged into the bottoms of the cells through perforated piping. Exiting through a drain pipe at the top, the water passes from one cell to another until it is clean and can be reused.

Constructed wetland's effectiveness in treating wastewater is determined by two main factors: temperature and the amount of time the water is retained within the system.

Constructed wetlands are basically microbial habitats. The metabolism of microbes speeds up or slows down proportionately to temperature. The warmer it is, the more efficiently the bacteria will clean the water, while their ability decreases as it gets cold. (See Cold Climates, page 110, for more on cold-weather designs.)

Bacteria need time to process wastewater. The larger a system is, the longer it takes for water to pass through it, and the more time bacteria have to work on it. Logically then, a big system with a small amount of water going into it will produce the cleanest finished water.

How clean water needs to be depends on its intended use and its point of discharge. If the wetland is located near a body of water such as a river, lake, or pond, it should be filtered to a higher level than if it is to be discharged onto soil far from any water. Also, water that is meant for irrigating food crops should be cleaner than water that just goes back into the ground.

PLANTS

While just about any water plant will work in a constructed wetland, certain types are preferable. The most important factors in choosing plants are rooting depth, speed of growth, and climate adaptability.

Proper rooting depth ensures that all water passing though a cell is exposed to aerobic activity. Plants with shallow roots do not effectively treat water at the bottom of a deep cell. Most plants do not send down roots further than two feet (with many only going down one foot), so a wetland cell should be no deeper. Fast-growing plants are preferred as they will more quickly colonize the cell. Bulrush, cattail, phragmites (or giant reed), and canna lily are all vigorous, deep-rooting plants. Other usable plants include taro, arrowhead, thalia, papyrus, horsetail, or any plants found growing in wet areas. All prefer full sun.

Plants can be bought at a nursery or can be collected from the wild. Collecting local plants is free and ensures that the species are adapted to the local climate. However, this should not be done if it would endanger a sensitive wetland area.

Digging up deeply rooted wetland plants is hard work. Loosen the roots by digging around all sides of the plant with a shovel. Try to damage the roots as little as possible. Keep the roots wet and transplant them into their new home as soon as possible.

BUILDING A CONSTRUCTED WETLAND TO FILTER WASHING MACHINE WASTEWATER

This section describes how to build a constructed wetland system out of three recycled bathtubs that is capable of treating the wastewater from a clothes washing machine. From the washing machine the water flows through a series of bathtubs filled with wetland plants which clean the water. After the last tub, the filtered water is

new graywater system while leaving the original drainage pipes in place. This allows for a sewer connection to be re-established quickly if need be.

It is important to be familiar with the basics of plumbing before attempting to implement any of these systems. Consult one of the many good how-to books written on the subject. (also see Codes & Zoning, page 72)

Wetlands support numerous and diverse forms of life, but they are rapidly disappearing in many areas. Considered by many to be undesirable, wetlands are frequently drained and bulldozed to make room for farms, suburbs, and strip malls. Careless harvesting in sensitive areas can cause great harm to the wetlands and the life they support. **Never take a plant if it is the only one of its kind in the area.** Don't take too many plants of any kind from a single area to avoid making a big gaping hole in the landscape.

Carbon Loads and Eutrophication

The nutrients in wastewater are fertilizers for algae. When wastewater enters a body of water, the algae "bloom," or rapidly proliferate. As the nutrient supplies are used up, the algae die and become food for bacteria. The bacteria then multiply and consume much of the oxygen in the water. This commonly results in mass die-offs of fish and other creatures dependent on that oxygen. Bodies of water with low levels of dissolved oxygen are **eutrophied**, and can support little life. Carbon load is the measure of how much of the kinds of organic matter that cause eutrophication are found in a given flow of wastewater. The primary purpose of passing water through a biological filtration system is to minimize its carbon load. It is particularly important to filter wastewater if it is draining near any body of water.

discharged through a hose that can lead to a garden bed, food tree, or just onto well-drained soil. Alternatively, the hose could lead to a 55-gallon storage barrel, from which water is scooped out as needed using buckets or pumps. In warm weather, this system can safely filter the water from a load of wash about every other day, making it suitable for use in irrigation. As washing machines use an average of 40 gallons per load, wastewater recycling can save a significant amount of water.

Washing machine water is one of the easiest types of wastewater to treat, as it contains few greases and food particles, two of the most difficult pollutants to process out of wastewater. A washing machine's drainage system is also easy to tap into: it's usually just a flexible hose coming out of the back. Another advantage to washing machines is that they are designed to sit in a basement and pump their water up to ground level, as much as eight feet. This allows the constructed wetland to be located either far away from, or vertically above the washing machine.

Bathtubs are ideal constructed wetland cells. Easily salvaged from houses being demolished or remodeled, these impermeable containers come with existing plumbing that can be utilized. Both plastic, porcelain, and metal bathtubs are usable. Bathtubs are also about the perfect depth for a wetland cell—plant roots typically won't go down much further than 2 feet. Cells can also be made from any impermeable container: sinks, 55-gallon plastic barrels cut in half, kiddie pools, galvanized metal stock tanks, or even in-ground structures like carpet sandwich ponds. Cells should not be more than 2 feet deep. (See Aquaculture, page 21.)

In order to prevent backflow and assist gravity, the cells should be staggered at different heights. In locations where space is not an issue, stacks of concrete blocks and bricks could be used to elevate the tubs. The diagram and photographs show a tiered structure that raises the bathtubs off of the ground. It is designed like a staircase, allowing gravity to pull water from one tub to another and letting

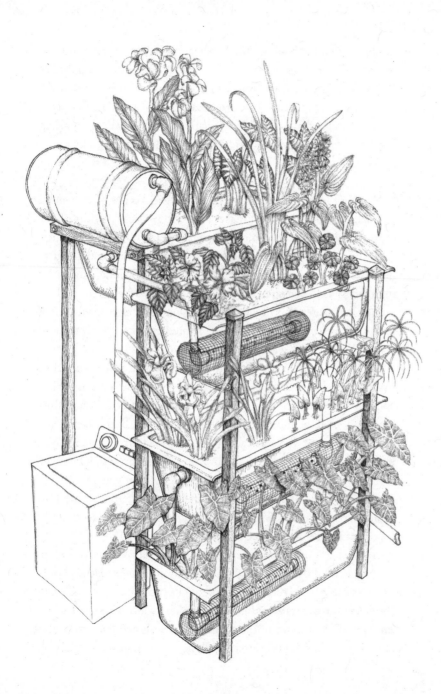

the plants in each tub receive full sunlight. The best materials to build the structure with are 4" x 4"s of rot-resistant wood (cedar, black locust, or white oak) held together with notches and lag bolts. If access to welding equipment is available, a steel structure could be fabricated.

In spaces where horizontal space is extremely limited, it is possible to build an entirely vertical structure to hold the tubs. With these designs, be sure that that there is enough space between tubs so that the ones on top do not completely shade out those beneath them and so that the plants have room to grow (bulrush and cattail each grows stalks five or more feet in height). The main disadvantage to a vertical tower is that a ladder must be used to access the tubs for maintenance.

Remember that a single bathtub full of gravel and water will weigh more than 440 pounds. Whatever structure is built to support them will need to be very strong and reliable.

The design below has an additional component called the surge tank. Surge tanks are 55-gallon barrels designed to take the initial gush of water that blasts out from a washing machine. This water might otherwise overwhelm the wetland and cause the washing machine to back up and burn out its pump. The surge tank allows the water to be slowly distributed into the first wetland cell and also gives hot water from the washing machine time to cool.

It is a good idea to filter washing machine graywater before it enters a constructed wetland system. Synthetic fibers, lint, and hair can prematurely clog a wetlands system. A nylon stocking tied across the end of the drain pipe that fills the surge tank works well. It must either be cleaned or replaced when full of debris as a blocked filter can burn out a washing machine's pump

Nearly all wetland plants need full sun in order to grow. The constructed wetland therefore needs to be placed in a sunny spot, ideally close to both the washing machine and the area where the water will be used.

How to:

1. Build a structure for the tubs.
2. For stacked structures put the tubs in position so that the overflow drains of tub #1 and #3 are above each other and the overflow drain of tub #2 is at the opposite end. For terraced designs arrange the tubs so the overflow drain of tub #1 is adjacent to where you want the water to enter tub #2 and the outflow of tub #2 is adjacent to the inflow of tub #3.
3. Plug the drain holes in the bottom of the bathtubs by sealing jar lids over them with silicone adhesive. If the drain holes are threaded, this can also be done with a threaded plumbing cap. It is important to get a good seal, because if a drain leaks later on it will be very difficult to repair.
4. Create an inflow for each tub:

    a. Cut a length of 2-inch pipe slightly shorter than the length of the bottom of the tub (about 4 feet). It is important that the pipe run along the bottom to ensure a complete exchange of water in the cell.

    b. Drill multiple ½-inch to ⅝-inch holes all around the pipe, spaced every few inches.

    c. Use the 2-inch cap to close off one end of the pipe, and connect the other end to a 90-degree elbow.

    d. Measure the depth of the tub. Cut a piece of pipe equal to this distance. Insert it into the other end of the elbow. Once inserted into the elbow, these pieces should stick out 4-6 inches over the top of the tub.
5. Create a screened diffuser around each inflow pipe to prevent plant roots from clogging its holes.

    a. Lay a piece of window screen lengthwise on the bottom of the tub. Place a 2-inch deep layer of 1-inch gravel on top of the screen.

    b. Place the perforated pipe down the middle of the tub on top of the rocks so that the capped end is on the same side as the tub's overflow drain. The smaller pipe attached to the elbow should be vertical and extend slightly above the top rim of the tub.

Supplies needed:

Materials to build support structure (cedar 4" x 4"s, steel, or concrete blocks)

Three bathtubs or other cell container

Three jar lids and silicone adhesive or three threaded plumbing caps

Three bathtub overflow tubes (if missing from the tubs)

Three adapters that connect bathtub overflow tubes to standard 2-inch pipe

Surge tank (a single plastic 55-gallon barrel)

One male-threaded 2-inch adapter

Nylon stocking filter and strong rubber bands or hose clamp

Utility knife or hole saw

Drill with ½ inch to ⅝-inch bit

Roughly 30 feet of 2-inch pipe, plastic or metal (See Pipes, page 105)

Three 4 foot by 3 foot pieces of window screen

Seven 2-inch 90-degree pipe elbows

Three 2-inch caps

30 gallons of 1-inch diameter rocks

90 gallons of ½-inch diameter gravel

Plants

c. Cover the pipe in a few more inches of gravel, pulling the edges of the screen up to hold it in place. When finished, the screen should be a cylinder, holding two inches of gravel all around the pipe. The weight of the rocks should keep the screen in place.

6. Empty the remaining 1-inch gravel around the diffusers, dividing it evenly between the three tubs.

7. Fill each cell halfway with ½-inch gravel.

8. Install bathtub overflow tubes if not already present. Overflow tubes are the part of the tub that excess water drains out to prevent the tub from overflowing. They drain toward the top of the tub with a pipe attached on the outside. Replacement overflow tubes can be purchased at hardware stores.

9. Attach the surge tank to tub #1:

a. Cut a hole in the bottom of the surge tank equal to the diameter of the washing machine drain hose.

b. Screw the male-threaded 2-inch adapter into the standard-threaded bunghole on the top of the 55-gallon barrel. Make sure that the coarse-threaded cap is screwed on tight. (See Barrels, Bungholes, and Bulkheads, page 80.)

Plants uptake nitrogen and phosphorus

Water level 3" below gravel

On to the next cell

Window screen wrapped around pipe blocks plant roots from blocking up holes

Water distributed through perforated pipe running along bottom of tub

Close-up of bacterial community living around the roots of the plants

c. Apply glue to the outside of the top of the vertical inflow pipe going into tub #1 (if using plastic pipe).

d. Turn the barrel upside down and slide the adapter over the inflow pipe, creating a seal.

e. The surge barrel will rest on the gravel once the tub is filled. In the meantime, it may be necessary to temporarily support the barrel with boards and bricks.

10. Connect the bathtubs:

a. Twist the overflow tubes out, so they are pointing toward the next tub

b. Connect the standard 2-inch pipe adapters to each overflow tube.

c. Join the outflow on tub #1 to the inflow on tub #2, and the outflow on tub #2 to the inflow on tub #3 using pipe and elbows.

d. Attach an irrigation hose to the outflow on tub #3.

11. Put in the plants.

12. Continue filling the cells with gravel, to a height a few inches above the top of the outflow pipe. The gravel should cover the plants' roots, but not too much of the stems. Initially, only a few plants are needed in each cell. Ideal spacing is about a foot apart. With sun, water, and nutrients, the plants will fill in the spaces.

13. Fill with non-chlorinated water. (A container of water can be dechlorinated if it is left sitting uncovered for a 24-hour period, during which time the chlorine will volatilize and escape into the air.)

14. Connect to the washing machine:

a. Make sure the washing machine drain hose is long enough to reach the top of the surge tank. If not, it will need to be extended.

b. Attach the nylon stocking filter by wrapping it around the end of the drain hose. Hold it in place with strong rubber bands or a hose clamp.

c. Insert drain hose into the hole on what is now the top of the surge tank.

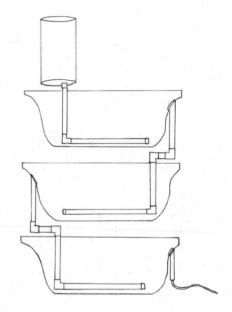

Plumbing diagram

Pipes (More Basic Plumbing)

The main types of pipes used in conventional plumbing are metal (copper, iron, and galvanized steel) and plastic (PVC and HDPE).

Metal piping is considerably more expensive than plastic. It is also more difficult to cut apart and join together. Copper pipe can be cut to length, but pieces must be sweated together, a process involving a torch. Iron and galvanized pipes have threaded ends. Because they are bought in precut lengths and cannot be cut to fit on site, they are a challenge to work with.

Plastic pipes can be easier to work with, but also have drawbacks. The manufacture of PVC (polyvinyl chloride) is a highly toxic process. When PVC is burned in incinerators or accidental fires, it creates dioxin, a known carcinogen and one of the most toxic synthetic compounds ever made. PVC is commonly used in everything from piping to toys.

Not only is the process of making PVC harmful, using it is far from pleasant. Standard PVC cement and primer releases a horrid vapor that burns eyes

Now that the system has been built, it will need time to develop before it can be used. Constructed wetlands need time to mature before they can be expected to effectively process wastewater. Bacteria have to multiply and self-organize, and plants need time to grow and establish their root systems. Following construction, allow the system to sit for two to three months, being sure that it remains full of water. Wastewater can be introduced in small quantities after this period. In six months, the system can be relied on to process full loads of wastewater.

INOCULATION

One way to jumpstart the microbial processes in a new wetland system is to **inoculate** it. This is done by deliberately introducing the bacteria and microorganisms that the wetland needs to function. While bacteria will likely arrive over time through plant roots and bird and insect droppings, the process can be accelerated. Inoculation could possibly shorten the time it takes for a wetland system to be ready for wastewater.

The best source for inoculants would be another constructed wetland, but a healthy pond, swamp, or river will work. Collect inoculants by inserting a turkey baster into the muck of the wetland or water body. Suck it up and inject it into the new system. The desired microorganisms will quickly multiply throughout the cells. Through exchange of DNA, introduced bacteria can give others the information needed to process wastes.[1]

WHAT SHOULD OR SHOULDN'T GO DOWN THE DRAIN INTO A WETLAND SYSTEM?

Biodegradable soaps are ideal because they are more easily broken down and leave fewer toxic residues. Regular shampoos and soaps won't kill a system right away, but are not good for its long-term health. Never use chlorine bleach or antibacterial soaps, as they will destroy a wetland's microbial community. If bleach must be used, hydrogen peroxide, while still harmful, is better to use than chlorine bleach. Avoid washing synthetic materials like fleece, as their fibers do not degrade and will eventually clog the system. Non-chlorinated water is ideal to use in connection with constructed wetlands. If chlorinated water is the only option, it may reduce the functioning of the system, but is not likely to destroy it.

MAINTENANCE

The wetland will require regular pruning and removal of dead plants. Any plant that has turned brown or whose stem has broken and fallen over should be taken out, as it will block sunlight from getting to growing plants. Dead plants can be composted.

After time, the constructed wetland may become clogged. This will be evident if water is no longer able to move through it. The most likely cause of clogging is plant roots that have grown so dense that water cannot move through them. The solution to this problem is to pull out about half of the plants in the cell, with their roots attached. If this fails to solve the problem, there may be a blockage in the discharge pipe that will need to be manually cleared.

IS IT WORKING?

Ideally, the water leaving a constructed wetland is clear and odorless. General criteria used to judge the quality of wastewater are:

- Total suspended solids (TSS)—how much floating gunk
- Carbon load—also called biological oxygen demand
- Total nitrates and phosphates

Elaborate pond-water testing kits (with instructions) that measure nitrates, ammonia, phosphates, hardness, fecal coliforms, and dissolved oxygen are available for purchase. Alternatively, a cheap

and nasal cavities. If PVC must be used, nontoxic glues are available.

Despite its drawbacks, PVC is cheap, available, and easy to work with, making it the most common type of drainage plumbing.

While not exactly environmentally friendly, HDPE (high-density polyethylene) is more benign than PVC. Because HDPE lacks chlorine in its molecular structure, its manufacture and burning release fewer toxins than that of PVC. Typically sold in the form of black flexible tubing, HDPE can be joined with "barbs" and hose clamps to meet plumbing needs. The cost of the fittings needed for HDPE make it less commonly used.

Constructed wetland at the Rhizome Collective

and simple test is to place a sample of fresh water, a sample of untreated wastewater, and a sample of treated wastewater in a dark place for five days. Then compare the three. The treated wastewater's color and odor should be closer to the fresh water's than to that of the untreated wastewater. If it's cloudy and stinky, it needs more filtration.

GOING BIGGER

In the system described above, water is cleaned as it sits in the bathtubs until it is displaced by new wastewater. Because it would give the water more time to be treated before it is displaced, a larger system would filter the same quantity of water to a higher quality.

A larger system is also capable of cleaning greater volumes of graywater. Below is a description of how to size a constructed wetland system to accommodate any volume of water use.

Because it takes a well-functioning wetland at least one day to clean water, the first step is to determine the number of gallons of graywater being produced daily. This can be done by measuring how many gallons leave a faucet in a minute and multiplying this by the length of its use. For example, if the water flowed out of the shower head at a rate of 2 gallons per minute and two people each took a six-minute shower every day then the shower would produce 24 gallons of graywater daily. Repeat for every major water-consuming activity, like dishwashing or laundry, that feeds the graywater system.

The second step is to plan the size of the system. The majority of the volume of a wetlands container is filled with gravel and plants. To determine how much water it can hold, multiply its total volume by 0.3. If a bathtub can normally hold 40 gallons, it will only take 12 when full of rocks and plants. So, if a house is producing 24 gallons of wastewater a day, two bathtubs would be needed to give all of the wastewater a full day of treatment.

Temporary graywater system
(Cancun, Mexico)

The system should be sized slightly larger than the approximate calculation to accommodate for periods of occasional high water usage. It is always possible to add on cells to the system if the finished water quality is less than desired. The only limitations are space, sun, and gravity.

FILTERING OTHER SOURCES OF GRAYWATER

Washing machine water is not the only wastewater that can be recycled. Showers and sinks certainly produce water that has the potential to be reused; however, treating these kinds of wastewater is trickier. Unlike a washing machine with its built-in pump, the water draining out of a shower or sinks must be elevated enough to have sufficient pressure, or **head**, to reach the graywater system. This can be a problem if the shower or sink is on the first floor. Some buildings, however, have sinks and showers on second floors, or have sloping yards. Another possible issue is gaining access to drainage plumbing, as many first-floor pipes lead directly into a cement block. Every building is unique in this regard and needs to be assessed for its graywater potential.

Graywater from sinks and showers often contain large amounts of grease, hair, food, and soap scum that can quickly clog a graywater system. These can be filtered out using a woodchip biofilter. A 5-gallon bucket with many small holes drilled into its bottom is placed between the drainpipe and the surge tank. A funnel slightly larger than the diameter of the bucket is placed below the bucket, leading into the surge tank. The bucket is filled with woodchips. Grease and large pieces of food stick to the woodchips as the wastewater passes through the bucket. If there are chickens around, they will pick out large food particles from the top of the biofilter. The soiled chips can be composted or used in a barrel breeder to cultivate insects for chickens. (See Insect Culture, page 55.)

Sizing a Constructed Wetland

1. Rate of flow from faucet x sum of length of activities = daily graywater produced

Ex.: 2 gallons/minute x (6 minutes + 6 minutes) = 24 gallons/day

2. Volume of empty cell x 0.3 = water volume of filled cells

Ex.: 40 gallons x 0.3 = 12 gallons

3. Daily graywater produced ÷ water volume of filled cells = cells needed

Ex.: 24 gallons produced ÷ 12 gallons per cell = 2 cells

COLD CLIMATES

Constructed wetlands are much easier to maintain when grown outdoors. It's wise to use plants that are well adapted to the climate and can tolerate extremes of temperatures. A wetland is a microbial habitat: its performance directly correlates with temperature. Water-cleansing bacteria are most active at higher temperatures; their activity comes to a standstill near freezing. Furthermore, plants only take up nutrients during active growth. A wetland that is frozen solid will not clean water until it thaws.

However, living in a cold climate does not make it impossible to have a wetland. The season can be extended by insulating the tops and sides of the cells with straw or dead plant stalks, burying the cells in the ground, or using bioshelters or cold frames. (See Bioshelters, page 50.) If a wetland is not frozen solid, some of its microbial processes will continue, although greatly slowed. In cold climates, it is important to build a system extra large to compensate for reduced activity. If freezing cannot be avoided, it is a good idea to have a backup method of wastewater disposal (like a sewer connection) for cold times. In most cases the freezing will not kill the microbes. The system could be back up and running pretty soon after it thaws.

LEGALITIES

The use of graywater and constructed wetland systems is legally ambiguous. Often, codes are different depending on the specific source of the wastewater and its method of discharge. Laws vary from state to state. The drier states are typically more permissive of alternative water systems and are more likely to have established codes. Other states expressly forbid it.

The obvious alternative to the legal permitting process is going under the radar. Officials tend to be unaware of these systems unless they receive complaints about them. The responsible and discreet use of graywater will hopefully avert problems. A constructed wetland could be explained as a water garden. Staying connected to the city sewer through a tee valve leaves the option of switching back if needed.

UNFILTERED DISCHARGE OF GRAYWATER

While in many places unprocessed graywater is discharged directly onto soil, this practice is generally not advised in cities. The high amount of impervious cover in cities often reduces the amount of soil with good drainage. This can lead to unfiltered graywater forming pools on the ground's surface, an undesirable condition.

In some emergency situations, unfiltered discharge may be the only option available. In this case, it is best to pour it into a pit filled with gravel. This will allow the water to be dispersed below ground where it will not cause as many odor problems. A pile of woodchips on top of the pit will help to remove some large particles, while also suppressing odors. If it is impossible to dig a pit, unfiltered graywater should be dumped in small amounts over as wide of an area as possible, preferably on well-drained soils.

COMPOSTING

Soil is the foundation of all land-based food production. The degradation of soils through unsustainable agricultural practices has been a contributing factor to the collapse of many civilizations. If food is to be grown in today's cities, the creation and maintenance of healthy soil is crucial. Most urban soils are compacted, contaminated, and nutrient deficient. Compost can improve soil conditions and make soil when there is none.

Compost, or humus, is decomposed organic matter that is rich in nutrients and microbiological life. Adding compost to soil has the following benefits:

- Improvement of soil structure
- Enhancement of moisture retention
- Neutralization of soil pH
- Fertilization
- Increase in microbiological diversity and activity
- Binding and degradation of toxins

Composting is a simple way for urban residents to reduce the amount of food wastes they throw into the garbage and to return nutrients to the soil. Small composting operations need little space and can fit into a backyard. Because sunlight is not required, compost piles can be located in fully shaded areas.

Composting involves mixing carbon-based materials, like dead leaves, woodchips, or straw, with nitrogen-based materials, like food scraps, into a pile. Within this mixture, there is a teeming population of microscopic life forms. These include bacteria, fungi, nematodes, protozoa, actinomycetes, and micro and macro arthropods. When the correct ratio of carbon and nitrogen is present, these organisms become activated and begin consuming the organic matter. Their metabolic processes produce considerable amounts of heat that raise the temperature of the compost pile. After sufficient time, the organic matter in the pile will have been largely consumed. Stable, nutrient-rich compost will be left. If done correctly, the process of composting will even degrade some contaminants, such as certain types of pesticides. (See Bioremediation, page 179.)

COLLECTING COMPOSTABLE MATERIALS IN THE CITY

Millions of tons of organic wastes are dumped in landfills each day, taking up a huge amount of space. When this material is buried, it decomposes anaerobically and produces methane, a major greenhouse gas. The process of collecting, transporting, and landfilling organic wastes is energy intensive. It also robs potential nutrients

Pedal People is a human-powered delivery and hauling service based in Northampton, Massachusetts, active since 2002. They haul trash, recyclables, and compost year-round on 6-foot trailers pulled behind bicycles, even in the cold of a northern winter. A worker-run and -owned cooperative corporation, they successfully compete with truck-based waste-collection operations. In addition to being a viable business, Pedal People has created a model for community-based waste pick-up that is independent of petroleum.[2]

from the soil. This organic matter should be diverted from the waste stream and turned into compost. If a community were to collect these materials, it could produce compost for its own needs and possibly develop a composting microenterprise.

Many cities have large-scale food processing facilities, like coffee brewers, tofu producers, beer breweries, and tortilla factories. Food waste disposal is a major expense for these types of businesses. Homes, restaurants, grocery stores, and cafeterias also produce huge volumes of food scraps. Local businesses may be eager to donate to a neighborhood composting operation. These food wastes could be regularly picked up, and some businesses may even pay for the service. Dumpstering is also an option. Some products are easier to handle than others. High-nitrogen foods that have been processed under high heat, like spent brewer's grains and tofu wastes, are especially prone to putrefaction and must be composted immediately in well-functioning compost piles.

Grass clippings are a good source of nitrogen. Green leaves and most yard trimmings are nitrogen rich. Horse and other animal manures are also high in nitrogen, and may be available from city stables or zoos.

Wood chips, a carbon source, may be collected for free from tree trimming businesses or city mulching operations. Dead leaves are another great carbon source. Many cities have a curbside leaf collection program. Brown bags of leaves on curbsides can be easily collected by composters. (Trash that often gets mixed in must be removed.) Shredded newspaper, brown paper bags, and cardboard are also acceptable.

A neighborhood composting operation is a great way to build community. It could make use of a vacant lot, or a section of a community garden. Residents could be encouraged to bring their food scraps, yard clippings, and leaves to the composting site. In exchange, donors could receive finished compost.

COMPOST BASICS

The key to successful composting is a proper ratio of carbon to nitrogen. Different materials have different proportions of carbon and nitrogen. Typically, brown, dry materials are high in carbon, and green, wet materials are rich in nitrogen. Ideally, for every part nitrogen in a compost pile, there should be 30 parts carbon. The chart below lists common types of organic matter and their carbon to nitrogen ratio. The number before the colon is the amount of carbon for each part nitrogen. The higher the first number, the more carbon-rich the material is.

HOW TO CALCULATE A PILE'S CARBON:NITROGEN RATIO

A pile's total C:N ratio is found by first multiplying the carbon to nitrogen ratio of each ingredient by the weight of that ingredient. Then, that total is added together to find the ratio for the entire pile. If the total ratio can be simplified to around 30:1, then the pile is balanced.

For example, if 10 pounds of food scraps were added, that is 15:1 multiplied by 10, or 150:10. Two pounds of leaves is 54:1 multiplied by 2, or 108:2; and 2 pounds of straw is 80:1 multiplied by 2, or 160:2. Then each side of those ratios is added together to get a total of 418:14. 418 divided by 14 is roughly 30, so the final ratio can be simplified to 30:1.

Most people don't actually weigh the materials going into the compost pile to calculate a ratio. Over time and with experience it will become intuitive.

When in doubt, it is better to err on the side of adding too much carbon. Excess carbon will just slow the composting process, but too many nitrogenous materials will cause the pile to stink.

Certain types of food break down more easily than others. Chopping food into smaller bits speeds up decomposition.

Material	C:N
Alfalfa hay	18:1
Blood	3:1
Cardboard	400–563:1
Coffee grounds	20:1
Corn cobs	56–123:1
Corn stalks	60:1
Farm manure	90:1
Fish scraps	3.6:1
Food scraps	15:1
Grass clippings	19:1
Humanure	5–10:1
Tree leaves	35–85:1
Newspaper	170:1
Pine needles	60–110:1
Poultry carcasses	5:1
Rotted manure	20:1
Sawdust weathered two months	625:1
Sawdust weathered three years	142:1
Seaweed	19:1
Shrimp residues	3.4:1
Straw	80:1
Telephone books	772:1
Urine	0.8:1
Vegetable produce	19:1
Water Hyacinth	20–30:1
Woodchips: hardwoods (Avg.)	560:1
Woodchips: softwoods (Avg.)	641:1

Sources: Humanure Handbook & University of California Cooperative Extension[3]

C:N ratio of ingredient X x weight of ingredient X

Ex.: Food scraps: 15:1 x 10 pounds = 150:10

C:N ratio of ingredient Y x weight of ingredient Y

Ex.: Leaves: 54:1 x 2 pounds = 108:2

C:N ratio of ingredient Z x weight of ingredient Z

Ex.: Straw: 80:1 x 2 pounds = 160:2

Total Pile Ratio = Total C of ingredient X + total C of ingredient Y + total C of ingredient Z : Total N of ingredient X + total N of ingredient Y + total N of ingredient Z

Ex.: 418 : 14 = 150 + 108 + 160 : 10 + 2 + 2

Simplify and compare to target ratio of 30:1

Ex.: 418÷14 = 29.9, or nearly 30:1. Pile is balanced.

Vegetables and breads degrade quickly. Meats, oils, and dairy products break down slowly and can potentially produce smells or attract vermin. Experienced composters can add them sparingly to a well-functioning pile.

Composting is an aerobic, or oxygen-using, process. If a compost pile is deprived of oxygen, it will turn anaerobic, smelling horribly and producing alcohol, which should not be put directly on plants. While oxygen can diffuse into the pile from the outside to some extent, the oxygen-filled spaces between ingredients are essential. Finished, mature compost should be dark brown in color, not black. Black compost is a sign that the compost went anaerobic at some point.

Moisture content is also important. When a handful of compost is squeezed, there should only be a few drops of moisture, like a moist sponge, not a wet one. Excess moisture can turn compost anaerobic, while the composting process will be hindered if it is too dry. A pile may need to be protected from rain or occasionally watered.

In some places, rats and dogs can cause problems by getting into compost piles. The key to thwarting them is to wrap metal hardware cloth around the pile and place a solid lid on top.

Finished compost should appear as dark brown, rich dirt. It will have a pleasant, earthy smell. There should be few to no remaining recognizable pieces of food. Small amounts of non–broken down materials like peach pits, nut shells, or woodchips can be sifted out and added back into a new compost pile for further composting. Finished compost can be added directly to gardens and put around the bases of food trees.

Composting methods primarily differ in the labor and the time needed to produce compost. Using passive composting, a properly layered pile left to sit may take a year or more. With the active method, manually turned compost that has its temperature monitored can be made in as little as several weeks.

PASSIVE COMPOSTING

In passive composting, carbon and nitrogen materials are layered into a pile and left to sit. This method involves no labor other than adding the materials. The tradeoff is that it can take up to a year to break down into finished compost.

The compost container can be a circular cage made from livestock panel fencing or a box constructed from wooden freight pallets. The container gives the pile shape, allowing it to build up vertically. It should be large enough that the volume of the compost can be at least three cubic feet. This volume is necessary to create sufficient internal heat. Ingredients are added over time, as they are collected. Once the container has been filled, it is left alone to break down. A second container can be built next to it and filled while the first is breaking down. After sufficient time has past (about a year), the container is opened and its contents removed. The container can be used again for a new pile.

ACTIVE COMPOSTING

Active composting produces finished compost far quicker than the passive method. In this labor-intensive method, the temperature of the pile is carefully monitored and it is regularly turned. It requires a composting thermometer—a thermometer with a long stem that can be inserted into the center of a compost pile to give internal temperature readings. Composting thermometers are available at nurseries and gardening supply stores.

In active composting, the compost materials are put in a pile that can be easily accessed for turning. When the temperature of the center of the pile reaches between 135 and 155 degrees Fahrenheit, it is turned: the contents are moved to a new pile with a pitchfork. Turning the pile brings the temperature down. When it rises again, it is turned again. Ideally, the pile should be turned five times in

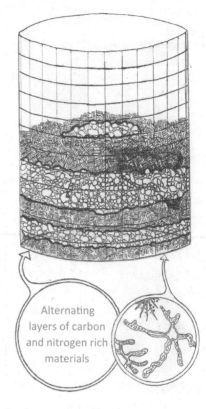

Alternating layers of carbon and nitrogen rich materials

Passive compost pile

the first 15 days. When the compost temperature stays equal to the outdoor temperature after turning, the compost is finished.

A pile that reaches temperatures above 160 degrees F can kill its beneficial microbial populations. Adding more carbon-rich material will bring the temperature of a pile down. Piles that fail to reach high temperatures need more nitrogen-rich material. (Urine is very nitrogen rich and can be added for a quick nitrogen boost.) If the temperature fails to increase even after more nitrogen is added, it may indicate that some of the materials have been treated with strong pesticides and the pile's contents should be landfilled.

COMPOST FIRST AID

It is not uncommon to find an existing compost pile that has been poorly maintained for years and smells badly whenever wind blows across it. In most cases, this is a result of people just piling up food scraps with little or no carbon material mixed in. Fortunately, these embarrassing piles can be salvaged. The contents of the pile will need to be shoveled out, and then put back with copious amounts of carbon material dumped in between shovel loads. This first aid treatment should turn a bad pile around. Noses should be held during the process, however.

SHEET COMPOSTING

Sheet composting is a method of quickly producing soil in areas with no or poor soil. It is a quick way to process large amounts of food scraps that doesn't involve making a pile, or having to turn anything. Sheets of cardboard are laid flat across an area, serving as a weed barrier. Layers of food wastes and nitrogen materials are piled on top of the cardboard. The pile is capped with brown leaves or straw. The sheet can be over a foot thick. It is watered and allowed to stand. The pile will break down into usable soil in a year.

Alternating layers of cardboard, foodscraps, and leaves

Sheet composting

BIOTHERMAL HEATING

The biological processes occurring inside a compost pile generate a considerable amount of heat. Referred to as biothermal heat, it can be used to heat water, or even a greenhouse or bioshelter. Water in a hose or tubing that is run through a compost pile will be heated, and can be used as a compost hand wash. A compost pile located in a bioshelter will produce considerable warmth that helps to moderate the internal temperature. (See Bioshelters, page 50.)

OTHER OPTIONS

Composting is an ideal process for moderate amounts of food waste. A flock of chickens can also rapidly reduce the volume of food waste and create valuable manure. (See Microlivestock, page 4.) Vermicomposting, discussed below, can process smaller amounts of food, yielding incredibly rich compost. A combination of all these methods can be tailored to meet differing needs while building soil.

VERMICOMPOSTING

Vermicomposting ("vermi" means worm) is a method of composting that uses worms to break down food wastes into a nutrient-rich manure that is excellent for gardens. Worm composting is great for urban residents because it can be done without access to land. Worm composting boxes can fit neatly underneath the kitchen sink. If done correctly, the process is odorless. Worms can eat their own weight in food during a 24-hour period under optimal conditions. When fed regularly, worms will multiply and can be used to start new worm boxes or be fed to birds or fish. Large operations are capable of processing institutional-scale food wastes.

The worm manure, or castings, is rich in nutrients and microbiological life. As a worm has no acids in its stomach, all the digestion is performed by bacteria living in its gut. These bacteria-rich castings are often used as an inoculant in compost tea. (See Compost Tea, page 185, for a definition.)

WORMS

Red wigglers (*Eisenia fetida*) are the type of worm most commonly used in vermicomposting. Unlike the common earthworm, which prefers a mineral-based environment like soil, red wigglers require a nutrient-rich environment like compost. Red wigglers wouldn't survive long in regular garden soil.

Red wigglers have another property that makes them ideal for treating food wastes: they secrete a substance that kills pathogenic bacteria. If placed on a Petri dish containing *E. coli* bacteria, a wiggler would not only kill all the bacteria it ate, it would kill any bacteria that touched its skin. For this reason, vermicomposting systems would be an ideal choice to process restaurant waste. Hundreds of worms wriggling about in the food scraps would disinfect them of any possible bacteria from customers' saliva.

The best place to get wigglers is from an existing vermicompost system. Simply dig through a friend's worm bin for a small container's worth. A pint of worms will soon multiply to create a healthy vermicomposting system. They can also be bought from bait stores or some garden supply stores.

BINS

The worm bin is a wood or plastic container with a lid. The dimensions can vary depending on the size of the operation. A guideline is 1 square foot of bin for every pound of food waste put in the box at any given time. Boxes should be shallow. Piled up food waste will begin to compost thermally, producing heat. Because the worms are trapped in the box, the heat can kill them.

The sides of the box should have holes covered with screen to allow for ventilation while preventing flies from becoming a problem.

The lid should keep light out, as worms prefer a dark environment. As the worms reproduce and the vermicompost system expands, bins can be added and stacked on top of each other.

Worm bins made of stacking, shallow trays are also commercially available and can probably be constructed with a little ingenuity.

BUILDING A CHEAP AND EASY WORM BIN

How to:

1. Using either a utility knife or hole saw, cut two, 2-inch holes on each of the long sides of the bin, near its top.
2. Cut pieces of window screen slightly larger than the holes.
3. Attach to the outside of the bin, over the holes, using silicone or other adhesive. Make sure a bead of adhesive spans the entire circumference of the hole so worms will not be able to escape.
4. Allow silicone to cure.
5. Add bedding, worms, and food.

Supplies needed:

Plastic or wood storage bin with
    removable, snug-fitting lid that
    measures roughly 18 inches wide,
    24 inches long, and 8 inches deep.
    Dimensions can vary.
Utility knife or 2-inch hole saw
Silicone or other adhesive
Window screen

BEDDING

Fill ¾ of the box with bedding. The bedding absorbs excess moisture and is something to bury the food under. The best bedding is shredded newspaper. It can also be made from cardboard, sawdust, old leaves, or straw. Bedding is a starting material: the worms will eventually eat the bedding and turn it into castings. More bedding can be added if moisture becomes a problem, but the worms are generally happy to live in their own castings.

FOODS

A worm has no teeth. It can only eat what it is able to pass its body through, making soft foods ideal. Smaller pieces of food are more quickly digested. Avocadoes, mangos, bananas, apples, melon, cof-

Worm bin

fee grounds, pasta, rice, tofu, and tomatoes are all favorite worm foods. Worms do not handle meat, dairy, oils, or spicy foods well. Initially, give the worms small amounts of food. Add more only when it has all been eaten.

MOISTURE AND TEMPERATURE

Moisture levels need to be monitored. A slight dampness is ideal. Too much liquid will make the box go anaerobic and kill all the worms. Too little moisture will dry them out.

As worms do best in temperatures in the human comfort range, indoor vermicomposting is easier. Outdoor operations must be insulated and heated.

HARVESTING AND USING THE CASTINGS

Periodically, the castings should be harvested for use as a fertilizer. The easiest way is to push all the material in the bin to one side and place fresh food and bedding on the other side. The worms will migrate to the new food, leaving the old castings worm-free and ready to harvest. Another method is to spread the finished compost on a screen with holes big enough for the worms to crawl through. Put the screen in the sun. The light-sensitive worms will burrow away from the top layer. Keep removing the wormless top layer until all the worms have crawled through the screen.

Worm castings can be applied directly as a fertilizer to gardens. They can also be used to make compost tea. (See Compost Tea, page 185.)

RECYCLING HUMAN WASTES

Nutrients exist in limited supplies in soil and are replenished at a very slow rate. When food is grown in soil, it removes nutrients from the ground. Unless those nutrients are returned to the dirt, there will be a net loss of nutrients. Eventually, the soils will become depleted and incapable of supporting agriculture. Nutrients can be returned in several ways. Food-scrap composting is one method, but since the majority of food gets eaten and not composted, the bulk of nutrients are not being returned in this way. Most nutrients pass through human digestive systems, are excreted, and flushed away. The creation of a truly closed-loop system, where the nutrients used to grow food are being returned to the soil, requires some form of human-waste recycling.

Throughout history, many cultures have returned their feces to the soils that grew their food. While this practice did restore soil fertility, in some cases it also was responsible for causing illness. In a raw, uncomposted state, human feces can spread disease if improperly handled or applied to agricultural soils. Today, with advances in the fields of microbiology and disease transmission, the knowledge exists to compost human manures safely, without chemicals or mechanical systems. When properly composted, human feces (or human manure or humanure) can add fertility to urban soils and create a truly closed loop of food production and nutrient replacement.

PROBLEMS WITH STANDARD SEWAGE TREATMENT

The typical municipal method of processing human feces is terribly wasteful on many levels. It begins with defecating into *clean water*. Not only is this an incredible waste of an increasingly scarce resource, but once harmful pathogens enter water they can proliferate and possibly make others sick.

Untreated sewage is pumped to a central processing facility and mixed with everything poured down the drain, flushed, or washed into the sewers: metals, pesticides, toxic household cleansers, and industrial and medical wastes. The sewage is treated with energy-

and chemically-intensive processes. Treated sewage is either incinerated, dumped at sea, or sprayed on golf courses. None of these disposal methods are environmentally sound. In some places it is resold as compost, which would be a better idea if it were not mixed with all the varieties of hazardous materials that also make their way into sewers.

The inefficiency of modern waste treatment systems only strengthens the argument for human manure composting.

CARBON AND COMPOSTING TOILETS

In a composting toilet, human manure is collected in a container and mixed with a carbon-based material. The mixture is allowed to sit for a two-year period to ensure that any possible pathogens are dead. (Pathogens cannot survive that length of time outside of a human host.) Following this two-year period, there are different choices for handling the finished compost. There are some who feel confident that the compost is now safe and choose to add it to garden soil. However, due to the small chance that some pathogen may have survived the composting process it is recommended that composted human manure be applied only to non-edible plants. Hopefully in the future, as more experiments are done and more data gathered, the absolute safety of applying human manure compost to food crops will be assured.

Success in composting relies on a proper balance of carbon and nitrogen. The same applies to human manure composting as well. Feces are high in nitrogen and need to be balanced with a high carbon material. Sawdust is most commonly used. It is carbon-rich, absorbent, and will soak up urine and other moisture. Sawdust comes in many varieties and using the right kind is important. The ideal sawdust is light and fluffy, closer to a shaving than a dust. Actual wood dust compacts and blocks oxygen from diffusing into the compost pile. Often wood mills or lumber yards are happy to give away sawdust. Be certain the sawdust is not from pressure-treated wood, as pressure treated wood contains arsenic and other toxic substances that are bad for compost.

Used toilet paper should be thrown into composting toilets, as well.

Other high-carbon materials suitable for use in a composting toilet include dead leaves, straw, and shredded paper. As a general rule, several handfuls of carbonaceous material should be added after every time someone poops. A well-managed composting toilet should not smell. Presence of odors indicates too little carbon and/or too much moisture. Make sure the poop is well covered, to prevent flies from getting to it. (Remember, flies pick up pathogens from feces and transmit them to what they land on next. This can be especially dangerous if they land on food someone is about to eat.) A tight-fitting lid will also help.

COMPOSTING TOILET DESIGNS

While there are many commercially available composting toilets, they are all fairly expensive and difficult to get permits for in cities. (See Legalities, page 126.) Discussed below are several designs for user-built composting toilet systems that can be built cheaply and out of recycled materials.

FIVE GALLON BUCKET-IN-A-BOX AND THERMOPHILIC METHOD

This simple composting toilet design consists of a wooden box with a toilet seat mounted on top. A 5-gallon bucket lined with a brown paper bag is placed beneath the seat. Full buckets are dumped into a designated human manure composting pile or a larger, separate container.

The main drawback to the bucket method is that it's fairly labor intensive: a 5-gallon bucket fills quickly and weighs around 40 pounds. While the paper bag minimizes splatter, there is some risk

It is important to make a distinction between composting toilets and outhouses. In a composting toilet, carbonaceous material is mixed in with the human manure, creating a balanced ration of carbon to nitrogen. Composting toilets keep human manure on the surface of the ground, where any pathogens in its leachate are deactivated by microorganisms living in the top few inches of the soil. Conventional septic tanks work on the same principle. In outhouses, or pit latrines, raw feces fall into a hole several feet deep in the ground and are not mixed with carbon. Because leachate from the feces does not pass through the most biologically active layer of soil, potential pathogens could find their way into groundwater. Also, when an outhouse's pit fills, it is covered with dirt and left. The composted material is not available for soil building.

of accidentally coming into contact with uncomposted fecal matter when the bucket is dumped.

The 5-gallon method works well for urban homes without space for a large composting pile: buckets can be transported to other locations. It also requires no plumbing, is quick to install, and easy to relocate if the landlord or inspectional services drops by.

It is possible to use the 5-gallon bucket method in a thermophilic composting process. The **thermophilic** process is based on the theory that heat and time kill pathogenic organisms. A temperature of 122 degrees Fahrenheit, maintained for one day, should be sufficient to kill all pathogens. When a compost pile is properly made, it can produce these temperatures. The temperature of the compost pile can be monitored with a long-probed compost thermometer. The microorganisms in a compost pile assist in the destruction of pathogens as well. This method is named for the thermophilic (heat-loving) bacteria that become active at these high temperatures.

According to Joseph Jenkins, author of *The Humanure Handbook*, feces processed by thermophilic composting can safely be used as a garden fertilizer. Even if thermophilic temperatures have been attained, it is still a good idea to allow the compost to sit for two years before use.

STRAW BALE VAULT

This human manure composting method requires a somewhat hidden outdoor location. Boards are placed on the ground in a rectangular shape. Straw bales are stacked on the boards to form a rectangular vault. A generous amount of sawdust is placed on the ground in the center space. An outhouse is constructed to sit on top of the straw bales. The roof must be wide enough to keep the bales dry. When the space between the bales is filled, a new vault is constructed next to the old one and the outhouse is moved onto it. The old vault is capped with loose straw and allowed to decompose.

A straw bale vault composting toilet

After two years, the remains of the bales are mixed with the vault's composted contents.

FIFTY-FIVE-GALLON BARREL

In this method, a housed toilet is built on a frame tall enough to fit a 55-gallon barrel underneath. Human manure falls into the open-top barrel, and is mixed with sawdust. Once the barrel is filled it is covered with a few inches of sawdust and then pulled out from under the structure (a barrel filled with composting human manure can be quite heavy and may require two people to move). A new barrel can then be put in the old one's place. The full barrel is then put aside and has a lid put on it. A sheet of plywood weighted with a rock makes a good lid. As the wood does not make a perfect seal with the barrel, it allows it to vent, yet keeps rain out. The barrel then has the date written on it, and it is allowed to stand for two years. After this time period, the human manure/sawdust mixture will have composted and can be applied to soil.

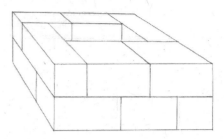

Diagram of placement for a straw bale vault

URBAN CAMOUFLAGE COMPOSTING TOILET

A plastic-shelled port-a-potty can be used to conceal a composting chamber with a 5-gallon bucket in it instead of a chemical bath. Such units could be displayed conspicuously, as they're being used for their intended purpose. No one needs to know that they've been "modified." The manure can be treated similarly to the 5-gallon bucket method above.

LEGALITIES

People's socialized resistance to human manure composting is high. Raised in a society that disassociates itself from its own wastes, most people are very squeamish about the subject. Feces are seen

as something deeply unclean that should immediately disappear. Overcoming these cultural obstacles is an enormous task.

Of all the sustainable systems outlined in this book, composting humanure may be the one that is least tolerated by authorities. Local health departments will likely shut down and fine human manure operations. For this reason, it is necessary to be completely clandestine while using unpermitted composting toilets. It is also important to do it right to create conditions for the laws to be challenged.

Most states have laws against composting human excrement in anything other than manufactured composting toilets with NSF (National Sanitation Foundation) certification. These toilets can cost thousands of dollars. Many use mechanical aerators and moistening systems that are energy intensive and unnecessary.

Legal approval for self-designed, owner-built composting toilets is typically a battle against bureaucracy. (See Codes, page 72.) Such systems need to have the signature of a professional engineer and be approved by city or state regulatory agencies. Creating permitted user-built composting toilets is noble work, as it sets a precedent for others wishing to do the same.

Composting toilet on wheels

URINE

Each day, millions of gallons of toilet water are used to flush away urine, a potentially beneficial human by-product. Urine contains high amounts of nitrogen, a valuable plant nutrient. Unlike feces, which are almost certain to contain pathogens, the urine of a healthy person is essentially sterile. Properly managed urine will produce no offensive odors.

Ideally, urine is separated from feces at the source. This is not always possible or practical, but fortunately, most composting toilet systems have sufficient carbon in them to handle some urine. Ideally, a separate system would be set up for urination alone.

For garden use, urine can be collected in containers and diluted to about 1 part urine to 7–15 parts water. (The high nitrogen levels in undiluted urine can burn plant roots.) Vegetables will benefit greatly from it.

Urinating on high-carbon materials, like dead leaves, straw bales, sawdust, or old books with their covers torn off will break these materials down into an odorless, nutrient-rich compost. This final product can be tilled into the ground or placed around vegetables.

Finally, urinating on a compost pile will add high levels of nitrogen to it, and can greatly accelerate the composting process. Just remember that a proper balance of carbon and nitrogen is essential for a successful compost pile.

THE ADVENTURES OF THE MOBILE COMPOSTING TOILET

Aside from tear gas, rubber bullets, and concussion grenades, a major discomfort suffered by global justice protesters during mass demonstrations is the lack of sanitary facilities. Propaganda about violent protesters leads many stores and restaurants in the vicinity of protests to close up, and few protesters ever bother to rent a port-a-potty. To find a place to poo while struggling to breathe through a gas mask is too much. Something has to be done. And something was—a mobile composting toilet.

The toilet was constructed in preparation for the 2003 anti-FTAA (Free Trade Area of the Americas) protest in Miami. The needed parts were assembled at the Rhizome Warehouse in Austin. The toilet was installed on a cargo tricycle, a hefty pedal-powered vehicle that had been used to transport employees around an auto manufacturing plant in Michigan. It could be biked to the scene of a street protest and be fast enough to ride away from an advancing police line. The tricycle also had an enormous load capacity and was able to handle the combined weight

Juniper on mobile toilet

of the tricycle rider, the pooper and a full container of poop. The human manure container was a plastic 55-gallon barrel. A hole was cut in the barrel's top, and a toilet seat was bolted into the barrel itself. The barrel was then hoisted on to the back of the tricycle. Using a 1,000-pound ratchet strap, the barrel was secured to the frame of an old hand truck that had been welded onto the tricycle. A blue tarp hung from a metal hoop above the barrel, providing some privacy for activists wanting to relieve their bowels. A fold-up ladder provided access to the toilet seat.

The mobile toilet was ferried via pickup truck to Miami, where it came in quite useful, serving as one of the main latrines at the protest convergence center. A cardboard sign was made for the toilet, painted bright yellow with the words "give a shit for the revolution" written across it in bold lettering. (The collected human manure was donated to a local gardener at the end of the action.) The mobile toilet brought a grounded, earth-focused element into the movement, highlighting the connections between global justice and local sustainability.

Near the end of the protest, Juniper, a compost toilet co-conspirator, and Scott were riding the toilet back from the "really free market," where it had again served its duty. All of a sudden, a bright red pickup truck pulled across the road in front of them. Several undercover cops all jumped out at once with their guns drawn. Surely the police imagined that this container of crap was going to be catapulted at them on the front lines of the protest.

"What's in that barrel?"

"It's filled with shit," Juniper calmly replied.

"Oh, that's all it is? We were sure it was full of bombs and explosives." The cops were quite glad to know that it only contained poop, "just like a port-a-potty."

Scott and Juniper biked away from the scene, the shit and their freedom intact.

PUTTING IT ALL TOGETHER

The creation of waste products is a trait common to all living organisms. Waste products should be seen as another phase in an ongoing cycle of nutrient use. Instead of being emptied into rivers to pollute the waters of downstream communities, waste products could build local soil fertility or irrigate crops. Along with food, water, and energy production, the intelligent processing and recycling of human-generated wastes is an integral component of a sustainable city.

ENERGY

Whether by eating food, burning wood, combusting oil, or splitting atoms, humans have always sought to extract energy from nature. Cheap and abundant energy fueled the growth of industrialism. This ascent was first powered by burning wood. Depleted forests spurred innovation, leading to the rise of coal, which was then largely replaced by petroleum, an even more energy-dense fuel. Society has now become entirely dependent on this black liquid. Not only has this addiction fueled the rate of global climate change, but our dependence upon it will cause the consequences of peak oil to be particularly severe. A transition into a culture that consumes drastically less and whose energy infrastructure is based on non-polluting, renewable, and decentralized energy sources is necessary to avert catastrophic collapse.

OIL

The global industrial economy and the society it supports are entirely reliant on the continued availability of cheap petroleum energy. Worldwide food production, the transportation infrastructure of global trading, the manufacture of medicines, mining and resource extraction, the military, and electricity generation all require oil. Petroleum has elevated the standard of living of an elite minority to levels never before experienced by humanity while accelerating the rate of planetary environmental destruction and resource depletion.

Oil, however, is a limited resource. It is a "fossil fuel," made from the bodies of ancient photosynthetic organisms. Over millions of years, their **biomass** was transformed by tremendous heat and pressure into coal and petroleum. The resulting products are incredibly energy dense. While the process of biomass being changed into oil is still ongoing, the speed at which fossil fuels are renewed is immeasurably small compared to the rate at which they are presently being consumed. In the scale of human lifetimes, fossil fuels are a finite, non-renewable resource.

The quantity of petroleum in the ground was a one-time supply. Driven by the desire for short-term profit in an economy based on infinite expansion, humans have consumed this resource in a remarkably short amount of time. Energy that could have been shared by hundreds of generations has been used up in only a few. Upon its completion, the petroleum era will have lasted for a mere 150–200 years.

In history it will be seen as the petroleum bubble, a brief period of tremendous energy expenditure used to power a wasteful civilization. Cultures of the future will be shocked by the current society's extreme selfishness and utter lack of regard for future generations.

PEAK OIL

Cheap oil will become unavailable long before oil reserves are exhausted. The **peak oil** theory predicts that the world will reach a point where all of its oil wells are at maximum production, following which they will go into irreversible decline. After this point, diminishing returns will make petroleum increasingly expensive: it will take more and more energy to extract less and less oil. The exact date of the peak is hotly debated. Some claim it has already happened, while others insist it is still years off. Even more uncertain is how quickly society will go into decline afterwards. In any scenario, the economic and social repercussions will be enormous.

At present levels of consumption, there are no sustainable energy sources available for the world today. No other fuel source presently known is capable of providing anywhere near oil's net return of energy. Even if the planet was covered with solar panels and windmills, it still wouldn't meet the needs of an economy based on infinite expansion. Without a drastic reduction of resource usage, no sustainable options exist.

When the massive energy inputs required by today's world are no longer available, humanity will be forced to transition into a low-energy society. If people are wise and have foresight, they will use the energy surpluses that exist today to invest in the development of a sustainable global infrastructure. If the greedy and arrogant path of today's political and economic leaders is continued, total collapse will be inevitable. The world will experience scarcity and starvation on levels before unknown.

GLOBAL WARMING

Fossil fuels are made up of carbon (from ancient organisms) that was on the surface of the planet millions of years ago. Since then, that carbon has been locked up underground. When oil and coal are brought to the surface of the planet and burned, that carbon binds with oxygen to form carbon dioxide. The practice of burning fossil fuels has led to a significant increase in the percentage of carbon dioxide in Earth's atmosphere. Carbon dioxide, along with methane, nitrous oxide, and other greenhouse gases, act as heat trappers: the sun's heat is allowed in, but is prevented from escaping back into space. This has created a 1.13 degree Fahrenheit increase in average global temperatures since the beginning of the industrial era.[1]

Slight increases in temperature have the potential to set off a chain of positive feedback loops that will accelerate the warming process. Glaciers' white surfaces reflect large amounts of the sun's radiant heat back into space. As they melt, that heat will instead be absorbed by dark oceans, further increasing planetary temperatures. As ocean temperatures rise, their capacity to absorb carbon dioxide is reduced, allowing more of it to accumulate in the atmosphere, furthering the heat-trapping effect.

By sequestering atmospheric carbon dioxide, the world's forests act as **carbon sinks**, critical to balancing the Earth's climate. Slight changes in temperature and weather patterns, however, can cause already imperiled forests to become drier and more prone to fire and desertification. Loss of these forests will have devastating repercussions.

These and other feedback cycles have the potential to create a runaway warming effect that could destabilize many of the underpinnings of civilization,

Climate Justice

It is tragic that the people who will be affected first and most severely by climate change contribute the least to worldwide carbon dioxide emissions. Global warming already disproportionately affects the world's poor. Those who inhabit low-lying flood- and hurricane-prone regions of the world are already suffering the effects of climate disruption as sea levels rise and weather becomes more severe. People producing food on a subsistence level are also particularly susceptible to the harm caused by erratic weather patterns. Unpredictability of seasonal temperature and precipitation patterns makes it difficult to successfully grow food. For these communities, survival is always at stake, especially when no safety net of surplus is available.

Meanwhile, residents of the Global North with the highest standards of living are the biggest emitters of carbon. With a carbon energy infrastructure that provides food, water, and thermal comfort, they will likely be the last to feel the worst effects of climate change.

Climate justice is a term for the movement that seeks to analyze the root causes of climate change and provide support to those most affected. It encourages genuine grassroots, community-based solutions to the challenge of global warming. Rising Tide (http://risingtidenorthamerica.org) is an international, decentralized organization that promotes the goals of the climate justice movement. The Environmental Justice Climate Change Initiative (http://www.ejcc.org) has developed a list of principles for climate justice.

such as agriculture, fishing, and potable water. Even if worldwide carbon emissions are reduced, continued warming is likely inevitable, as many of these feedback cycles are already in motion. Climate change is a certainty. Nonetheless, humanity must do whatever it can to reduce its carbon emissions to mitigate the damage of global warming and avoid its worst consequences.

RESPONSES AND AUTONOMOUS ENERGY

The actions taken in the near future will be critical. A "descent culture" must be created—one that is capable of functioning on the lower energy provided by renewable sources. This low-energy life needn't be a grim existence. Instead, it could be an opportunity to redesign society and to eliminate the gross disparities between the haves and have-nots.

Energy is strategically important. The global elite have engineered a highly centralized and technically complicated method of energy extraction, refinement, and distribution. Through enforced economic dependence and military coercion, dominant powers maintain an energy monopoly, keeping a stranglehold on the rest of the world.

Energy self-reliance would allow communities and nations to be free of the monopolies. An infrastructure based on small-scale biofuels and wind power could offer self-sufficiency. A country independent of oil imports is not easily controllable. For this reason, those in power greatly discourage energy autonomy.

It is in the interest of sustainable communities to develop autonomous energy. Autonomous energy comes from sources where the means of extraction, development, maintenance, and disposal can be managed completely on the scale of a village-sized community, or by an equivalently sized neighborhood in a city. The energy source must be renewable and non-polluting in nature, decentralized in structure, and most importantly, give total control of its processes to the people who are using it.

Sources of energy may vary from community to community, depending on available natural resources. Some regions receive abundant sunshine, while others have consistently strong winds. Fertile parts of the world are rich in biomass. Regardless, it will be in every community's interest to reduce energy demand at the household level and supply as much energy as possible from as close by as possible. As with many other things, local is better when it comes to energy.

Autonomous energy is different from monopolized energy sources such as oil, coal, natural gas, nuclear, and big hydroelectric dams. These types of energy require extremely centralized and technically complicated means of extraction, refinement, and distribution. Their operations are dangerous, polluting, and environmentally destructive. They cannot be managed on a sustainable scale.

Energy sources such as solar panels, big wind farms, tidal power, and large-scale biofuels production are examples of technologies that utilize renewable resources to some degree, yet are still highly centralized in their means of production. While they may be a transition into a more sustainable future, they have considerable social and ecological shortcomings.

This chapter covers some examples of autonomous energy sources that are appropriate for the urban environment: small wind turbines, passive solar technology, biochar, biogas, and small-scale biofuels. A section on building efficient rocket stoves is also included.

BIOFUELS

Biofuels are fuels that come from biological material, or **biomass**, harvested from the surface of the planet. One defining property of biofuels is that the biomass used to produce them was recently growing on the surface of the planet (wood, agricultural plants, algae, and manure). While this broad definition of biofuels includes energy sources like biogas, the gas made through **pyrolitic gasification**, and wood, the public discussion of biofuels is generally focused on fuels that can power vehicles, such as vegetable oil, biodiesel, and ethanol. Therefore, this section is about these vehicular fuels. (Pyrolitic gasification is discussed in the biochar section and biogas in the biogas section.)

With the price of oil rising and the correlation between climate change and auto emissions becoming harder to refute, society has begun to look for alternatives to petroleum. Biofuels, particularly biodiesel and ethanol, are among the options that are being proposed. Some argue that biofuels are preferable to petroleum because their use results in fewer carbon emissions and allows independence from oil-exporting nations. However, when considering the world's current and projected energy demands, biofuels would need to be produced on a gigantic scale to meet any part of this need. Growing fuel crops in such massive quantities would require putting an enormous amount of the world's surface area into agricultural production. Forests would be replaced with a monoculture of chemically dependent, genetically modified soy, corn, palm, and canola farms. Any benefit in reduced carbon emissions from biofuels would be offset by the destruction of the world's forests, a crucial carbon sink. Considering the huge petroleum energy inputs needed to plant, fertilize, apply pesticides, harvest, process, and distribute biofuels, it is debatable whether they are a viable energy option. The energy needed for their production could exceed the energy produced, making them **energy negative**. As petroleum resources become scarcer, large-scale biofuel production may not even be possible. There is also concern that wealthier nations' demands for biofuels will create food shortages for the world's poor. If resources used to grow corn and other crops are reallocated for biofuels, food production could decline.

The world's energy problems will not be solved by biofuels, hybrids, hydrogen, clean coal, nuclear power, or any other energy source. Humanity's current demand for energy is fundamentally unsustainable. The only feasible choice is to conduct a massive downscaling of all economic, industrial, and political operations. A decentralized, autonomous, and locally-based energy infra-structure is ultimately the only sustainable option.

However, small-scale, sustainable production of biofuels is possible. In a society making a transition to a low-energy future, automobiles, farm equipment, generators, and other machines will likely still play a role, albeit reduced. These machines re-quire liquid fuel in order to operate. Starchy and sugary plants can be made into ethanol to power gasoline engines, and plant oils can run diesel engines. Both can be made from a variety of surface-grown crops in an organic, **energy positive** way. The wastes left behind from their processing can be returned to the soil or used as a livestock feed. (It is important to remember that although the wastes may be returned to the ground, the most energy-rich elements have been burned off. As with any crop, continued biofuel production will eventually deplete soils if they are not replenished from external sources or given time to lie fallow.) Biofuels can be made in a small space, making it pos-sible for them to be locally produced in cities. The rest of this section applies only to the sustainable production of biofuels on a small scale—planted and harvested by hand, manually pressed, and used locally.

Nuclear

In response to growing fears over global warming and oil depletion, a desperate search has begun for an energy source that can prolong industrial society while producing fewer greenhouse-gas emissions. Nuclear power is being held up by many, including some so-called environmentalists, as the answer to world energy problems. However, nuclear power is far from being the solution. Among all energy sources, nuclear power is the most dangerous, environmentally destructive, polluting, and centrally managed. Contrary to the propaganda of the nuclear industry, the entire cycle of nuclear power production is responsible for considerable greenhouse-gas emissions. Furthermore, as global uranium supplies will peak in the near future, nuclear power may soon be facing severe geological limitations, just as petroleum is now.

Nuclear power is made when uranium fuel rods are exposed to each other. Atomic particles flying off the rods bounce off one another and create a chain reaction that generates tremendous heat, boiling water that powers an electricity-producing turbine.

The fuel rods used in a nuclear reactor are made from uranium, a mined resource. In the Americas, Australia, China, India, and in other countries, many uranium mines are located on the lands of indigenous and traditional peoples. These mines were often built by taking advantage of the local people's exclusion from political power and without first informing them about the dangers of uranium mining.

As only a very small amount of usable uranium is present in uranium ore, gigantic quantities of material must be excavated. This process, along with many other aspects of the nuclear fuel cycle, requires enormous amounts of conventional energy to be used and results in significant greenhouse-gas emissions. To get to the enriched uranium that is needed for fuel rods, the ore must be crushed and treated with chemicals, producing highly radioactive tailings as a by-product. In the past, these tailings were dumped directly into rivers and lakes. Today, they are stored on-site at the mines, where they frequently leak into surface water and groundwater and create windblown radioactive dust.

BIOFUELS AND THE CLOSED-LOOP CARBON CYCLE

The production and combustion of biofuels creates a **closed-loop carbon cycle**—the amount of carbon dioxide that is used to grow the plants from which the biofuel is made is equal to the amount that is released when the fuel is burned.

For example, a crop of sunflowers takes carbon dioxide out of the atmosphere as it grows. The plants are harvested, and the oil containing that carbon is extracted from the plants. The oil is burned as a biofuel and the carbon forms carbon dioxide again and is released back into the atmosphere. When the next crop of sunflowers is grown, it will absorb the same amount of carbon dioxide that was released when the prior crop's oil was burned.

In theory, if the plants are then replanted, burning biofuels does not contribute to global warming, because levels of carbon dioxide, a major greenhouse gas, remain constant in the atmosphere. Sources of energy with this characteristic are referred to as being **carbon neu-**

tral and create closed-loop carbon cycles. Because large-scale biofuel production, as described in the introductory paragraph, involves petroleum energy inputs, it is not truly carbon neutral.

Petroleum, coal, natural gas, and peat are not carbon neutral. When burned, these fuels release ancient sources of carbon dioxide into the air, contributing to global warming.

VEGGIE DIESEL: BIOFUEL FOR THE DIESEL ENGINE

The diesel engine was invented in 1892 by German engineer Rudolf Diesel. It was designed to run off a variety of fuels including mineral oil, coal dust, and peanut oil. Diesel hoped that farmers would be able to run equipment off waste products produced on their farms, chiefly plant oils.

In a gasoline engine, explosive gasoline vapors are ignited by the engine's spark plugs. Diesel fuel and vegetable oils are more difficult to ignite, needing much greater temperatures and pressures in order to combust. A regular gas engine is not capable of creating these conditions. Only a diesel engine, which uses pistons to compress fuels instead of having spark plugs, can burn oils.

With some modifications to the fuel and the vehicle, today's diesel engines are capable of running off vegetable oils. Because petroleum-based diesel gas is considerably less viscous than vegetable oil and can turn into a gel at low temperatures, vegetable oil must be made less viscous to burn properly in the diesel engine. This is done in two ways: through chemical processes and through heat. These methods produce **biodiesel** and straight vegetable oil/waste vegetable oil (**SVO/WVO**), respectively. Biodiesel and SVO/WVO are collectively referred to as **veggie diesels**.

With modification to the equipment, veggie diesels also can be burned in oil burners to heat homes and can run electric power generators.

Communities exposed to radioactive tailings suffer from high instances of cancer and birth defects. Resistance, however, is strong. In 2006, people from all over the world who were opposed to uranium mining came together at the Indigenous World Uranium Summit. Calling for a global ban on environmentally racist uranium mining on native lands, they demanded that mining companies leave uranium in the ground.

After fuel rods have been used, they are extremely radioactive, and will remain so for millions of years. They are currently most commonly stored at reactor sites, where they are vulnerable to attack or leakage. In the US, the nuclear industry is looking to create a long-term storage facility for this high-level radioactive waste. The proposed site is Yucca Mountain, a location on native lands in Nevada that is on seismic lines and prone to leakage. Any high-level waste will need to be guarded into the indefinite future to protect it from theft or from anyone accidentally coming upon it. The energy needed to run even so much as a light bulb, let alone a full security operation guarding spent fuel, for the duration of nuclear waste's radioactivity would rival that of all of the energy ever produced by all of the world's nuclear power plants combined. This fact alone makes nuclear power a complete energy loser: over time, more energy must be put into its production and waste disposal than will ever be made from it. The waste produced today by nuclear power will remain a threat to every future generation of humans, as well as most of the life on the planet, for ages to come.

Uranium itself is a finite resource. Just like oil, there is only so much of it in the ground, and when it's gone, that's it. The concept of "peak uranium" is becoming known. At current usage rates there is estimated to be only 50 years worth of extractable uranium in the ground. If all current electricity demands were to be met by nuclear power, that would drop to a three year supply. In consideration of this, and all the other negative aspects of nuclear power, it makes little sense to build more nuclear reactors just to allow a high-consumption society to continue its wasteful extravagance for a few more years.

BIODIESEL

Biodiesel is vegetable oil that has undergone a chemical process called transesterfication to make it permanently less viscous. Biodiesel has a low gelling point, meaning it stays in a liquid state at relatively low temperatures (usually down to around 30 degrees Fahrenheit). Provided the temperature is above freezing, biodiesel can be put into a diesel engine and used as a fuel with no supplemental heating. When temperatures drop below freezing, biodiesel can be mixed with petroleum diesel to lower its gelling point. Many individuals and small cooperatives are successfully producing biodiesel even though the process of making it is fairly complex and time consuming (and beyond the scope of this book). Transesterfication involves working with lye and methanol; both are quite dangerous.

If biodiesel is used in older vehicles, old rubber fuel lines and seals must be replaced by synthetic materials (either viton or polyurethane). Biodiesel degrades natural rubber, causing rubber hoses to turn mushy and collapse.

Biodiesel can now be purchased from fuel pumps across North America at a price comparable to standard diesel fuel.

SVO/WVO

Heated vegetable oil that has not been chemically processed can also be used to run diesel engines. **SVO**, or straight vegetable oil, is new oil that has not been used to cook food. Oil that has already been used to cook food is called **WVO**, or waste vegetable oil.

Vegetable oil gels at a much higher temperature than diesel fuel and biodiesel. When it is cold, it turns solid and will not flow through a fuel line. When it is heated, the oil becomes less viscous and can flow through a vehicle's fuel system. In an SVO/WVO system, waste heat is captured from the vehicle's engine cooling system and is used to heat the vegetable oil. When the oil is warmed to around 70 degrees Fahrenheit it is brought to a fluid liquid state and can be burned as a fuel. For long-term engine health, the optimal temperature for SVO/WVO when used as a fuel is 160 degrees Fahrenheit.

SVO can be purchased as cooking oil or pressed from plants. WVO can be collected for free from restaurants and food processing facilities. It must be filtered to remove residual amounts of food that would otherwise clog an engine's injectors and filters.

BASICS FOR CONVERSION OF A CAR TO RUN ON SVO/WVO

To start with, the vehicle must have a diesel engine. With the exception of big trucks and Volkswagens, not many new diesels are sold in the United States today. Other new foreign diesels are available, but are extremely difficult to legally import and register in the United States. Compared to today, there were many more diesel models made in the 1980s, many of which can still be found in reasonable condition. Don't be put off by high miles on a diesel engine, they are far more robust than gasoline engines and can run for 500,000 miles or more. They typically also get many more miles per gallon than gasoline vehicles.

A vehicle is converted to run off SVO/WVO by installing a second fuel tank for the vegetable oil. Hot coolant from the engine is redirected through a heat exchanger in the second fuel tank, where it heats up the vegetable oil.

The original tank, filled with diesel or biodiesel, is used to start the engine. Once the vehicle's waste heat (carried by the coolant) has sufficiently warmed the oil in the second tank, it can then be used to power the engine. Before the vehicle is turned off, diesel from the first tank is used to purge the fuel system of vegetable oil to prevent it from congealing in the lines.

The materials needed to convert a vehicle can be conveniently bought as a kit or can be purchased for less money as individual components. There are several companies that sell conversion equipment and do professional conversions.

While simple in theory, converting and maintaining a SVO/WVO vehicle requires an understanding of mechanics. Incorrect modifications can cause serious damage to vehicles. Using SVO/WVO is also messy and requires a significant time commitment.

COLLECTING AND FILTERING WVO

WVO is most frequently collected from restaurants. It is much easier to transport if the kitchen staff put the oil back into the plastic 5-gallon containers it was purchased in. Used oil is often mixed with impurities such as hydrogenated oils, food particles, and water. These contaminants must be removed by filtration. Failure to do so will cause the fuel filters in the engine to clog very quickly. Generally, the darker an oil is, the more times it has been cooked with and the more likely it is to have impurities. Light-colored oil is ideal.

Hydrogenated oils and even animal fats can be burned in a diesel engine, but their use is not ideal. These fats congeal at a much higher temperature than vegetable oils and can lead to clogged fuel lines and filters if sufficient temperatures are not being reached in the WVO system. Hydrogenated oils and animal fats can be recognized as cloudy patches in oil and should be rejected.

Containers should be allowed to sit for at least a week (although longer is better) in a reasonably warm space to allow time for the oil to separate into visibly stratified layers. Water and large food particles will settle to the bottom of the container. Smaller food particles may remain in suspension. The WVO must now be filtered, as even small food particles can clog an engine's injectors. Once filtered, WVO should be stored in a sealed container to keep out dirt and moisture.

GRAVITY FILTER BAGS

The simplest filtering method is to pour the oil through a hanging filter bag. This is an inexpensive, easy way to filter oil. Filter bags made of synthetic materials are available, and come rated for their ability to remove different size particles. Oil should be filtered down to at least 10 microns, although finer filtration is preferable. When pouring WVO into a filter bag don't try to get every last drop, leave the sludge of water and large food particles at the bottom of the container. The quality of oil determines the life of a filter bag. Dirty oil quickly clogs filters. A filter bag can be reused as long as oil still passes through it. The warmer the oil is, the faster it will filter. Oil can be warmed by bringing it indoors close to a heat source, by using an electric fish-aquarium water heater, or by building a cold frame sized to your barrel (see Bioshelter, page 50). Unfiltered oil should not be heated above 90 degrees Fahrenheit, as any waxes present will melt and pass through the filter, carrying along small impurities.

ENVIRONMENTAL EFFECTS

As far as fuels go, veggie diesels are among the safest. Unlike petroleum-based fuels, veggie fuels are non-toxic and degrade easily in the environment if spilled. With the exception of nitrogen oxide emissions, which may be higher, veggie diesels also have considerably fewer harmful emissions than regular diesel. They have no explosive fumes like gasoline and need a much higher temperature flame to cause them to ignite. Nonetheless, they still can create a fire hazard, especially when being stored in large quantities. Grease fires burn very hot and are difficult to extinguish. Always keep an ABC fire extinguisher on hand—never attempt to put a grease fire out with water as that will only spread burning oil around.

Any town or city produces only enough waste vegetable oil to keep a limited number of veggie diesel cars on the road. The huge

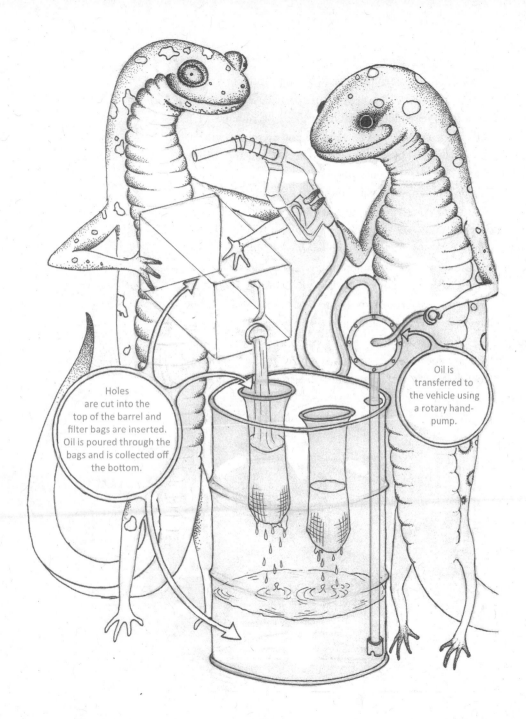

amounts of waste oil that currently exist are a by-product of the excesses of petroleum culture. As oil prices rise, surpluses of anything will become scarce. Vegetable oil will most likely become far more valued as a food than a fuel. But for now, veggie diesels provide a way for a few resourceful people to save money on fuel and utilize a waste product, riding out the end of the petroleum era.

A sustainable, but labor-intensive method of creating veggie diesel fuel would be to extract oils from small plots of oil-producing crops. A portion of the harvest can be set aside for fuel, with the oils pressed out by hand. Examples of oily crops include corn, olives, soy, palms, sunflowers, sesame, safflower, rapeseed, canola (a type of rapeseed), and many nuts. More adventurous people could experiment with certain types of molds, maggots (see Insect Culture, page 55), and algae (see Aquaculture, page 21).

Veggie diesels may make the act of driving somewhat less offensive, but their use does nothing to change one of the least sustainable and most destructive aspects of the modern world—automobile culture. It is important that mass transportation and bicycles be emphasized over any alternatively fueled automobile.

ETHANOL

Ethanol is alcohol produced by the fermentation of starchy or sugary plants. When distilled to a high concentration, it can fuel modified gasoline engines. The waste products of the fermentation process can be composted or used as a livestock feed. Limited quantities of ethanol can be produced on a small scale.

FERMENTATION AND DISTILLATION

Ethanol is a flammable and explosive fuel. Treat it with the same respect and caution given to gasoline. While the process for making ethanol fuel and moonshine are the same, don't ever drink ethanol made by an inexperienced moonshiner, as it can contain harmful, non-alcoholic compounds that can cause blindness or death.

Making ethanol begins with selection of a plant crop. While grains and corn are most typically used, many different crops are suitable: sugarcane, sugar beets, potatoes, apples, and even Jerusalem artichokes. The higher the sugar content of the crop, the more ethanol it will make. Sometimes these crops can be obtained as "seconds," crops considered not of sellable quality, from a food distributor or from farmers. As with crops used for veggie diesels, it is also possible to grow these crops inside of city limits. While their sugar content is low, Jerusalem artichokes grow expansively in many places with minimal energy on the grower's part. Cattail tubers, harvested from constructed wetlands, are a starchy root that can be made into alcohol. In drier climates, cacti and mesquite seeds are also an option.

The plants are ground and mixed with water making a slurry, or mash. Enzymes that convert starches into sugars (similar to the ones found in human saliva) are added to the mash. Yeasts, microscopic fungi, are then added. In anaerobic conditions like those found in the mash, yeasts convert sugar into alcohol and carbon dioxide. When the alcohol concentration reaches the point where it kills off the yeast, the mash is ready for distillation, that is, it's time to separate the alcohol from water.

The mash is distilled by carefully heating it to vaporize its liquids. The water/alcohol fumes are passed through a condenser column. The temperature cools as the gases pass through the column. Because water vapors condense at higher temperatures than alcohol, they condense first and are separated from the alcohol vapors. The remaining vapors leave the column, where they are further cooled back into a liquid form and collected in a separate vessel. If the distillation process is done correctly, the liquid in this vessel will contain a high percentage of alcohol and can be burned in an engine.

USE IN VEHICLES

Ethanol was the fuel used in the internal combustion engine before refined gasoline became available. Today however, modern engines are designed specifically for gas and need to be modified to run off ethanol. (Exceptions are the new flex fuel vehicles designed to run off either ethanol or gasoline.)

Alcohol is a less energy-dense fuel than gasoline. An engine needs more alcohol available to it than gasoline. This modification is achieved by increasing the size of carburetor jets by 40 percent (best done by a machinist with precision drills) in older cars or by altering the onboard computer in newer cars.

OTHER USES

If distilled sufficiently, and if organic crops are used, an organic grade alcohol can be produced. This alcohol can be used to make herbal tinctures, which can then be sold at a premium. The government regulates production and sale of alcohol, but it is possible to obtain licenses to produce alcohol on a small scale, especially if it is for use as a fuel and not consumption. City ordinances may still prohibit distillation, so clandestine operations may be required.

BIOCHAR AND GASIFICATION

A GRASSROOTS TACTIC FOR PRODUCING POWER AND FIGHTING GLOBAL WARMING?

Recently, a lot of research has been conducted on the *terra preta* (dark soil), a type of soil found in parts of the Amazon jungle. It is theorized that the ancient peoples of the Amazon made the terra preta by adding charcoal to compost, which was then used to amend the soil.[4] Full of nutrients, the terra preta continues to support agriculture today, centuries after its creation. Its richness and staying power is believed to be due to its high content of charcoal made from biomass, or **biochar**. Biochar's greatest attributes as a soil amendment are its nutrient affinity, surface area, and stability.

Biochar has the ability to bind many nutrients to its surface (a process called **adsorption**) and make them available to plants over a long period of time. Biochar's ability to retain nutrients apparently exceeds that of compost, potentially making it an excellent soil additive.

Under a microscope, a charcoal particle resembles a coral reef, with many nooks, crannies, and crevices. Similar to a reef, charcoal's many cracks and holes create a habitat for an abundant and diverse array of life forms, albeit microbiological rather than marine. The community of bacteria, fungi, and other microbes supported by the charcoal play important roles in making nutrients available to plants and in the development of new soils. (Charcoal is also used in water filters because the many notches in its large surface area are able to trap water-borne contaminants.)

Lastly, biochar is an extremely persistent form of organic matter. It has the ability to remain stable in soil for perhaps thousands of years, unlike other types of organic matter that may degrade or be leached away in much less time.

Biochar is made through a process called **pyrolysis**: heating in the absence of oxygen. Produced in special burners that can be built out of natural materials, biochar is made from biomass like wood, grass, rice, or grain. Pyrolysis is essential to the production of biochar. Simply burning organic matter will only produce ash. Although ash can be added to soil as a source of potassium, it has none of biochar's desirable properties.

During pyrolysis, organic matter is broken down into its component gases of methane, hydrogen, and carbon monoxide in a process called **gasification**. All three of these combustible gases can be directed away from the pyrolysis chamber and burned together to produce heat, electricity, or mechanical power. It is even possible to modify a vehicle to run off these gases. During the later years of World War II, most of civilian Germany was powered off of wood gasifiers that were attached to cars.[5] (Inconvenient and large, the gasifiers were mostly disposed of following the war. Technical innovations have made modern gasifiers easier to use.)

Following pyrolysis, the biochar contains up to 50 percent of the carbon that was in the original source material. Mixing biochar with soil takes carbon out of the atmosphere. Due to biochar's great stability, that carbon will be locked up for many years. For this reason, biochar has the potential to be used as a carbon sink and could possibly reduce the effect of global warming.

Acting as a carbon sink, biochar/gasification has the rare property of being **carbon negative**, where its manufacture and use takes more carbon dioxide out of the atmosphere than it adds. Comparatively, carbon-neutral fuels return an equal amount of CO_2 to the air, and fossil fuels actually increase atmospheric CO_2 levels. (For a more detailed explanation of carbon-neutral fuels, see Biofuels, page 139)

Combined with gasification, the production of biochar creates a connected cycle of building fertile soils, combating global warming, and providing a source of autonomous energy. Urban communities can produce biochar by putting biomass grown or collected in cities into home-built, low-tech pyrolizers/gasifiers. The biochar can be added as an amendment to garden soils, while the gas is used for energy production.

Production of biochar and its use in agriculture is a potentially promising way for people to be actively working against global warming on an autonomous grassroots level: a global citizens' movement for a decentralized CO_2 drawdown.

While it has great potential, it is important to know that biochar's application is still experimental. Studies using biochar as a soil amendment have had mixed success—the unique microbiological combination of the terra preta has eluded replication. Also, the level at which biochar production would significantly mitigate global warming is uncertain. Despite these unknowns, biochar production offers a hopeful addition to the toolbox of tactics for building community autonomy.

BIOGAS AND METHANE GENERATION

The primary component of natural gas is methane. Extracted from below ground, natural gas is pressurized and pumped through pipelines. It is used for heating, cooking, generating electricity, fueling vehicles, and manufacturing synthetic products.

Like petroleum, the extraction, refinement, and distribution of natural gas has resulted in a number of negative environmental and social consequences. Also like petroleum, natural gas is considered a non-renewable strategic resource and is fought over by governments of the world. However, methane's combustion, while it still produces pollutants, is considerably cleaner than the burning of oil or coal. Methane itself is a potent greenhouse gas if released directly into the atmosphere, but when methane is burned it becomes carbon dioxide, a much less harmful gas.

METHANE DIGESTERS

Much like plants give off oxygen and animals breathe out carbon dioxide, biogas is a waste product of **anaerobic bacteria**. Anaerobic bacteria thrive in the absence of oxygen. They live in places like landfills, the muck in the bottom of a pond, and the large intestine. Thrusting a stick into the mud in a pond will release biogas bubbles.

Biogas consists of descending percentages of methane, carbon dioxide, hydrogen sulfide, and other gases. (The small amounts of hydrogen sulfide produced in biogas give it its distinctive rotten eggs smell.) When the carbon dioxide has been bled off from the biogas, mostly methane remains.

For years, entire villages in Asia have been producing much of their energy needs from methane digesters: large containers that collect animal manure and break it down anaerobically.[6] Methane digesters recreate the conditions found in pond muck. In a sealed container of water, anaerobic bacteria are given food to eat and permitted to proliferate.

The scale of a methane digester can vary. A giant facility could ferment the waste of an entire city and feed gas back into its pipelines, or a 5-gallon bucket filled with rotting plants could make a 6-inch flame. The biogas made from these systems can be used for just about everything that natural gas is used for in the home, primarily cooking and heating. There is also potential to use it for powering electrical generators. As is the case with many energy sources, the scale and size of the system will determine how sustainable it is overall. When made on a small, backyard scale, biogas can be used with none of the undesirable political and environmental consequences that plague natural gas production.

MANURE AND GREEN MANURE

Biogas can be made from nearly any biological material. Each will produce varying percentages of methane and carbon dioxide. Anaerobic decomposition, like composting, requires a 30 to 1 carbon to nitrogen ratio. Be sure that the materials used are properly balanced. (see Composting, page 111)

Animal manure is an option, but unless the livestock is kept in close quarters, more energy may be spent collecting the manure than is derived from the gas produced. It is possible to use humanure for biogas production. Great care, however, would need to be taken to ensure that pathogens were not spread in the process. (See Recycling Human Wastes, page 121.)

Fast-growing water plants produce one of the highest concentrations of methane. Water plants can be easily grown in ponds as small as a 55-gallon drum or a kiddie pool. (See Aquaculture, page 21.) Plants can be regularly scooped off the pond surface and thrown into a digester. Duckweed and azolla are two fast-growing native North American water plants. Green algae, or spirogyra, is also abundant in ponds and lakes and can be harvested in large quantities.

Biogas production can also be used to turn problem plants into a resource. The water hyacinth is a rapidly growing, aggressive aquatic species. In some warmer regions, it forms dense mats that harm the diversity of native ecosystems, prevent sunlight from penetrating the water's surface, and interfere with boat navigation. Affected communities could harvest it for energy production.

BIOGAS IN THE HOME

Since biogas is mostly methane, the primary component of natural gas, anything in a home that runs off natural gas theoretically could be powered by biogas as well. The main obstacle is pressurizing the gas sufficiently. When natural gas goes into a home, it is under considerable pressure. This pressure is needed to force the gas through gas lines and out through appliances. Without adequate gas pressure, stoves and heaters will not work properly. Pressurized gas is extremely dangerous—working with it requires advanced skills and knowledge.

BIOGAS IN VEHICLES

Any vehicle that has been modified to run off of natural gas can be powered by biogas as well. Similar to home use, the main difficulty in using biogas as a fuel is pressure. Natural gas pumped into a vehicle's fuel tank is under enormous pressure. When unpressurized, biogas takes up a great volume. A car powered by non-pressurized gas would require an enormous storage tank to make it a few miles down the road. Because a fuel tank as large as the vehicle itself is impractical, and gas pressurization is technically complicated, there is limited use for biogas in powering cars.

INSTRUCTIONS FOR BUILDING A SMALL-SCALE 5-GALLON BIOGAS DIGESTER

In this system, a 5-gallon bucket is filled with the material to be digested and non-chlorinated water. A clear, bottomless 5-gallon water jug slides into the bucket, covering the material. After the material ferments for two to three weeks in a sunny spot, gas will form, causing the water jug to rise. The gas is forced out a hose in the top by depressing the jug.

WARNING: Exercise caution when working with methane. It is highly combustible when mixed with oxygen. Never smoke or produce open flames or sparks where methane is being stored.

Supplies needed:

5-gallon bucket

Handsaw or jigsaw

Clear plastic 5-gallon water jug (the
kind used for office water dispensers)

Bungcap: a cap from a 55-gallon barrel
with a female ¾-inch adapter in the
center

Garden hose faucet with ¾-inch inlet
and outlet

Flexible metal gas hose with ¾-inch
ends

Tube of adhesive sealant, like Liquid
Nails

Organic matter to be digested

How to:

1. Cut the bottom off of the 5-gallon jug with a handsaw or jigsaw. Because the jug must be able to slide up and down in the bucket without getting jammed, the cut should be above the bottom rim on the jug, which is its widest part. If the jug gets stuck, gas will bubble up around the edges and the container won't rise. It is okay if the jug isn't tight against the sides as long as the biomass is contained within it.
2. Fit the bungcap over the opening on the top of the jug. Apply the adhesive sealant around the joint to form an airtight seal. Allow it to dry.
3. Punch out the center of the threaded part of the bungcap and thread the garden faucet into it. Attach the metal gas hose to the end of the faucet.
4. Fill ¾ of the bucket with the digestible matter. (Chop any large plant matter into small parts first. The smaller the particles, the quicker the bacteria can break it down.)
5. Fill the rest of the bucket with non-chlorinated water. Use rain water or spring water, or allow tap water to sit out in an open container for 24 hours to evaporate its chlorine. Tap water contains chlorine, a microbicide that kills the anaerobic bacteria you are trying to culture.
6. Agitate and blend the material with a stick so that it mixes in the water, forming a slurry.
7. Open the faucet valve. Put the open bottom end of the jug inside of the open top of the bucket. Push down on the jug until it almost touches the bottom of the bucket, allowing the air to escape in the process. Make sure that the digestible material is inside of the jug. Close the valve tightly, making sure no air is getting into the container.
8. Place the whole container in the sun. Depending on the temperature, gas production will begin in two to three weeks, and the jug will rise up in the bucket. The air temperature surrounding the container, either indoors or outside, should be between 70 and 90 degrees Fahrenheit. Temperatures above or below will result in little gas being produced. In cold climates, gas production can be extended by placing the biogas container inside

a greenhouse or cold frame. Be sure either structure is regularly ventilated to prevent methane from building up to dangerous levels.

9. Bleed the container: open the valve slightly and push down on the jug, allowing the gas to escape. When the jug has been pushed back to the bottom of the bucket, close the valve. (The gas causing the jug to rise initially should be rejected. Carbon dioxide, a non-flammable gas, is the predominant gas produced during the early stages of anaerobic decomposition. Methane is more prevalent in the later stages.)

10. Restart the process by putting the container back in the sun and wait for the jug to rise a second time.

11. Bleed the container again.

12. When the jug rises a third time it will be filled with a sufficient percentage of methane to be burned! As one person holds the end of the metal hose away from the container with a lighter or a sparker under the open end, the other person applies light downward pressure on the top of the jug and opens the valve. If it has worked correctly, the methane will ignite, creating a bluish flame.

13. To ensure that the flame does not travel up the line and into the bucket, keep constant pressure on the jug. The amount of gas coming out and the size of the flame will be proportional to the pressure applied.

14. Close the valve to stop the gas flow and put out the flame.

15. When the gas is emptied, step 12 can be repeated. It may be possible to get several batches of gas from one round of material.

A 5-gallon biogas digester

This is an extremely small-scale system. The amount of gas produced in one batch is hardly useful for more than warming a pot of water, let alone bringing it to boil. The point is experimentation. After gaining experience with the 5-gallon version, bigger batches in 35- or 55-gallon barrels can be tried. Small batches are also good for testing the viability of different materials for gas production.

BACKFLOW PREVENTER

This simple device prevents a flame from traveling backward through the gas line to the gas source, where it could cause an explosion. While the positive pressure from the flow of gas from the source is usually sufficient to prevent a flame from traveling back, a backflow preventer is a wise precaution when burning gas from a source container larger than 5 gallons. This design is appropriate only for gas kept under low pressure, like in the systems described in this section.

The backflow preventer is made of a sealed bucket filled mostly with water. Gas enters the bucket through a line that pushes it out at the bottom of the bucket, underwater. It then bubbles upward, through the water into the airspace at the top of the bucket, and then travels on through the exit pipe to the stove. The water prevents any flame from traveling past it back to the stored gas.

While small inline backflow preventers can be purchased at gas and plumbing supply stores, the water bucket design also helps clean the homemade gas. Because carbon dioxide is much more soluble in water than methane, the water "scrubs" out any residual carbon dioxide as the gas bubbles up. It will also remove any hydrogen sulfide that may be in the biogas. For long-term use, it is ideal to remove hydrogen sulfide as it is highly corrosive and will eventually rust out metal parts.

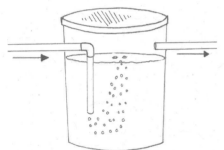

Backflow preventer

LEFTOVER SLURRY

When the material in the digester no longer produces gas, dispose of the spent slurry. Slurry can be composted in a compost pile.

Keep in mind that human pathogens breed in anaerobic conditions. Anaerobic bacteria can also produce compounds that are harmful to plants. While the temperatures reached in a biogas digester are high enough to kill some pathogens, there could be some harmful pathogens left in the spent slurry. Spent manures are likely to have started with more pathogens than plant material and should be handled with particular care. Use caution when handling any spent slurry and never apply it directly to plants.

WIND POWER

Winds are created by the uneven heating of the Earth's surface. When the sun shines on a particular part of the atmosphere, it heats the air and causes it to rise, creating a low-pressure area. When air from a higher pressure area moves into the lower one, wind is created.

Wind power has great potential to provide renewable energy to people while resulting in relatively little pollution or environmental damage. Centuries before the discovery of electricity, wind was used to power mechanical equipment and for sailing. Today, **wind turbines** convert wind power into electrical energy. The size and scale of turbines range widely, from massive wind farms with gigantic towers to tiny turbines made from recycled parts.

Wind power is an excellent example of autonomous energy. Small wind turbines can be made cheaply from locally available materials. They are simple enough to be constructed and maintained by persons with minimal technical expertise and with tools that can be commonly found in a city. Users building a turbine from scratch will be familiar with all of its workings and be able to easily troubleshoot and repair any problems that may arise. Wind turbines can provide independent power to autonomous communities in many regions of the world.

HOW TURBINES WORK

Turbines have blades that spin when the wind moves through them. The blades are connected to a component called a rotor, which has magnets attached to it. The rotor spins around another part called the stator, which is made up of copper coils. The ro-

tor and the stator together create what is called an alternator. The magnets and the coils are spaced in a particular way in the alternator such that when they cross each other, electrical current is produced. This electricity can be stored in batteries or used to power equipment directly.

Wind is stronger at higher altitudes, as it loses power to friction against the Earth's surface. Buildings and trees also weaken wind strength. For this reason, small turbines may not produce as much power in cities as they might in rural areas. The trick to getting a turbine to perform optimally is to place it as high off the ground as possible, and ideally as far away from any large buildings or trees as possible. While many places in cities are obstructed, the rooftops of tall buildings or the tops of hills would be good sites for placing a turbine in the city.

Wind strength varies greatly in different parts of the world. Some regions may experience consistently strong winds throughout the year, while others barely receive a calm breeze. As a result, wind power may be more practical in some places than others. The map below shows average wind strengths for different parts of the United States. Similar maps exist for most places in the world.

In many areas, wind strength can change with the seasons, making it necessary to have redundant sources of power. Wind turbines can be used in conjunction with other power systems, like solar, to ensure year-round electricity. Conveniently, during cloudy, stormy times when the sun is obscured, wind strength may pick up. Wind and active solar systems can share the same network of charge controllers, wires, inverters, and batteries.

DESIGNS FOR SMALL-SCALE TURBINES

Building a small-scale turbine that produces a significant amount of power and that is safe is not a simple task. While the skills and tools needed to build one are drastically less than those needed to construct a solar panel, a fair degree of handiness and a decent knowledge of mechanical and electrical systems are needed. Complete instructions for building a turbine are too large and detailed to be included in this book. This section contains basic overviews of different existing designs and suggestions of where to find more information.

Safety is an important factor in constructing a turbine. Turbines contain moving parts that are spinning at high velocities and are placed at high altitudes. In a crowded city, this could create a very dangerous situation. It is critical that all parts of a turbine be firmly attached and that the turbine itself is securely mounted. Keep a turbine on the ground and test it for reliability before mounting. Once mounted, regular safety inspections are required.

AXIAL-FLUX WINDMILL

The axial-flux windmill is a turbine that can produce a 100-watt output under optimal conditions. Its blades are carved from wood and are mounted onto the hub from a wheel of a car. This in turn is connected to welded steel components that are mounted to a pole. Constructing the turbine requires access to specialized tools including a 120-volt welder, drill press, and grinder. Machine shops, which are common in cities, will have these tools and can fabricate the needed components for a fee. Building an alternator and mounting unit calls for purchasing neodymium magnets, copper magnet wire, and steel disks, all of which can add up to a price of several hundred dollars. The advantage to building this turbine is that a good percentage of its parts can be made from recycled materials, and the end product is sturdy, safe, and efficient.

THE RECYCLED BICYCLE-PART WIND TURBINE

This design was inspired by the turbines built at the Gaviotas community in Colombia. However, instead of being built from new

Scavenging Magnets and Wire

Neodymium magnets are one of the most expensive components used in a wind turbine. Fortunately, they can be easily scavenged. Every computer hard drive contains two small but powerful neodymium magnets. They can be removed by taking apart the hard drive and prying the magnets out. An alternator can be constructed after accumulating enough of these magnets. Hard drives can be pulled from discarded computers or sometimes gotten for free from computer repair stores, where they often sit in piles. Copper magnet wire, also used in alternators, can be pulled from broken microwave ovens.

machined parts, this turbine was constructed largely from recycled bicycle parts for under $50. The turbine is mounted onto the bottom bracket of a bicycle, the strong component where the pedals attach. Poles made of bent electrical conduit are bolted onto a flat metal disk, about ¼ inch thick and around 10 inches in diameter. This disk is mounted on to the bottom bracket of the bicycle. The blades are made from sheet metal bent in the shape of an air foil and are screwed onto the conduit poles. The entire unit is mounted onto a car axle, which is welded onto the steel frame of the building upon which it sits. The car axle allows the turbine to spin freely 360 degrees as the wind changes directions.

The rear end of the bottom bracket is connected to a dynahub, a tiny alternator that is normally used on bicycles. In its usual use, as the bicycle's wheels spin, the dynahub produces enough voltage to power a bicycle light. Similarly, when the wind turns this turbine, the dynahub lights a light bulb. (A cool feature when the wind blows at night!)

The Rhizome's wind turbine constructed with recycled bicycle parts

Despite its intrigue, this turbine still has design flaws. The chain ring frequently cracks, which causes the whole machine to fail. A more reliable steel plate should be used in its place. Tinkering with such an inexpensive design is a good way for a beginner to become familiar with turbines and build up the confidence necessary in order to construct a larger one.

SAVONIUS WINDMILLS

Savonius turbines differ from traditional ones in that they are built on a vertical axis, rather than a horizontal one. They can be made very simply by slicing metal 55-gallon barrels in half and attaching them to a central steel rod. Savonius turbines are often used for pumping water as well as for electricity production.

Overall, with some ingenuity, wind turbines can provide a considerable amount of electrical power to an urban community looking to become independent from a non-renewable power grid. They are one of the few means of producing electricity from a common resource using machines that can be built and repaired by people having intermediate level skills and access to minimal technical infrastructure.

PASSIVE SOLAR

The sun is a source of abundant, non-polluting energy that powers many biological, atmospheric, and oceanic systems on the planet. For centuries, humans have built their settlements in relationship with the sun and its cycles in order to benefit from its light and heat. The sun's energy can heat and light a living space and can be harnessed for cooking and heating water. The utilization of the direct radiance of the sun is called **passive solar design**. Devices made to capture the sun's direct energy are **passive solar technologies**, and buildings designed to incorporate passive solar design are examples of **passive solar architecture**.

PASSIVE SOLAR TECHNOLOGIES

Passive solar technologies utilize glazing, mirrors, thermal mass, and insulation to maximize solar energy for cooking and heating. These decentralized and non-polluting technologies meet the criteria for autonomous energy. Passive solar devices can be built largely out of recycled materials such as refrigerators, glass windows, broken mirrors, and old satellite dishes. Passive solar technologies can be applied all over the world. They are particularly important in places where deforestation has occurred as a result of high demands for wood as a cooking fuel. Using the sun for cooking can dramatically reduce the amount of wood fuel that needs to be burned. In cold northern cities, passive solar designs can heat buildings, reducing the amount of fossil fuels that need to be burned.

Direct sunshine is necessary for most passive solar technologies to function. For this reason, they will perform better in sunnier climates. They are still useful in less sunny regions, however, as when the sun is shining they can significantly reduce or supplement people's reliance on other energy sources.

Passive solar technologies differ from active solar technology, or photovoltaic panels (PV). While PV uses semiconductors to transform the sun's rays into electricity, passive solar has no electronic components. Although solar panels can provide power "off the grid" and utilize the sun's renewable energy, they are not examples of autonomous energy. The manufacture of solar panels is an expensive, energy-intensive, polluting, and technically complicated process. Few people have the expertise or the access to the technical infrastructure needed to build solar panels. Panels have a limited lifespan and are subject to damage by falling objects. Once their period of usefulness is used up, they have little potential to be repaired or reused. Most DIY-built solar panels are terribly inefficient and hardly worth the effort. Photovoltaics are not the magic bullet solution to world energy problems that many hope they are. Despite their limitations, however, PVs are enormously preferable to coal or nuclear power for electricity generation and can be useful tools in the transition to a more sustainable future.

Many different low-tech passive solar designs have been invented and are in use by people worldwide. Designs using passive solar technology to provide clean water and maintain a bioshelter have been discussed. This section describes how to build a few simple devices: a solar oven, a parabolic solar cooker, and a passive solar water heater.

SOLAR OVEN

Solar ovens cook food over the course of a day. Although it may take several hours to bake a potato, slow cooking's conversion of starches to sugars makes up for the wait. Food cooked in this way is especially tasty. Solar ovens produce deliciously cooked food with no energy inputs other than the sun and are great for tasks from cooking vegetables and tofu to toasting nuts. In their most basic form, solar ovens are boxes covered by **glazing** that heat up when set in the sun. Their designs can be highly elaborate or plain and simple. Solar ovens can be constructed out of wood or even layers of cardboard.

The sheet of glazing that covers a solar oven allows sun rays in, but doesn't let heat back out. This trapped high heat sometimes nears 200 degrees and will crack regular glass. Tempered glass must be used for glazing. Store-bought tempered glass is very expensive. However, one salvageable source of tempered glass is the heat-resistant glass doors found on some ovens. Another cheap option is to use baking bags—plastic bags designed to roast turkey. These can be cut open and stretched across a solar oven. For the same reason that regular glass can't be used for glazing, only oven-safe cookware can be used inside of a solar oven.

Below are instructions for building a simple solar oven. The dimensions given are just suggestions; it is best to size an oven according to what size cookware and glazing are available.

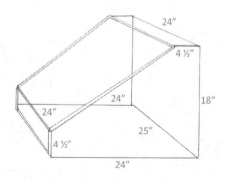

Diagram of solar oven

Supplies needed:

4 foot x 4 foot sheet of ½-inch plywood

4 foot x 4 foot sheet of rigid foam
  board insulation

24 inch x 25 inch piece of glazing

Grill rack smaller than 2 feet x 2 feet
  and two bricks

98 inches of weather stripping or
  silicone

Heat-resistant black paint

Wood saw

Utility knife

Hammer, nails, and glue; or screws and
  screw gun

Optional: sandpaper

How to:

1. Cut out pieces of wood according to the dimensions in the diagram.
2. Attach the wood with screws or nails and glue to construct the box.
3. Using a utility knife, cut pieces of rigid foam insulation to line the inside of the box. Put the pieces in place. They should fit together snugly, sealing the corners.
4. Paint the exposed face of insulation with heat-resistant black paint to help absorb the heat.
5. Put the bricks in the oven and place the grill rack on top of them. The rack will allow hot air to circulate beneath the pot.
6. Place weather stripping around the perimeter of the top of the box.
7. Add glazing to the top of the box, making an airtight seal. If the glazing is glass, its weight will make a seal. If a lighter material is used for glazing, it can be sealed using duct tape. Wetting the weather stripping can help make a seal.
8. To put in or take out cookware, the glazing can be lifted off or a simple hinged door can be made in the back of the box. If a door is cut, the glazing can be permanently attached with silicone sealant and less heat will escape when pots are accessed.

COOKING WITH A SOLAR OVEN

Place the solar oven in a sunny spot with the glazing angled towards the sun. An oven thermometer can be used to track the temperature inside the oven. Generally, the hotter it is, the better. The temperature can be regulated if necessary by moving the stove into the shade or covering it with a shading object. As some foods take many hours to cook, planning ahead is necessary. Check periodically throughout the course of the day to be sure that the sun is still shining on the oven.

Solar oven

PARABOLIC SOLAR COOKER

Dark sunglasses or welding goggles should be worn to protect eyes when using this cooker. Never look directly into the reflective side of the dish when it is facing the sun.

This device focuses the sun's rays onto a small area, producing highly concentrated heat capable of cooking, lighting fires, or producing steam. It is made by lining the concave side of an old satellite dish with reflective material. The object to be heated is placed at the dish's focal point.

While any size dish will work, a larger dish will produce more heat, boiling a gallon of water in about ten minutes. Older 8-foot diameter models can be found in rural areas and at metal scrap yards. Smaller, 30-inch dishes are more commonly used today, and are more likely to be scavenged in urban areas. Lightweight and portable, the 30-inch dishes may be a smarter option for non-homeowners.

Mirror-plated aluminum sheets, Mylar plastic, or mirror shards can be used as reflective materials. The aluminum sheeting will create a perfectly smooth surface, but is fairly expensive. Mylar plastic is inexpensive, but degrades in the sun fairly rapidly. Tin foil has low reflectivity and easily becomes dented. The dents create distortions in light that equal inefficiency. Mirror shards can be broken into small pieces and made into a mosaic on the dish's surface with an adhesive, similar to a disco ball. The smaller the mirror pieces, the more concentrated the heat will be. Broken mirrors can be easily scavenged. Use gloves when handling the dish and broken mirror shards, as they can be quite sharp. To avoid a continuous dusty mess of tiny mirror shards tile grout can be used to seal between the pieces.

TESTING THE DISH

Before taking this step, protect eyes with dark sunglasses or welding goggles. Again, never look directly into the reflective side of the dish when it is facing the sun.

The dish needs to be used in nearly direct sunlight with little to no cloud cover to function correctly. To align the dish create a small hole directly in the center of the dish and aim it at the sun. Hold a piece of paper directly beneath the hole on the shaded side of the disk. The light shining on the paper should run perpendicularly through the dish. This will indicate that the disk is keyed in properly. If it is not correctly aligned, the light will shine off to an angle. This step will need to be taken every time the cooker is used.

The next step is to find the focal point of the cooker. The focal point is exactly where the receiving apparatus sits. If the apparatus is missing, the focal point can still be easily found. Face the dish toward the sun and hold a piece of cardboard up to its face. As the cardboard is moved toward and away from the dish, the light reflected on it will appear more concentrated or scattered. The focal point is where the light appears about the size of a quarter. Hold the cardboard in place for 30 seconds. It should begin to darken, smoke, and burst into flames. If the cardboard ignites, you've found the focal point. The focal point is where you want to place objects to be heated.

To use the dish for cooking, a stand must be constructed that will hold a pot exactly at the dish's focal point. The stand can be independent of the dish, or can be connected to it.

As the sun moves across the sky, the focal point shifts. The dish must be moved every 10 minutes or so in order to properly track the sun. This feature can be a benefit as a forgotten pot will cool instead of burn.

· A small parabolic dish solar cooker

A large parabolic dish solar cooker

SOLAR WATER HEATER

This simple device uses the sun to heat large quantities of water for cooking or washing. It is made by placing a recycled hot water heating tank inside of a refrigerator and covering it with a sheet of glazing. Sun rays pass through the glazing, heating the tank and the air

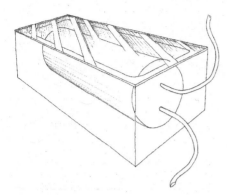

Solar hot water heater using a reclaimed refrigerator

around it. The glazing and the insulation in the refrigerator slow the heat from being lost after the sun has gone down.

The performance of the solar water heater, as with any passive solar device, is subject to climate conditions. The seasonal angle of the sun, outside air temperature, and relative cloud cover are all variables in determining how quickly the water will heat, how hot it will get, and how long it will stay warm for. A clear, hot day in the summer would be the optimal time to use one.

There are many designs for passive solar hot water heaters. This model makes use of two items that are frequently thrown away—refrigerators and household water heating tanks. Refrigerators are a major waste problem. They are bulky and create a hazard for children when not properly disposed of. However, they make excellent storage boxes for solar water heating. Because they are made mostly of painted metal and plastic, they are not prone to rot or rust and therefore can be kept outdoors. They are also insulated. A layer of household fiberglass insulation lies inside the fridge's walls. Keep it there. It will help the hot water tank retain its heat once the sun has gone away. Using refrigerators for solar heaters keeps them out of the landfill and gives them a second life.

Refrigerators use gases called refrigerants for cooling. Some refrigerants, like Freon, are potent greenhouse gases and others may be toxic. When working with a fridge, it's easy to rupture a refrigerant line and release the gas. Before modifying one, bring the refrigerator to a waste management facility and have its refrigerant gas safely drained.

Hot water heating tanks consist of a black, iron tank inside of an aluminum shell, with insulation in between. They are also commonly thrown away and easy to find. Many tanks are thrown out because they leak—reject any tank with visible rust spots: they will only worsen. As a precaution before using a tank, fill it with water to make sure that it does not leak.

How to:

1. Strip off the outer layers of aluminum and insulation from the hot water heater to reveal the black iron tank inside.
2. Remove the refrigerator door and any shelving inside.
3. Place a piece of reflective sheet metal inside the fridge, curving it with the contour of the interior. It will reflect sunlight back onto the tank, adding heat:
4. Construct a frame with 2"x4"s inside the fridge that will hold the tank toward the side where the door was. The frame should hold the tank steady and prevent it from rolling or sliding.
5. Put the tank on the frame inside the fridge.
6. Plumb the tank: hose or pipe can be used. Tanks are fitted with threaded connections. Hot water rises, so the inflow should be at the bottom of the tank and the outflow at the top. The pipes or hose can come into and leave the fridge through the existing holes in the back. Cut holes if needed. The inflow can be from municipal water or water from an on-site source, such as a pressurized rainwater tank.
7. Place a layer of silicone or weather stripping around the perimeter of the front of the fridge. Put the glazing on top of the weather stripping or silicone (where the door was), making an airtight seal.
8. Place the unit in an area with good sun exposure—a sturdy rooftop or sunny backyard. Face it south and set it at an angle where it will receive a balance of summer and winter sun. It is best to have the tank lying parallel to the ground, as it will receive more sun. If space is limited, it is acceptable to stand it vertically.
9. Run the outflow to its point of use. It can be attached to existing house plumbing or used nearby as hot water for hand washing or for an outdoor shower. (See Rainwater Harvesting: Adding a Delivery System, page 66.)

Supplies needed:

Hot water heating tank: Any size is fine as long as it fits inside the refrigerator
Old scavenged refrigerator drained of refrigerants
Glazing: Heat-resistant glass, Plexiglas, or twin-wall polycarbonate (a material used for greenhouses)
Silicone sealant or weather stripping
Reflective sheet metal
Pipe or hose
2"x4"s

With the widespread use of fossil fuels, designing with the sun has been mostly abandoned. The majority of structures in today's cities were built at a time when fossil fuels and wood were perceived as being cheap and abundant. As a result, many buildings are horribly inefficient in regard to heating. Spaces with few or no windows that face the sun have been built in the shadows of other structures. Insulation is minimal or non-existent. Once fuel prices begin to escalate, this lack of foresight on the part of architects and city planners will condemn many structures to be uninhabitable. Urban residents of the future will need to redesign their neighborhoods, demolishing some sun-blocking buildings and knocking large holes in others for sun-facing windows.

PASSIVE SOLAR ARCHITECTURE

Passive solar architecture designs structures that are either entirely or partially heated by the sun. Most passive solar homes have large windows on their sun-facing sides that let the sun's rays enter the building and heat the interior air space. Efficient insulation and abundant thermal mass keep the heat inside. Even in extremely cold and cloudy environments, a well-designed building can remain comfortably warm with only minimal supplemental heating.

Passive solar design is easiest to incorporate into new construction. Passive solar retrofits on old buildings typically involve adding huge windows, which can be prohibitively expensive. Constructing a sun-collecting bioshelter on the sun-facing side of a building and making sure the building is well insulated are more economical ways to take advantage of passive solar energy. (See Bioshelters, page 50.)

ROCKET STOVES

Rocket stoves are high-efficiency cooking stoves that can bring water to a boil or cook food using minimal amounts of wood. They can be made almost entirely from salvaged materials and are just as useful in an urban outdoor kitchen as they are in a campground. Using a rocket stove can help communities reduce their reliance on natural gas, a non-renewable energy source.

Boiling water on an open fire pit is a terribly inefficient process. Very little of the heat produced by this type of fire is actually transferred to the cooking pot: most is lost to the surrounding air, earth, and space. Large amounts of wood are burned, contributing to deforestation. Open pit fires also produce a lot of smoke, which can cause respiratory ailments in the people working around them.

On the other hand, rocket stoves are highly efficient cookers. Their combustion chamber (where the fuel burns) is insulated, ensuring that minimal heat is lost to space and maximum heat is directed to the cooking pot. Only small amounts of wood are needed to bring a pot of water to a boil—a handful of dry sticks is usually enough. Designed to give the fire an unobstructed flow of oxygen, rocket stoves also burn very hot. Hot fires with plenty of oxygen burn clean, producing little smoke or soot. This makes them much healthier to work around than open pit fires.

MAKING A ROCKET STOVE

A rocket stove can be made by joining together horizontal and vertical lengths of stovepipe with a 90-degree elbow. The base of the 90-degree elbow serves as the combustion chamber, where the wood is burned. The joined pipes are inserted inside of a 5-gallon metal vegetable-oil container. Wood ash is packed in around them to insulate the combustion chamber. The cooking pot is placed directly on top of the vertical length of stove pipe.

Rocket stove

How to:

1. Identify the "crimped" end of the stovepipe. This is the end with the wavy, bumpy appearance. The crimped part is designed to slide inside of the normal end of stovepipe.
2. Open up the stovepipe and lay it out flat.
3. Cut a 4 inch piece of pipe off the non-crimped end of the stovepipe. (Be sure to wear gloves: cut metal is razor sharp.) This will become the horizontal section.
4. Cut a 7 inch piece off the crimped end of the stovepipe. This will be the vertical section.
5. Make both pieces into round pipes by popping them closed along their seams.
6. Hold one section of pipe against the face of the oil container, centered and 2 inches off its bottom. Trace the circumference of the pipe on the can. Cut out the hole with snips.

Supplies needed:

5-gallon rectangular metal vegetable-oil container (often found behind restaurants)
24 inch length of 4-inch diameter metal stovepipe
4-inch stovepipe with a 90-degree elbow
Empty tin can
Burner grate from a gas stove or metal grill
Tin snips
Can opener
Work gloves
About 7 gallons of wood ash

7. Trace the circumference of the pipe on the center of the top side of the oil can. Draw a second ring 1 inch wider around the first one. (The wider circle's diameter should be 2 inches larger.) Cut out the wider circle.

8. Stick the crimped end of the vertical section into the non-crimped end of the 90-degree elbow, and insert both pieces into the oil container through the hole on the top.

9. Slide the horizontal section through the hole on the side so that it sleeves over the crimped end of the 90-degree elbow.

10. Pour wood ash into the oil can through the 1 inch gap between the top of the container and the vertical pipe. Tamp it occasionally as it fills by shaking the container. Fill the can to its top.

11. If the vertical section protrudes more than an inch above the top of the can, trim it. If desired, a metal flange can be cut from sheet metal that slides around the vertical pipe and seals off the gap on the top, preventing ash from getting out.

12. Make a tray to insert into the opening of the horizontal run:

    a. Take a soup can and cut off both its lids with a can opener.

    b. Cut the can lengthwise with snips.

    c. Open the can, flattening it into a rectangular section of metal.

    d. Cut the metal so that its width is equal to the diameter of the horizontal section of pipe.

    e. Cut tabs into the sides of the metal and fold them down to be legs that will hold the metal at about half the height of the horizontal opening. The tray provides a platform to put sticks on as they are slid into the combustion chamber. The space beneath the tray remains unobstructed and allows oxygen to flow freely into the combustion chamber. As the air enters the chamber, it is heated by the burning sticks above. When oxygen is preheated, it burns more efficiently.

13. Put the burner grate or metal grill over the top of the rocket stove to place a pot on. Make sure that there is at least a half inch between the bottom of the pot and the top of the vertical stovepipe. If there is not enough space, raise the grill up using rocks.

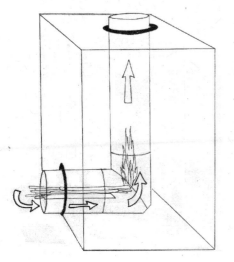

Rocket stove: insulated with ash around the pipe, the chimney sends most of its heat to the pot used for cooking.

LIGHTING THE STOVE

To light the stove, drop a few loosely crumpled pieces of paper down the vertical pipe. Insert dry sticks into the horizontal pipe by placing them on the tray and pushing them to the back of the chamber. Light the paper by dropping a match on it. The stove should light very quickly—it takes off like a rocket.

PUTTING IT ALL TOGETHER

When people today are confronted with climate change, peak oil, and other energy issues, often their main concern is how their standard of living can be maintained. Questions such as "How will I drive?" or "How can I keep my air conditioning?" are more frequently asked than the important ones like "Where will our food and water come from?" or "How will our waste be processed?" Energy is necessary for providing society with its most basic needs. This is commonly forgotten in an age when energy is primarily associated with the electricity that powers the television.

In the near future, enormous investments will be made trying to develop energy sources that can maintain the status quo. Since no known energy source is capable of this, the only rational option is for everyone to get by with less. While many of the autonomous technologies described in this book are helpful transitional tools, they will be of no use unless an ethic of conservation, efficiency, and reduced consumption is adopted. Ultimately, the best way to harness energy is to grow food for feeding people, thereby producing human power. While underrepresented in this book, bikes, wheels, gears, flywheels, levers, and pulleys are all enormous labor-saving devices that can maximize human energy. Their intelligent use can reduce reliance on external power source.

A Word About Wood Ash

Wood ash is made from burning wood in a fire pit or a wood stove. An excellent insulator, ash has particles that trap small air pockets, which help to slow the loss of heat. Wood ash can be collected from a fire pit or from a wood stove. In a pinch, it is possible to use vermiculite (a potting soil amendment) as an insulator for a rocket stove, although the fact that wood ash is naturally produced and is generally considered a waste product makes it greatly preferable.

Materials such as sand or dirt are not good insulators and should not be used with a rocket stove. Sand and dirt have good thermal mass properties—they are good at soaking up and storing heat—but they are poor at slowing down the loss of it.

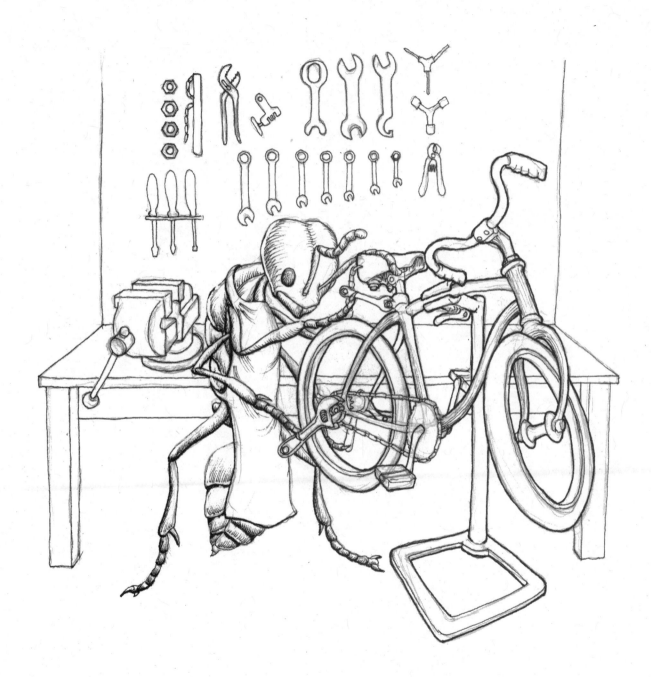

BIOREMEDIATION

Rhizomecollective.org   Juan Martinez

Today's urban soils have been poisoned by years of the irresponsible use of toxic metals and chemicals. These contaminants pose a great risk to human health and have rendered much of the land that could potentially be used for urban food production dangerously unfit. Not only can plants grown in polluted soil pass pollutants on to those who eat them, but mere exposure to contaminated dirt and dust can be hazardous. The problem is so extensive that along with gaining access to land, contaminated soil is one of the greatest obstacles to growing food in the city.

The approaching era of declining energy resources will most likely necessitate a relocalization of food production. The increasing urbanization of the world's population makes this issue particularly significant to cities. If cities are to become potential centers of food production, current available resources must be used to begin erasing industrialism's toxic urban legacy.

Fortunately, there is hope for doing this work. Bioremediation is the process of using the natural abilities of living organisms (typically plants, bacteria, and fungi) to speed the degradation of or assist in the removal of contaminants. In relatively short periods of time, bioremediation can break down chemicals or absorb metals that otherwise might persist indefinitely or take years to degrade.

Using bioremediation to treat contamination is not radical in and of itself—it is an accepted method in mainstream engineering. What is radical is an approach that uses techniques that are cheap and simple and can be carried out by people with little to no background in science and without being dependent on engineers and massive funding. These techniques give people a genuine hope of proactively cleaning the soil in their backyards, community gardens, playgrounds, and parks.

Bioremediation differs greatly from conventional **ex-situ** (off-site) methods of soil remediation. Typically, such methods destructively excavate huge amounts of contaminated soil. The soil is then either landfilled and replaced with sterile fill dirt or transported to a facility for chemical- and energy-intensive treatment and then returned, all at great financial cost. Such investments tend not to benefit poor communities. In contrast, bioremediation is an **in-situ** (on-site) process. All treatments are done on location. No soil is removed from the site. Bioremediation's processes result in an improvement of the overall quality and health of the soil.

CAVEAT

Most bioremediation research has been done in controlled laboratory settings. Community-based, DIY applications of bioremediation have been few. The interactions between molecules, micro-organisms, and human bodies are complex and not entirely understood. Much of the information in this chapter is still of an experimental nature. At minimum, these treatments will not cause harm to the soil or to people applying them. There is no guarantee that soils will be safe following remediation. It will take many people participating in this experiment and recording their results to create a more complete picture of what processes work in what concentrations, against what contaminants, and under what conditions.

POLLUTANTS

The two most general categories of soil contaminants are **heavy metals** and **molecular contaminants**.

Heavy metals are elements. Elements are the basic building blocks of matter. They cannot be broken down any further by regular natural processes. The Periodic Table lists all known elements, including oxygen, hydrogen, carbon. The elements lead, cadmium, mercury, chromium, and arsenic are called heavy metals. If left alone, heavy metals present in soils remain indefinitely.

While some heavy metals, like iron and magnesium, are essential nutrients in small amounts, humans and most other life forms did not evolve with heavy metals present in the high concentrations found today. Fueled by the demands of industry, enormous amounts of heavy metals have been brought to the surface of the planet by extractive mining and concentrated through smelting and refining. Excessive exposure to heavy metals can result in a number of negative health effects, including organ damage, birth defects, and immune system disorders.

Since they cannot be destroyed, there are limited methods for treating elemental contaminants. **Phytoremediation** and **compost remediation** are the bioremediation methods most commonly used to treat heavy metal contamination. Phytoremediation accumulates metals in certain metal-loving plants that are then removed and disposed of elsewhere. Compost binds up metals with organic molecules in the soil, reducing the percentage that is absorbed by plants or human tissue.

Molecular contaminants are made up of molecules: elements bound together in different ways to create substances with varying chemical properties. Some molecular contaminants found in soils are pesticides (dieldrin and chlordane), fuels (diesel and gasoline), and by-products of industry (**PCBs** and **dioxin**). Others, like **polycyclic aromatic hydrocarbons**, can result from either human or natural events, such as fires or volcanic eruptions.

The industrialized world is a virtual toxic soup. Poisons pervade almost all environments, from air to soil to water. Potential health effects from exposure to these contaminants include cancer, reproductive disorders, and liver and nerve damage. Even when present in relatively low concentrations, toxins pose a health risk over a lifetime of exposure.

Mycoremediation, **bacterial remediation**, and compost bioremediation are the most appropriate methods for treating molecular contaminants. The natural metabolic processes of bacteria and fungi are capable of ripping apart molecular contaminants into benign components, which they then use as food. These processes occur naturally over time, but the rate of degradation can be accelerated by adding beneficial organisms to a site and providing the proper habitat and nutrients.

DEVELOPING A REMEDIATION STRATEGY

Once a site has been identified as being possibly contaminated, it will be necessary to come up with a remediation plan. Different contaminants require different treatment methods, and unique site conditions require consideration. Background research on the site history will give clues to its past uses and possible pollutants. Towns often keep historical records and aerial photographs. These can be used to identify potential hazards such as factories, fuel storage tanks, or landfills. Past building permits can reveal previous site conditions and uses of the property. Knowing the land and what pollutants are present is the first step in crafting an effective cleanup plan.

TO TEST OR NOT TO TEST?

Soil tests tell which pollutants are present at which concentrations. Testing may even reveal that dangerous levels of toxins are *not* present and that no action is necessary.

With the exception of lead, it is typically expensive to test for contaminants in soil. There is no one single test that will comprehensively tell which toxins are present. Each suspected contaminant must be tested for individually. A single soil test can potentially cost hundreds of dollars, so narrowing the range of possible contaminants saves money! Sometimes universities or agricultural extensions are able to conduct tests cheaply or free, or sympathetic engineering firms may be convinced to donate their services. DIY testing options are limited.

The other option is to not test and assume the site is contaminated. In this case, utilizing a variety of methods to cover a number of potential toxins is a good idea. At a minimum, building soil health and microbial diversity through regular applications of compost and other organic matter provides some degree of protection.

TYPES OF BIOREMEDIATION

Bioremediation can be broken down into four categories: bacterial remediation, mycoremediation, phytoremediation, and compost bioremediation.

BACTERIAL REMEDIATION

Bacterial remediation is the process of using bacteria to break down molecular contaminants like hydrocarbons into simpler, safer components. It can be accomplished by culturing (breeding) bacteria in high numbers and then introducing them into a contaminated area, and/or by turning the affected soil into an ideal habitat for bacterial growth.

Large numbers of beneficial bacteria can be introduced into soil by brewing something called **compost tea** or through use of a product called Effective Microorganisms.

THE ECOLOGY OF BACTERIA

Bacteria are simple, single-celled organisms found in abundance in almost all regions of the world. They are found in diverse environments, from extremes like the human intestine to hot oceanic sulfur vents. A single teaspoon of healthy garden soil contains over a billion of them. Although often associated with disease, most bacteria are not harmful to humans. Many are essential to human health. Ten percent of human body mass is made of bacterial cells.[1]

Bacteria may be aerobic (oxygen using), anaerobic (non-oxygen using), or somewhere between the two on an overlapping continuum. Aerobic bacteria are typically found in healthy soil. Anaerobic bacteria are found in low-oxygen environments such as pond muck, poorly maintained compost piles, and intestinal tracts. While some anaerobes are pathogenic (disease-causing) organisms, many, like acidophilus and lactobacillus, are essential to effective human digestion.

COMPOST TEA

Compost tea is a water-based, oxygen-rich culture containing large populations of beneficial aerobic bacteria, nematodes, fungi, and protozoa, which can be used to bioremediate toxins. It is made by adding an inoculant and a food source to non-chlorinated water and aerating it. The microorganisms present in the inoculant rapidly multiply when put in oxygen-rich water with ample food. This brew is applied to contaminated soil, where the microbial populations go to work breaking down certain types of molecular contaminants. The ease and low cost of making compost tea make it a method of bioremediation with the potential for widespread application.

THE COMPONENTS OF COMPOST TEA

INOCULANTS

A cup of worm castings make an ideal inoculant for compost tea. The castings can be harvested from a worm composting box or bought from a specialty nursery. Worms have no digestive acids in their stomachs. Instead, they use bacteria to break down food. Worm excretion is an excellent fertilizer in itself, rich in beneficial bacteria, fungi, protozoa, and nematodes. Another inoculant choice is aerobic compost, teeming with microbial life. It is important for the compost to have been well-made, or few beneficial critters will be present.

The inoculant is put into a nylon stocking that is suspended into the water. This allows the microbes to enter, but prevents the passage of larger objects that could clog a sprayer's screen filter during application.

FOOD

Rapidly reproducing organisms need food to fuel their cellular divisions. Microbial foods are added to compost tea to help the process along. The most commonly used foods are molasses, humic acid, and fish hydrolase. The molasses, which should be unsulfured, is widely available at grocery stores. Humic acid and fish hydrolase, both fertilizers, need to be purchased from garden stores.

Molasses primarily feeds bacteria, while humic acid and fish hydrolase feed fungi. Bacterial teas enhance annual gardens, while trees prefer fungal teas. A mixture of these foods will create a finished tea with both bacteria and fungi, which is ideal for remediation of contaminants.

WATER

Chlorine, a powerful microbicide found in municipal water, will kill the microbial life being cultivated in compost tea. While it is far preferable to use collected rainwater or healthy pond water, municipal water can also be dechlorinated by allowing it to sit uncovered for at least 24 hours. Most of the chlorine will volatilize during this period. Aerating the water speeds up the process.

AERATION

Proper aeration is critical. As compost tea is being brewed, the population of microorganisms is rapidly expanding. Like humans, aerobic bacteria need oxygen for survival. There needs to be enough oxygen present in the water to keep the bacteria alive. If too little

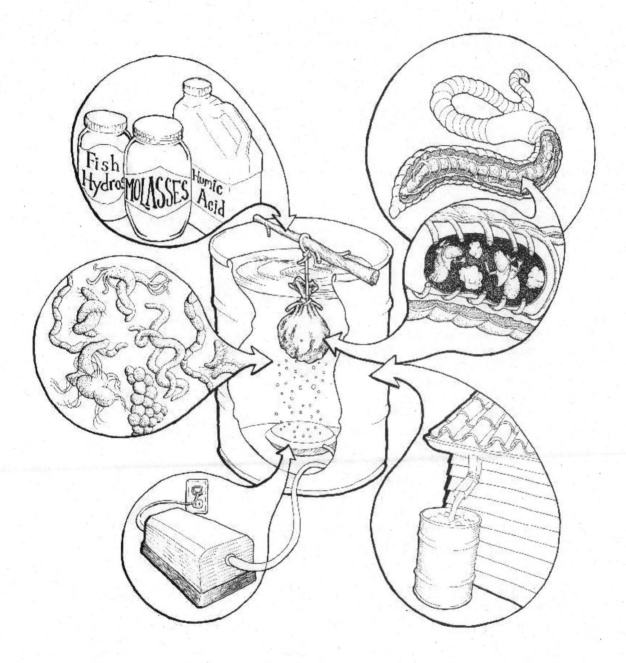

oxygen is available, anaerobic organisms will begin to grow instead. Some anaerobes produce alcohol as a by-product, which is harmful to plants. A small aquarium pump connected to an **airstone** will supply sufficient aeration for a 5-gallon batch of compost tea.

BREWING AND APPLYING THE TEA

This simple recipe for 5 gallons of compost tea can be multiplied for larger batches.

How to:

1. Fill the bucket with non-chlorinated water. (If using tap water follow the instructions above first.) Water temperature is ideally between 55 and 80 degrees Fahrenheit.
2. Put the airstone in the bottom of the bucket, attach the air pump, and let it start to bubble.
3. Put the inoculant in the stocking, tie off the end and suspend it in the water. Squeeze the stocking gently to release the organisms into the water.
4. After an hour or so, add the food.
5. Let the whole brew bubble for 24 to 36 hours. After 36 hours, the microbes begin to die, oxygen levels drop, and the tea can become dangerously anaerobic. If the tea received insufficient oxygen or too much food, anaerobic organisms will overcome the beneficial aerobic organisms. It will be obvious if the tea went anaerobic, because it will stink! If that has happened, pour it out away from garden plants and start over.
6. Pour the mixture through a strainer to remove large debris.

Supplies needed:

5-gallon bucket
One aquarium pump with airstone (bubbler)
¼ cup of food
1 cup of inoculant
One nylon stocking
Watering can or backpack sprayer

APPLICATION

Once the tea has been brewed and removed from the oxygen, it must be applied within four hours, before it starts to go anaerobic.

The tea can be applied to the soil with a watering can or a backpack sprayer. Applying to moist soil is ideal. Directly following a rainstorm is a perfect time. Remember, these are living organisms that need to be put in an environment capable of supporting life. If it is dry, spray the ground with non-chlorinated water prior to applying the tea.

If the tea is for bioremediation, apply it straight. For general soil conditioning where contamination is not a concern, dilute the tea with five to ten parts non-chlorinated water.

For bioremediation, a minimum application rate would be 1 gallon on 1,000 square feet of soil, though a heavier application rate would not be harmful. As there have been few studies done on using compost tea for remediating toxins, it is not known exactly how quickly or how effectively the treatment will work. It would be best to apply the tea several times, with a period of a month or two in between applications. If testing is to be done, it should be conducted before spraying the tea and at intervals between applications to chart the treatment's effectiveness.

SOIL CONDITIONING
USES FOR COMPOST TEA

The weight of a building or parking lot severely compacts the soil underneath it. With the air squeezed out and deprived of moisture, these soils are nearly devoid of beneficial bacterial life. After the soil is exposed (see Depave the Planet, page 47), compost tea is an easy way to quickly reintroduce the healthy microbes necessary for soil building and gardening.

Compost tea is also regularly used by organic farmers as a fertilizer and foliar spray. Plants benefit greatly from the nutrients made available to them by the microbes in the tea. It is equally beneficial for use in urban gardens or on houseplants.

EFFECTIVE MICROORGANISMS

Effective Microorganisms (EM) is a trademarked product made by several different companies. It is basically a liquid culture of microorganisms consisting of yeasts, anaerobic bacteria, and photosynthetic bacteria. There are many claims for EM uses, from enhancement of agricultural production to wastewater treatment and remediation of toxins. What sets it apart from compost tea is that EM bacteria are **facultative anaerobes**. Unlike the strictly aerobic bacteria found in compost tea, facultative anaerobes can survive in both oxygenated and oxygen-lacking environments. This allows EM to be bottled with a long shelf life, unlike compost tea, which must be applied shortly after being brewed. EM microbes include the bacterium *lactobacillus*, which is found in our gastrointestinal tract and helps us digest dairy, and the yeast *Saccharomyces cerevisiae*, which is used to ferment beer. Containers of EM can be purchased at specialty nurseries or over the internet.

EM is an effective alternative to chlorine bleach for mold abatement. It was used successfully for mold remediation in New Orleans following Hurricane Katrina. After leaks in mold-stricken homes were repaired and mold was scraped off of surfaces, EM was sprayed. The organisms in the EM competed for space on the surfaces with the mold spores, and either slowed or stopped regrowth of mold.

Compost tea and EM differ in that EM only contains 8 to 12 types of organisms, while compost tea contains thousands. Compost tea's diversity is what makes it desirable for use in remediating toxins—it is more likely that one of those thousands of organisms will be able to break down a particular toxin.

MYCOREMEDIATION

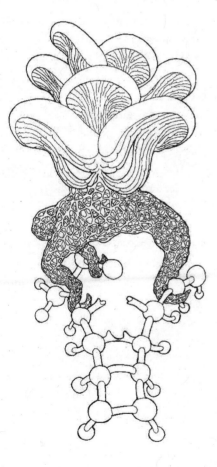

Mycoremediation ("myco" means fungus) is the process of using fungi to degrade toxic compounds. Fungi are nature's decomposers. They are often found digesting dense, woody materials. This ability to break down tough materials is what makes them effective at degrading certain persistent environmental pollutants.

The majority of fungi's biomass grows underground in the form of white, ropy threads called **mycelia**. The mycelia secrete powerful enzymes capable of breaking down not only wood, but also molecular contaminants. The enzymes can literally tear molecules apart, reducing them to safer, smaller components. Fungi can degrade hydrocarbons and are capable of breaking down toxins, like PCBs and even dioxins, that bacteria cannot.[4] Fungi can be used to clean up toxic sites if an environment suitable for the expansion of mycelia is created.

Mycoremediation is a discipline in relative infancy. Various strains of fungi have been shown to break down certain contaminants in controlled laboratory settings. These discoveries hold much promise, but with few exceptions, they have not been demonstrated to be practical outside of the lab. A challenge of mycoremediation is getting desired strains of fungi to grow expansively in the outdoors among competing organisms. Mycelial growth is also constrained by seasonal and climatic factors. For these reasons, mycoremediation's potential for broad-scale, community-based applications has yet to be proven. However, the possibility of cleaning pollutants using only natural processes deserves exploration. It is a worthy experiment for autonomous communities wanting to remediate small oil or fuel spills in localized areas. Below is a description of how to conduct a small-scale mycoremediation project.

GROWING OYSTER MUSHROOMS TO BREAK DOWN PETROLEUM PRODUCTS

Oyster mushrooms (*Pleurotus ostreatus*) are an edible species of fungus found in most places in the world. In experiments, oyster mushrooms have been grown on soil heavily contaminated with diesel fuel. Diesel fuel, a hydrocarbon, is made up of chains of hydrogen and carbon. In experiments, the fungi grew through the soil and tore apart the hydrocarbon chains, eating the carbon and offgassing the hydrogen. After a few weeks of fungi growth, the soil's diesel levels were reduced by 95 percent.[5] This method could be used to clean places where cars have been worked on or fuel has been spilled near urban gardens.

Oyster mushrooms can be cultivated with relative ease, making them ideal for cleaning up small spills. Because there may be residual contaminants, and because fungi accumulate metals (common in urban soils), eating mushrooms from a mycoremediation

Oyster mushrooms growing on jute twine

What Are Fungi?

Fungi are a distinct taxonomic kingdom, different from plants, animals, or protists (single-celled algae and bacteria). Mushrooms, molds, and yeasts are all considered fungi. Mushrooms are referred to as upper fungi, while molds (the things that grow on old food in refrigerators) and yeasts (the organisms that make bread rise) are the lower fungi. Like animals, fungi take in oxygen and give off carbon dioxide. Fungi differ in that they are saprophytic—they have evolved to digest food on the outside of their bodies, rather than inside. Lacking chlorophyll, the pigment that allows plants to photosynthesize, fungi secrete enzymes to break down materials in their environment and use them for nutrients.

Fungi can be microscopic or enormous. It is possible that the largest organism in the world is a mass of honey fungi in Oregon. It covers an area of 2,200 acres and is estimated to weigh 605 tons.[2] Recent studies have shown that some melanin-containing fungi may be capable of using ionizing radiation as an energy source, a unique ability indeed.[3]

project is not advised. If it is certain that no metals were present in the soil, the mushrooms may be composted. Otherwise, they should be landfilled like plants used for metal extraction. (See Phytoremediation, page 198.)

Climate is an important factor in successful mushroom growing. Oyster mushrooms can be grown indoors or out, and generally prefer high humidity and temperatures in the area of 65–85 degrees Fahrenheit. Temperatures below this range will slow or stop the growth of the fungi, while higher temperatures will also slow growth and increase the likelihood of contamination by foreign molds and mushrooms. Mycoremediation experiments should be put on hold until a several-month window of time is available under which these conditions can be met.

Successful mycoremediation requires getting fungi to grow across the contaminated area. This is done by mixing **spawn** (mycelia that has grown and colonized a material) with wood chips on top of the affected soil. There are often many other microorganisms living in the soil and wood chips that will compete with the remediating fungi. In order for the fungi to survive and grow expansively, large quantities of spawn need to be introduced initially—the more spawn, the better the chance for the fungi to fight off competitors.

Described below are two methods of growing spawn: from sterile sawdust spawn mixed with coffee grounds and rhizomorphs mixed with cardboard. The sterile spawn–coffee ground method has a higher success rate at producing large volumes of spawn than the rhizomorph–cardboard method. However, once on the ground, the spawn made using the rhizomorph method has a better chance of surviving the hurdles and growing expansively in a mycoremediation project, because it uses locally adapted strains of oysters.

STERILE SPAWN–COFFEE GROUND BUCKET METHOD

The easiest way to generate oyster fungi spawn is to begin with a bag of sterile spawn. Sterile spawn is mycelia that has colonized straw, grain, or sawdust and has been grown in laboratory conditions. It can be purchased from a number of companies and arrives in a sealed plastic bag. Large quantities of oyster fungi spawn can be grown from a single bag of sterile spawn.

When a fungus has been grown in a sterile environment, its "immune system" is weak. It has never had to compete with other organisms to survive. Because it has so few defenses, fungi directly from the lab would stand little chance of surviving if mixed into outdoor soil right away. One strategy to encourage fungi growth and nurture its defenses is to first cultivate it on a **substrate**. Substrates are the nutrient-rich materials on which mycelia grow—for example, straw, sawdust, coffee grounds, coffee hulls, and cardboard. As the mycelia grow, they break the substrate down and absorb its nutrients. Coffee grounds are an ideal substrate. When coffee is brewed, the heat sterilizes the grounds, killing any competing organisms in it. By growing in a sterile substrate, yet exposed to open air, fungi can slowly build up their immune system while still being pampered.

Once the fungi have colonized the substrate, they can be mixed with denser, non-sterilized materials (like woodchips) in a "wilder" environment.

How to:

1. Drill six ¼-inch drainage holes in the bottom of the bucket.
2. In the bucket, mix the sterile spawn with the coffee grounds by breaking apart the block of spawn.
3. Wet the mixture with non-chlorinated water. Keep it moist, but not saturated. Placing a plastic bag with holes poked into it over the top of the bucket will help retain humidity in dry climates.

Supplies needed:

5-gallon bucket
1 gallon bag of oyster mushroom spawn (*Pleurotus ostreatus*)
4 gallons of used coffee grounds (filters are okay)
1 gallon non-chlorinated water
Drill with ¼-inch bit
Plastic bag large enough to cover bucket

A note about coffee grounds: It is important that the coffee grounds do not sit around long enough for mold to grow on them. If a large amount can't be obtained all at once from a local coffee shop, small amounts can be stored in the freezer until enough are gathered. Reject any grounds with mold growing on them. While harder to find, coffee chaff (the hull of the bean) is also a great substrate. It is completely dehydrated so it won't get moldy.

4. Put the bucket in a shady (but not lightless) spot.
5. After three to six weeks, the mycelia will colonize the grounds and mushrooms will begin to form. Because the coffee grounds are clean, these mushrooms can be picked and eaten or sold.
6. Successive regrowths of mushrooms, or flushes, can occur. Mushrooms will keep growing as long as there are nutrients available to them. When mushrooms have stopped forming, the contents of the bucket can be further propagated by mixing the colonized grounds in with other buckets of fresh grounds.
7. Once enough spawn has been made, it can be used for remediation. (See Remediation Using Mycelia, page 197.) Because the final spawn should be used for remediation as soon as possible after the bucket is colonized, the final batch of spawn should be cultured all at the same time. For example, if 15 gallons are needed, the first 5 gallon batch can be mixed in with three other 5 gallon buckets of coffee grounds to produce a final batch of 15 gallons.

RHIZOMORPH–CARDBOARD METHOD

Bypassing the need to purchase sterile spawn, the rhizomorph method uses native varieties of fungi to generate spawn. **Rhizomorphs** are root-like fungal structures. Like stem cells, they are capable of regeneration and can send out mycelia of their own. Gathered from wild mushrooms, rhizomorphs are used to colonize cardboard and turn it into spawn usable for mycoremediation.

Rhizomorphs are found at the bases of the stems of mushrooms. When a mushroom is dug out of the ground or a log, dangling, thread-like roots are attached to its base. These roots are the rhizomorphs, and can be cut off from the stem.

Oyster mushrooms can be found in woody areas in urban parks, often growing on logs or the ground. A good time to hunt for them is several days after a heavy rain, when the temperature is between 55 and 85 degrees. A mushroom field guide is needed for identification. There are many poisonous mushrooms—correct identification is extremely important!

To collect rhizomorphs from a log, cut out a chunk of the rotten wood at the base of the mushroom with a knife and remove it in a whole piece. If the mushroom is growing on the ground, carefully dig up the dirt under the stem with a hand trowel. Separate the rhizomorphs from the dirt or wood and the mushroom stem, being careful not to damage them. Be sure that they do not dry out while being handled.

How to:

1. Soak the cardboard in non-chlorinated water for a few minutes.
2. Tear the cardboard open to expose the corrugated curls. Place the rhizomorph on the open face of one piece of cardboard, and cover it with a second one.
3. Rewet, being careful not to damage or wash away the rhizomorph, and place the cardboard in shady location. Keep damp.
4. Check once a week to see if the mycelia have colonized the cardboard. The length of time this will take will vary depending on many factors. It will be obvious when the ropy white fans of mycelia cover the inside area of the cardboard. There are two possible next steps:
5a. After the mycelia have thoroughly colonized the cardboard, they can be mixed with more cardboard. A cardboard box filled with sheets of opened wet cardboard works well. Eventually, mushrooms will sprout from the box. Because the cardboard is not contaminated, these mushrooms can be eaten.
5b. Alternatively, a piece of colonized cardboard can be mixed in with a bucket of coffee grounds, as in the coffee ground–spawn method. (See Sterile Spawn–Coffee Ground Bucket Method, page 194.)

Once enough spawn has been made, they should be used for remediation as soon as possible.

Supplies needed:

Handful of oyster mushroom rhizomorphs
Corrugated cardboard
Non-chlorinated water

There is debate over whether it is necessary to use pasteurized woodchips. Pasteurizing the chips will kill off some competing organisms, increasing the likelihood that the remediating fungi will colonize the woodchip bed. Woodchips can be pasteurized by heating them in a bath of water to a temperature of 170 degrees Fahrenheit for a 1–2 hour period and then allowing them to cool. Containers such as a metal 55-gallon barrel or a metal bathtub would be suitable. They can be heated by either a wood fire or a gas burner. On the other hand, mycoremediation trials have been successful using unpasteurized chips. As pasteurization is an energy-intensive process, it may be acceptable to skip it.

Supplies needed to remediate a 10 x 10 foot area:

15 gallons of coffee ground spawn, or the equivalent volume of colonized cardboard
Two wheelbarrows full of woodchips

REMEDIATION USING MYCELIA

Roughly 15 gallons of coffee ground spawn or the equivalent amount of colonized cardboard is needed to remediate a 10 foot by 10 foot area. The basic idea is to create a woodchip sandwich (a layer of woodchips, then a layer of spawn, then another layer of woodchips) on top of the contaminated area. The mycelia in the spawn will colonize the woodchips and eventually work their way down into the soil, where they can begin degrading the pollutants in the spill. The more spawn, the faster it will colonize the woodchips.

How to:

1. If the spill is on compacted soil, aerate the dirt with a pitchfork.
2. Spread woodchips across the area affected by the spill.
3. Pour the spawn across the area and mix in lightly with the wood chips and the contaminated soil. If using the rhizomorph–cardboard method, tear the cardboard into pieces and mix in with the woodchips.
4. Cover the mix with another layer of woodchips.
5. Spray the area down with non-chlorinated water. Keep it moist but not saturated through the duration of the experiment.

After a few weeks, examine the sandwich to see if the mycelia have begun to grow. This will be evident if there are white, thread-like growths fanning off of the spawn onto the woodchips. Don't disturb the fungi too much, as this will only hinder its growth. Stand back and let the pile of chips be colonized. Mushrooms may eventually be formed, but it is more important that the mycelia grow. With luck, the mycelia will continue to expand and eventually start breaking down the petroleum wastes. Even if the mycelia fail to colonize the woodchips, there will still be some benefit from simply having applied the spawn, as rain will carry the active enzymes produced by the mycelia into the affected area, where they will work to degrade the contaminants.

HAS IT WORKED?

Laboratory testing of contamination levels in the soil pre and post remediation can measure success. However, if testing is prohibitively expensive, the soil can be examined for color, texture, and smell. Areas contaminated by oil or fuel will often be dark, oily, and have a chemical odor. Evidence of success would be a lightening of the soil and a reduction in odor and oily texture. Regrowth of plants in the area and development of mushrooms are also indicators that some degree of remediation has occurred. Always wear latex gloves when handling soil that may be contaminated.

While significant reductions in toxicity will take place in the first few months, full remediation will happen over years. Leave the sandwich intact and allow it to fully decompose naturally. Watering it during dry periods will assist in its decomposition.

PHYTOREMEDIATION

Heavy metals are elements, so unlike molecular contaminants, they cannot be broken down into any simpler forms. Once they are present in soil, they will remain there. When they are accidentally ingested or inhaled, they can cause a variety of adverse health effects. Areas of contamination in cities can include old factories and waste storage sites, places where batteries or tires may have been dumped or burned, and around old buildings where lead paint may have chipped off. Also, in many cities blocks have been built over old orchards. Arsenic was commonly used as an insecticide and may still be present in the soil.

Phytoremediation ("phyto" means plant) is the process of using plants to take up heavy metals from soil, reducing contamination levels. While very much a new technology in its experimental phase, phytoremediation has the potential of being a low-tech, low-cost

The Worcester Roots Project and its youth program, Toxic Soil Busters, are inspiring examples of community organizing and direct action to combat soil contamination in inner-city Worcester, Massachusetts. They have taken action to remediate community gardens and yards in low-income neighborhoods using pelargoniums (geraniums), compost applications, and groundcovers. Importantly, the group has been testing the soil and building data for future bioremediation projects. The youth program has created remediation kits with information about lead, seeds, and instructions for minimizing contact. They also host workshops on environmental health and racism.[7]

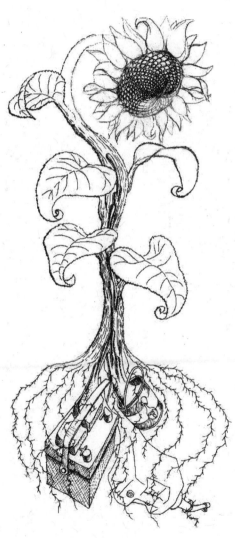

method of soil cleanup that could be accessible to urban communities. In one study, plants grown on land heavily contaminated by old car batteries in New Jersey drastically reduced lead levels in the soil.[6]

In nature there are certain types of plants known as **dynamic accumulators**. These plants have the ability to take up specific elements and minerals and store them in their roots, stems, or leaves. Certain plants are known to be able to take up toxic metals. Phytoremediation projects typically involve planting several successive crops of selected dynamic accumulators.

The problematic aspect of phytoremediation is the disposal of the harvested plants. They must be treated as hazardous waste because of their high levels of toxic metals. Currently, the most common methods of plant disposal are either incineration or adding them to a landfill. Incineration creates a toxic ash dust, bringing the risk of accumulation to another area. While also concentrating toxins in another location, double-bagging the plants and landfilling them unfortunately is the most practical option. For some precious metals like silver and gold, it can be cost-effective to extract them from the plants by smelting.

Overall, phytoremediation is a very new and experimental practice which requires significant scientific monitoring and frequent costly soil tests. The strategies explained here will do no harm to the soil, but it is strongly recommended that any experiments are conducted on small, controlled test patches. Clear signs should be posted warning people not to eat the plants.

SOIL ACIDITY AND METAL SOLUBILITY

In case it wasn't complex enough, the acidity of the soil affects the ability of plants to take up metals. Metals fall into two general categories: **cationic** and **anionic**. Each one is remediated differently.

Cationic metals donate electrons in chemical reactions, forming cations, or positively charged ions. Common toxic cationic metals include lead, cadmium, and mercury. Cationic metals are more soluble, and therefore more easily absorbed by plants, in acidic soils.

Conversely, anionic metals receive electrons in chemical reactions, forming anions, or negatively charged ions. Examples are arsenic and chromium. Anionic metals are more soluble (absorbable) in alkaline soils.

These factors can make phytoremediation more challenging. When phytoremediating soil contaminated with arsenic, it is helpful to add lime to increase the pH and make the soil more alkaline. On the other hand, adding sulfur will acidify the soil and help with removing mercury or lead. If both cationic and anionic metals are present, two separate rounds of phytoremediation may be needed, one using acidic soil additives and another with alkaline additives.

Following the same logic, if phytoremediation is *not* planned for soil that is contaminated with cationic metals, it would make sense to limit the danger posed by the contamination by making the soil alkaline to bind up the metals, and vice versa for anionic contamination.

Lead

Lead is a particularly insidious metal, and its sources include car batteries, smelters, old paint, old pipes, and leaded gasoline. It is found in dangerously high concentrations in the soils of most urban neighborhoods. Lead-based paint on older buildings can become dust-borne and is either inhaled or ingested. Some old paint is more than 50 percent lead. Lead impairs neurological development by readily binding to fat cells in our bodies, particularly brain cells. This can severely affect children's brain development. Also disturbing, lead is more easily absorbed into the blood on an empty stomach. Lead poisoning is a serious problem, disproportionately affecting low-income inner city youth.

Interestingly, the primary danger of gardening in heavy-metal contaminated soils comes not from eating contaminated food, but from prolonged contact with the dirt itself. Therefore, another strategy for dealing with heavy metals is to create a barrier between people and the contaminated soil. Groundcover crops, woodchips, gravel, and paver stones all block contact with soil. It is particularly important to concentrate on the area a few feet around the outsides of older buildings, where lead paint chips probably fell for years.

Cationic Metals

Cadmium (Cd)
Chromium (Cr)
Copper (Cu)
Lead (Pb)
Manganese (Mn)
Mercury (Hg)
Nickel (Ni)
Zinc (Zn)

Anionic Metals

Arsenic (As)
Boron (B)
Molybdenum (Mo)
Selenium (Se)

PLANTS USED FOR PHYTOREMEDIATION

Lead (in order of effectiveness): Indian and Japanese Mustard, Scented Geranium, Corn, Pumpkins, Sunflowers, Penny Cress, Amaranth, Nettles, Tomatoes

Arsenic: Chinese Brake Ferns

Nickel and Cadmium: Scented Geranium[8]

COMPOST BIOREMEDIATION

The most direct and easiest method of treating contaminated soil is to simply add compost—which is just great for gardens no matter what! Many toxic metals will readily form compounds with the organic particles found in compost. When this occurs, the metals essentially get "locked up" and are less likely to be absorbed into the bodies of plants, making them in turn less likely to be eaten. Compost high in phosphates will bind with lead to form a stable compound called chloropyromorphite. In one study, the addition of compost reduced lead **bioavailability** by 39 percent.[9] To some extent, the microbes living in compost will act to break down chemical pollutants, particularly hydrocarbons.

Adding compost to soil complements other bioremediation techniques. It creates habitat and provides nutrients for many of the organisms cultivated by other strategies. It will also facilitate future plant growth.

A good use for a piece of possibly contaminated land is a community composting operation. The land may be unfit for growing food, but suitable for surface compost piles. Finished compost can be shared with neighbors, and unused compost can be raked across the surface of the property. Not only will the organisms present in the compost assist with remediating toxins, the compost itself will act as a physical barrier between the contaminated soil and people. In time, a sufficient depth of compost may allow people to garden there. If it is too much work to run a composting operation, consider spreading wood mulch, which can often be acquired for free from tree mulching businesses. Although not as rich in bacterial life as compost, wood mulch is an excellent habitat for fungi, provides a barrier, and will eventually turn into soil.

While soil is in the process of being remediated, it is safer to grow food in raised containers, like old bathtubs or pots, filled with soil that is known to be clean.

AIR PURIFICATION

Air is the most immediate of all human needs. Unfortunately, the air of most urban areas can be difficult to breathe, if not eye-searing. Exhaust from vehicles, industry, and power generation creates a toxic smog. The short-term health effects of breathing polluted air include headaches and eye and lung irritation. Long-term effects include asthma, emphysema, and cancer. As a gas, air transports pollution over large distances. While water and soil contamination tend to be localized, the origin of air contamination could be miles away and possibly be from numerous sources. Controlling and remediating air pollution is an important political struggle and public

Air enters through the surface of the soil and passes by the roots of the plants, where bacteria break down toxins present in the air.

While most plants have some capability of removing toxins from the air, these do at accelerated rates:

Reca palm
Corn plant
Lady palm
Bamboo palm
Ficus/Weeping fig
Boston fern
English ivy
Mum
Umbrella tree
Peace lily

health issue, particularly as poorer, inner city communities suffer disproportionately from poor air quality.

Next to stopping pollution at its source, the most basic defense against outdoor air pollution is to plant more trees. Aside from producing oxygen, tree leaves act as filters. Leaves catch particulate matter on their surfaces and prevent people from inhaling them.

Less commonly considered is indoor air pollution. Typical building materials contain all kinds of toxins, including the volatile organic compounds (**VOCs**) benzene, xylene, and chloroform. Particle board and plywood release formaldehyde, a carcinogenic gas. Paints and adhesives also release VOCs. The release of these toxins into the air is called **offgassing**. Many buildings are built to be nearly airtight. While airtightness is great for heat retention in cold weather, ventilation is important. With no exchange of outside air, toxins (and mold) can build up and cause the health-threatening situation known as **sick building syndrome**.

Humans themselves offgas. Over time, humans will render a hermetically sealed space unlivable because of the excretion of **bioeffluents**. These airborne chemicals include alcohols, ammonia, and acetones.

Indoor plants can greatly reduce the amount of chemicals inhaled. Plants have the ability to remove offgassed toxins and bioeffluents from the air. This discovery was made by NASA during a search for a low-energy means of air purification on space ships.

Plants' purification mechanism is facilitated by the process of **transpiration**. As water droplets and oxygen are emitted from plant leaves, a convective effect is produced that draws carbon dioxide and other gases through the soil of the plants into the root zone, or the rhizosphere. Soil microbes in the rhizosphere break down toxic chemicals and convert them into useful nutrients for the plants.

Designs exist that use plants to filter a building's entire ventilation system. All incoming air is forced to pass through plant roots before being inhaled. It is theorized that such systems could remove life-threatening bacteria, like the kind that causes legionnaires' disease, from the air. Simply keeping houseplants can help improve indoor air quality.

Houseplants come in many shapes and sizes, each needing varying levels of sun and water. Tropical plants are typically easy to care for, preferring low light and little water, similar to conditions on a rainforest floor. A little research into specific needs will make for a much happier plant. Applications of vermicompost will help them thrive. A common cause of death for houseplants is overwatering. Plants can develop root rot from sitting in water. Cat feces and urine are also deadly to most plants. Covering the soil surface with stones can discourage cats from using the plant as a litter box.

Often, businesses that provide and maintain plants for office buildings throw them out after their first year—a possible houseplant goldmine!

PUTTING IT ALL TOGETHER

It can be a challenge to determine the most appropriate bioremediation strategy for any given site. Information about contaminant levels may not be available, and the idea of culturing remediative organisms may seem daunting. As with most things, it makes sense to begin on a small scale, and become more ambitious as confidence is gained. Consider this simple strategy: Begin with importing large amounts of compost to make a suitable habitat for organisms that will later be introduced. Next apply compost tea. Treatments with fungi and plants can then follow. If conducting soil tests is not possible, it is likely that this broad approach will degrade or bind up some of the toxins that may be present, though there is no guarantee that the soil will be safe for gardening. At a minimum, however, it will greatly improve the overall quality of the soil.

Toxic soil is an unfortunate reality of urban living. Through intelligent intervention on our part, we can improve the quality of soils for the benefit of generations to come.

HURRICANE KATRINA: A CASE STUDY IN APPLIED BIOREMEDIATION

Hurricane Katrina devastated the Gulf Coast and the city of New Orleans in September 2005. It left numerous oil spills, toxic hot spots, and biological pollution (sewage) in its wake, compounding the multitude of social and environmental problems already plaguing the region.

One of the ironic consequences of the flood was that it brought the nation's attention to the area after years of neglect. In New Orleans, grassroots organizations were able to receive donations of testing supplies from laboratories eager to contribute to the relief effort. One of the greatest limitations to implementing community-based bioremediation technologies is the cost of conducting soil and water tests, and these donations allowed groups without academic

A snapshot of the damage caused by Hurricane Katrina.

or governmental financial support the rare opportunity to get a clearer picture of the extent of the contamination.

One such organization is the Meg Perry Bioremediation Project, part of the Common Ground Collective. The group mapped New Orleans' toxic profile using independently collected soil and water samples. This map verified the official data presented by government authorities, whose data in the past has been known to be inaccurate.

The group has also worked to create the infrastructure for a community-based bioremediation project. It built compost tea brewers to make tea for application in the yards of residents and distributed sunflower seeds for lead remediation. The toxicological data collected from these remediation experiments will give a better picture of the effectiveness of different methods.

The lessons learned here will not only benefit the people of New Orleans by assisting them in cleaning the soil in their backyards, but will be applicable to residents of contaminated cities all over the world.

ACCESS TO LAND

Creating and building sustainable systems in a city requires a considerable amount of time, energy, and love. A person's reluctance to make investments into a property they don't own is understandable. It is absolutely heartbreaking to be evicted from a rented or squatted property after putting in years of work. Money is also a concern. While the systems in this book are designed to be affordable, it makes little sense to spend money to improve a landlord's property on top of paying rent. Systems like those that reuse graywater sometimes involve extensive retrofits that could jeopardize a renter's security deposit.

Secured access to land is desirable when creating long-lasting projects worthy of a significant investment of resources. Land pro-

Tempoculture

Many of the systems described in this book are portable or small enough to be brought with a person when they move. Others, such as garden beds, ponds, or constructed wetlands, can be designed to be detached and moved. Food can be grown in containers like pots, bathtubs, old toilets, and truck beds. Attaching wheels to the bottom of a container is an easy way to make it transportable. Easier still would be access to a forklift and a pickup truck.

vides the basis for community self-reliance, equality, and justice. Security of place also encourages people to take the effort that it takes to build real community. The struggle for land is at the center of many revolutionary movements. Although acquiring land or space in a city can be quite difficult, individuals and community groups have used creative strategies to successfully acquire or secure access to property.

BUYING LAND

The legal purchase of property can be confusing: whether or not to hire a real estate agent, how to make a bid, what inspections should be done, how to arrange financing, how much does a closing cost, etc. Many homeowner advocacy organizations or governmental agencies offer classes to help first-time home-buyers navigate the complex process. The right real estate agent can also be very helpful.

In most cases, financing the purchase of a building will necessitate a mortgage. An investigation of local resources could be fruitful—cities often have grant programs to help first-time homeowners. Also, the Permaculture Credit Union in Santa Fe, New Mexico, gives loans for permaculture inspired projects.

Many times abandoned or neglected buildings and vacant lots can be bought relatively cheaply. Counties seize properties from people who have not paid their property taxes and auction them off to the highest bidder. Information on properties and upcoming auctions can be found at county tax offices. Counties may also be willing to sell the buildings to non-profits for cost (back taxes) outside of an auction. Depending on the neighborhood, consideration should be given to the issue of gentrification in the seizure and purchasing of properties.

Non-profit groups can conduct capital campaigns to raise the money to buy property. Capital campaigns are intense fundraising efforts for a specific project, often property-related.

ADVERSE POSSESSION

Adverse possession is a process that allows people to claim legal title to a piece of land after openly occupying it for an extended period of time. The person doing so must be obvious about the fact that they are using the property, and must be the only ones using it. The details of the law, including the period of time, vary from state to state.

SQUATTING

A less secure method to access land is squatting or guerilla gardening on abandoned property. While it runs the risk of eviction and, on occasion, arrest, it could begin the process of adverse possession.

The MST, the Brasilian landless workers movement, provides a stand out example of people gaining access to millions of acres of land. Over 530,000 families have peacefully occupied unused lands, and over half of them have received legal title to those lands. Their occupations are working to create people-centered socio-economic structures. Schools, clinics, and cooperative farms have been built. MST chapters have sprung up across Latin America, making it the largest social movement in the region.

PROPERTY DONATIONS

One of the greatest advantages of being a non-profit is the ability to receive donations in exchange for tax write-offs. Landowners are more likely to donate property to a legal charity. A developer or individual may make more money from a write-off than they would dealing with a particular property, or they may really support the cause.

City governments often own many buildings and lots and can be convinced to donate outright, or at least donate the use of urban space for non-profit projects that benefit city residents. Similarly, county governments can donate foreclosed buildings and lots to non-profits.

More Gardens!

The New York City based organization More Gardens! is committed to creating community garden space and to protecting existing gardens. Since 1998, they have worked to save hundreds of garden spaces in New York City that have been threatened by developers, using tactics ranging from legislative appeals to direct action. Recognizing the importance of education and community outreach, More Gardens! also brings gardening workshops to local schools.

Mill Creek Farm

The Philadelphia Water Department put out a request in 2005 for proposals for projects on a 2-acre piece of land they owned in the Mill Creek Neighborhood of West Philadelphia. For the past 15 years a community garden had been located on part of the lot and the rest was vacant. The Mill Creek Farm's proposal to create a cooperatively-run urban educational farm was chosen and given a 99-year lease. It was the only proposal to incorporate the existing community garden. The Mill Creek Farm is dedicated to improving food security and access to nutritious foods, while educating school groups and the public about urban agriculture, natural resource management, and sustainable living. They have displays of a biodiesel operation, and a cob cottage with solar panels, a living roof, a composting toilet, and graywater collection. They are committed to improving the wellbeing of the neighborhood and partnering elder community gardeners with local youth. They are funded through donations, grants, and income from produce sales.

THE RHIZOME COLLECTIVE'S GROVE BROWNFIELD

Brownfield: A property that reuse of is complicated by the presence or potential presence of a hazardous substance, pollutant, or contaminant.

In 2002, we visited the City of Austin Brownfield Redevelopment Office and learned about the 9.8-acre Grove Brownfield, which had been a legally-operated, privately-owned landfill from 1967 to 1970. Following the closure of the landfill an additional 5,000 cubic yards of debris had been illegally dumped. The owner decided it was more economical to donate the land than to clean and sell it and was looking for a non-profit to take it on.

In 2004, the Rhizome Collective was donated the Grove Brownfield. We applied for and received a $200,000 EPA Brownfield Cleanup Award to clean the property. The grant provides federal funding to clean contaminated properties. In our application we outlined a vision to use innovative sustainable technologies to clean the debris from the site. Instead of just moving the trash to another landfill, it would be utilized to build infrastructure for the park we wished to create.

The cleanup officially began in January 2005 when the multi-person crew and generous volunteers took on the formidable task of taking down the 25-foot-high by 600-foot-long wall of debris. The wall was a giant jigsaw puzzle that needed to be undone piece by piece; crew members carefully dismantled this monolithic mountain of trash. A tractor powered by vegetable oil expedited the cleanup by extracting tires and tangled unidentifiable metal objects, and by pulling down concrete blocks.

All debris was separated into piles based on its potential to be recycled: metal, asphalt shingles, wood scraps, tires, concrete, glass, and mixed trash. All the metal and glass were taken to local recycling facilities. Some wood was put through a chipper/shredder to create mulch for trails while some was used as erosion control to fill in a badly eroded gully. Concrete was consolidated and kept onsite to be used in building infrastructure for the park in the future. We searched for a local recycler of asphalt shingles, but found none. The only option was to landfill the shingles along with the mixed household trash pulled off the pile. From January 2005 to July 2006, we removed 680 tires, 10.1 tons and 36.5 cubic yards of trash, and 31.6 tons of recyclable metal from the site. Huge amounts of wood scrap and concrete were diverted from landfills and used for erosion control.

As there is no power on the site, combinations of biofuel generators and solar panels were set up to power equipment. Other examples of sustainable technologies employed included chainsaws inoculated with fungi-spore-laden oil (used to assist in the degradation of residual pollutants) and the construction of floating islands made from recovered soda bottles. (See Floating Islands page 84) The islands create habitat for diverse aquatic life forms that bioremediate toxins flowing through the retention pond on the property.

The process of turning the brownfield into an Ecological Justice Education Park has begun.

SUSTAINABILITY AND GENTRIFICATION

Gentrification is a process where historically working-class neighborhoods or communities of color are transformed to the benefit of middle- and upper-class people. Although it occurs most commonly in inner cities, gentrification happens in rural locations as well. Generally, gentrification begins with a coalition of landowners, business owners, banks, and city planners that strategize to profit off the increase of property values in a neighborhood where they plan to invest. This is often done by creating new up-scale real estate and business developments and "cleaning up" a neighborhood—reducing crime rates through increased police oppression.

These changes are designed to make an area more attractive to wealthier people who will support high-end businesses and be able to afford expensive rents.

The increase of property values creates economic pressure in a neighborhood that usually results in the displacement of a neighborhood's poorer residents, many times families that have been living in an area for generations. Not able to afford increased rents or pay property taxes at reassessed higher rates, displaced people often end up moving to the outskirts of cities, or becoming homeless. One of the most tragic consequences of displacement is the destruction of communities. The networks and relationships formed over years are easily lost when people are relocated.

Gentrification can have a rippling effect. Development that is initially concentrated to one neighborhood can cause surrounding areas to become attractive to speculators as well. Although the exact form that gentrification takes can vary greatly from place to place, the end result is almost always that the poor lose while the wealthy plunder.

Working-class neighborhoods deserve community gardens, green spaces, and easy access to healthy food, transportation, and services. It is a deplorable catch-22 that these quality of life improvements often put a community at risk of being gentrified.

There has been a recent trend to use the term *sustainability* and its alleged principles to promote gentrifying developments. Programs that go under the names *smart growth* and *new urbanism* are often agents of gentrification masquerading themselves in the rosy language of sustainable development. Many high-income housing projects are promoted as being *green* and *sustainable* because they have incorporated a few environmental features in their design, such as natural building methods or solar panels. It is a horrible abuse of the term "sustainability" to use it to describe developments that proceed without regard to issues of class and race, or concern about the destruction of communities. In a radical analysis of sustainability, nothing that displaces a neighborhood's poorer residents can be considered sustainable.

In a capitalist society, economic forces push for gentrification, making it difficult to challenge. There are many differing opinions on the causes of gentrification and appropriate strategies to combat it. As it can manifest differently in every community, responses must be formed locally. While abolishing gentrification may seem impossible, it can be fought against, and in some cases, stopped.

Recently, gentrifiers have attempted to recast gentrification as having a positive social influence, or to assert its inevitability. As many people are entirely unfamiliar with gentrification, creating community dialogue about its existence and negative consequences is an important first step. Positive resistance to gentrification can take several forms. Rent controls, tax limitations, and land trust programs that support low-income home owners can work to combat gentrification. An awareness of and resistance to gentrification is critical to autonomous urban communities.

CONCLUSION

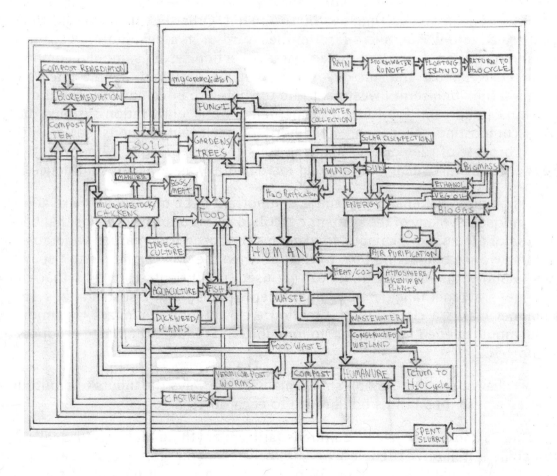

This book is chockful of information about a variety of different systems that can be applied on a range of scales. Deciding which systems to build and how to link them together is a decision that depends on goals and available resources.

Some people may be focused on their desire to live in a more environmentally sustainable way. Practical beginning options for this goal might include using worms to compost kitchen scraps and keeping some indoor mushroom logs—simple systems that can be done in an apartment without sunlight. Other people may want to create a small-scale, zero-waste, micro-farm in their yard or in a neighboring vacant lot. A gardening operation supported by rainwater collection systems, mound composting, constructed wetlands, and microlivestock could be designed. People interested in making a large, long-term investment into a whole urban community could develop aquaculture ponds and food forests, emergency water purification systems, human manure composting toilets, and neighborhood-scale autonomous power sources. The long process of remediating toxins in soils could also begin. With most things it makes sense to start small and build up incrementally as you gain confidence.

When designing a sustainable system, it is important to be mindful of the relationship of its components. Many of the systems described in this book have yields that become the inputs of others. For example, food scraps produced from garden vegetables can be put in a worm composting box, worms grown in the box can be fed to fish, whose wastes (along with worm castings) can be used as nutrients by plants that can be used to generate methane gas. Cycling nutrients throughout a sustainable system in this manner makes a **closed loop**. Creating a closed loop minimizes the amount of external inputs needed for a system to function, and reduces the waste products that are exported.

The chart that opens this section shows many of the ways the inputs and outputs of the systems described in this book relate to each other.

Today's world and industrialized culture is far from anything that could be called true sustainability—millions of people are completely reliant on a fossil fuel driven economy to provide them with their needs. Were this system to fail without a sustainable alternative in place, as is likely to happen with society's current trajectory, millions would perish. As it would be the world's landless poor who would suffer most, to wish for a sudden and dramatic collapse is misanthropic and untenable. A transition towards a sustainable society that is both rapid and urgent, yet still accounting for human needs, must begin. The process of building sustainable infrastructure can be started by implementing the technologies described in this book on as broad of a scale as possible. As a large percentage of the world's landless poor live in cities, constructing these systems in urban environments can minimize their suffering, and with enough work may even create conditions of prosperity.

While it is most likely that we will not see "true sustainability" in our lifetimes, it is a goal that must be worked towards. The enormous task given to our generation is to figure out how to repair the damage that has been done to our natural systems, to undo the social structures that act as blockades to self-reliance, and begin building communities and networks that are founded in the values of sustainability and egalitarianism.

RESOURCES

FOOD

AQUACULTURE

Aquaponics.com (Basic information)
www.aquaponics.com

Fox, Ripley D. *Spirulina: Production and Potential*. Aix-en-Province, France: Editions Edisud, 1996. (Explains a low-tech, low-cost method to grow spirulina that is used in the Global South.)

Furuno, Takao. *The Power of Duck*. Sisters Creek, Australia: Tagari Publications, 2001. (Duck-azolla-tilapia-rice-loach fish polyculture manual.)

Hutchinson, Laurence. *Ecological Aquaculture*. East Meon, UK: Permanent Publications, 2005. (More appropriate for owners of larger land parcels, but still useful for urban applications.)

Logsdon, Gene. *Getting Food From Water.* Emmaus, PA: Rodale Press, 1978. (One of the best books on small-scale aquaculture.)

Molyneaux, Paul. *Swimming in Circles: Aquaculture and the End of Wild Oceans*. New York: Thunder's Mouth Press, 2006.

The New Alchemy Institute
www.vsb.cape.com/~nature/greencenter/aquaculture.html (A list of all publications on aquaculture by the New Alchemy Institute, which researched aquaculture and sustainable systems from 1971 to 1991, with an order form for print copies.)

Romanowski, Nick. *Sustainable Freshwater Aquaculture*. Sydney, Australia: University of New South Wales Press, 2007.

ENDNOTES
ONE—FOOD

1. "Greenhouse Earth map insert," *National Geographic* (October 2007).

2. Charles C. Mann, *1491: New Revelations of the Americas Before Columbus* (New York: Vintage Books, 2006).

3. Karma Glos, *Humane and Healthy Poultry Production: A Manual for Organic Growers*. Organic Principles and Practices Handbook Series, Northeast Organic Farming Association (Athol, MA: Highland Press, 2004).

4. Cheryl Long and Tabitha Alterman, "Meet Real Free-Range Eggs," *Mother Earth News,* October/November 2007.

5. Slow Food U.S.A., 20 Jay St., No. 313, Brooklyn, NY 11201; www.slowfood.org.

6. Erik Millstone and Tim Lang, *Penguin Atlas of Food: Who Eats What, Where, and Why* (New York: Penguin Books, 2003), 52.

7. Boris Worm et al., "Impacts of Biodiversity Loss on Ocean Ecosystem Services," *Science* 314, no. 5800 (2006): 787–790.

8. For more information on determining which fish are safe to

eat in what quantities, see "Safe Sustainable Seafood" by Coop America at www.coopamerica.org/pubs/realmoney/articles/seafood.cfm; the Environmental Working Group at ewg.org; and Paul Johnson, *Fish Forever: The Definitive Guide to Understanding, Selecting, and Preparing Healthy, Delicious, and Environmentally Sustainable Seafood* (Hoboken, NJ: Wiley, 2007).

9. George Kling, "The Flow of Energy: Primary Production to Higher Trophic Levels" (lecture, Global Change Curriculum, University of Michigan, Nov. 15, 2005), www.globalchange.umich.edu/globalchange1/current/lectures/kling/energyflow/energyflow.html.

10. Frank Allmer, "Duckweed Soup," *Futureframe: International Webzine for Science and Culture,* March 13, 2000, www.morgenwelt.de/futureframe/000313-duckweed.htm.

11. From 1978 to 1996, the US Department of Energy conducted an experiment called the Aquatic Species Program, extensively researching algae's oil-producing potential. Their final report is: John Sheehan et al., *A Look Back at the U.S. Department of Energy's Aquatic Species Program—Biodiesel From Algae* (Golden, CO: National Renewable Energy Laboratory, US Department of Energy, Midwest Research Institute, 1998), www.nrel.gov/docs/legosti/fy98/24190.pdf.

Todd, John. "Ecological Aquaculture at Ocean Arks," *Annals of Earth 18, no. 2 (2000),* available at http://oceanarks.org/annals/articles/aquaculture/.

Van Gorder, Steven D. *Small Scale Aquaculture*. Breinigsville, PA: The Alternative Aquaculture Association, 2000. (Great introduction to basic aquaculture.)

Woods, Jonathan. The Urban Aquaculture Manual. www.webofcreation.org/BuildingGrounds/aqua/TOC.html.

BIOSHELTERS

Freeman, Mark. *Building Your Own Greenhouse*. Mechanicsburg, PA: Stackpole Books, 1997.

McCullagh, James C. *Solar Greenhouse Book*. Emmaus, PA: Rodale Press, 1978.

DOMESTICATED ANIMALS AND DISEASE RESISTANCE

Crosby, Alfred. *Ecological Imperialism: The Biological Expansion of Europe*. Cambridge University Press, 2004.

Diamond, Jared. *Guns, Germs, and Steel*. New York: W. W. Norton, 2005.

Mann, Charles C. *1491: New Revelations of the Americas Before Columbus*. New York: Vintage Books, 2006.

INSECT CULTIVATION

Gordon, David George. *Eat-a-Bug Cookbook*. Berkeley, CA: Ten Speed Press, 1998.

Menzel, Peter and Faith D'Alusio. *Man Eating Bugs: The Art and Science of Eating Insects*. Berkeley, CA: Ten Speed Press, 1998.

Ramos-Elorduy, Julieta. *Creepy Crawly Cuisine: A Gourmet Guide to Edible Insects*. Rochester, VT: Park Street Press, 1998.

FOOD TREES

Jacke, Dave with Eric Toensmeier. *Edible Forest Gardens*. White River Junction, VT: Chelsea Green, 2005. An encyclopedia-length two-volume set describing food forests and their design.

Toensmeier, Eric. *Perennial Vegetables*. White River Junction, VT: Chelsea Green, 2007.

GARDENING

Ellis, Barbara W. and Fern Marshall Bradley, eds. *The Organic Gardener's Handbook of Natural Insect and Disease Control*. Emmaus, PA: Rodale Press, 1996.

Jeavons, John. *How to Grow More Vegetables: And Fruits, Nuts, Berries, Grains, and Other Crops*. Berkeley, CA: Ten Speed Press, 2006.

Pears, Pauline, ed. *Rodale's Illustrated Encyclopedia of Organic Gardening*. New York: DK Publishing, 2002.

GENERAL

Pfeiffer, Dale Allen. *Eating Fossil Fuels*. Gabriola Island, BC: New Society Publishers, 2006.

Woelfle-Erskine, Cleo. *Urban Wilds*. Oakland, CA: water/under/ground publications, 2003.

MICROLIVESTOCK

Lee, Andy and Pat Foreman. *Chicken Tractor: The Permaculture Guide to Happy Hens and Healthy Soil*. Buena Vista, VA: Good Earth Publications, 2000.

MUSHROOM LOGS

McCoy, Jenn. *A Guide to Outdoor Mushroom Log Cultivation: Highlighting Shiitake, Reishi, and Tree Oyster Mushrooms*. Dorchester, NH: D Acres of New Hampshire, 2004, available at www.dacres.org/pdfs/MushroomCultivationGuide.pdf. (Great guide to making mushroom logs.)

12. US Environmental Protection Agency, "Fact Sheet: Final Rule to Reduce Toxic Air Emissions From Asphalt Processing and Asphalt Roofing Manufacturing Facilities" (Washington, DC: US Environmental Protection Agency, February 28, 2003).

13. See www.hud.gov/offices/lead/training/LBPguide.pdf

14. Peter Menzel and Faith D'Aluisio, *Man Eating Bugs: The Art and Science of Eating Insects* (Berkeley, CA: Ten Speed Press, 1998).

TWO—WATER

1. Robin Clarke and Janet King, *The Water Atlas: A Unique Visual Analysis of the World's Most Critical Resource* (New York: The New Press, 2004), 20.

2. For a thorough examination of dams and their consequences, see Cleo Woelfle-Erskine, July Oskar Cole, and Laura Allen, eds., *Dam Nation: Dispatches From the Water Underground* (New York: Soft Skull Press, 2007).

3. Alexander Cockburn and Jeffrey St. Claire. "To the Last Drop: Why the Colorado River Doesn't Meet the Sea" *CounterPunch* 3/14/01 http://www.counterpunch.org/colorado.html.

4. Clarke and King, (2004), 24.

5. Peter H. Gleick, *Dirty Water: Estimated Deaths from Water-Related Disease 2000–2020* (Oakland, CA: Pacific Institute for Studies in Development, Environment, and Security, 2002), 4.

6. Committee on Fluoride in Drinking Water, Board on Environmental Studies and Toxicology, Division on Earth and Life Studies, National Research Council of the National Academies, *Fluoride in Drinking Water: A Scientific Review of EPA's Standards*. (Washington, DC: The National Academies Press, 2006).

7. American Dental Association, *ADA eGRAM: Interim Guidance on Reconstituted Infant Formula*, (Chicago: ADA, November 9, 2006), www.ada.org/prof/resources/pubs/epubs/egram/egram_061109.pdf.

8. Fluoride Action Network, "Communities Which Have Rejected Fluoridation Since 1990," www.fluoridealert.org/communities.htm (accessed Jan. 3, 2008).

9. Certain strains of hepatitis can live up to a half hour in boiling water, and bacterial endospores can survive for hours. Some bacteria have the ability to turn into endospores and essentially hibernate. These inactive cells have strong coats and are very hard to kill. Thousands-of-years-old endospores have been discovered and coaxed back into living cells. Gerard Tortora, Berdell Funke, and Christine

Stamets, Paul. *Mycellium Running*. Berkeley, CA: Ten Speed Press, 2005. (Contains basic information on log culture, as well as other mushroom-growing techniques.)

WATER

FLOATING ISLANDS

Ocean Arks International
http://oceanarks.org/restorer/
This Massachusetts-based operation is an innovator of floating-island restorer technology.

RAINWATER COLLECTION/PURIFICATION

Banks, Suzy and Richard Heinichen. *Rainwater Collection for the Mechanically Challenged*. Dripping Springs, TX: Tank Town, 2006.

Huisman, L. and W. E. Wood. *Slow Sand Filtration*. Geneva: World Health Organization, 1974.

Lancaster, Brad. *Rainwater Harvesting for Drylands (Vol. 1): Guiding Principles to Welcome Rain into Your Life and Landscape.* White River Junction, VT: Chelsea Green Publishing, 2006.

Ludwig, Art. *Water Storage: Tanks, Cisterns, Aquifers and Ponds*. Santa Barbara, CA: Oasis Design, 2005.

Sand Filtration
www.oasisdesign.net/water/treatment/slowsandfilter.htm

Solar Water Disinfection
Swiss Federal Institute for Environmental Science and Technology
www.sodis.ch

WATER PRIVATIZATION

Barlow, Maude and Tony Clark. *Blue Gold*. New York: New Press, 2003.

Olivera, Oscar and Tom Lewis. *¡Cochabamba!: Water War in Bolivia*. Cambridge, MA: South End Press, 2004.

Reisner, Marc. *Cadillac Desert*. London: Pimlico, 2001.

Shiva, Vandana. *Water Wars: Privatization, Pollution, and Profit*. Cambridge, MA: South End Press, 2002.

Woelfle-Erskine, Cleo, July Oskar Cole, and Laura Allen. *Dam Nation: Dispatches from the Water Underground*. New York: Soft Skull Press, 2007.

WASTE

AIR PURIFICATION

Wolverton, B.C. *How to Grow Fresh Air: 50 House Plants that Purify Your Home or Office*. New York: Penguin, 1997.

COMPOSTING

Gershuny, Grace and Deborah L. Martin. *The Rodale Book of Composting*. New York: Rodale Press, 1990.

HUMAN WASTE RECYCLING

Jenkins, Joseph. *The Humanure Handbook*. White River Junction, VT: Chelsea Green Publishing, 1999.

Steinfeld, Carol. *Liquid Gold*. New Bedford, MA: Ecowaters Publishing, 2004.

VERMICOMPOSTING

Appelhof, Mary. *Worms Eat My Garbage*. Kalamazoo, MI: Flower Press, 1997.

WASTEWATER RECYCLING

Woelfle-Erskine, Cleo, July Oskar Cole, and Laura Allen. *Dam Nation: Dispatches from the Water Underground*. New York: Soft Skull Press, 2007.

Campbell, Craig S. and Michael H. Ogden. *Constructed Wetlands in the Sustainable Landscape*. New York: John Wiley and Sons Inc, 1999.

Case, *Microbiology: An Introduction* (San Francisco: Pearson Education, Inc., 2004).

10. The Swiss Federal Institute for Environmental Science and Technology (EAWAG) has conducted numerous tests on solar disinfection. For more information, including charts of pathogens killed and lists of research studies, see www.sodis.ch.

THREE—WASTE

1. Lynn Margulis and Dorian Sagan, *Microcosmos: Four Billion Years of Microbial Evolution* (Berkeley: University of California Press, 1997), 88, and http://en.wikipedia.org/wiki/Pilus.

2. Pedal People Cooperative, Inc., PO Box 415, Northampton, MA 01061; www.pedalpeople.com.

3. University of California Cooperative Extension, Placer and Nevada counties, *Composting 101: Carbon and Nitrogen*, http://ucce.ucdavis.edu/files/filelibrary/1808/353.PDF; and Joseph Jenkins, *The Humanure Handbook: A Guide to Composting Human Manure,* Second Edition (Grove City, PA: Jenkins Publishing, 1999), 56.

FOUR—ENERGY

1. Thomas Flannery, *The Weather Makers: How Man Is Changing the*

Climate and What It Means for Life on Earth (New York: Atlantic Monthly Press, 2006), 162.

2. Helen Caldicott, *Nuclear Power Is Not the Answer* (New York: New Press, 2006), 8.

3. Ibid.

4. http://www.css.cornell.edu/faculty/lehmann/terra_preta/TerraPretahome.htm.

5. http://www.green-trust.org/woodgas.htm.

6. Michael Crook, *A Chinese Biogas Manual*. (London: Intermediate Technology Publications, 1976), 11.

FIVE—BIOREMEDIATION

1. Lynn Margulis and Dorian Sagan, *Microcosmos: Four Billion Years of Microbial Evolution*. (Berkeley: University of California Press, 1997).

2. Jeff Barnard, "Oregon's Monster Mushroom is World's Biggest Living Thing," *The London Independent*, August 6, 2000.

3. Ekaterina Dadachova, et al., "Ionizing Radiation Changes the Electronic Properties of Melanin and Enhances the Growth of Melanized Fungi," *PLoS ONE* 2(5): e457 (2007), www.plosone.org/article/fetchArticle.action?art

Ludwig, Art. *The New Create an Oasis With Greywater: Choosing, Building and Using Greywater Systems —Includes Branched Drains*. Santa Barbara, CA: Oasis Designs, 2006.

ENERGY

BIOGAS

Crook, Michael. *A Chinese Biogas Manual*. London: Intermediate Technology Publications Ltd., 1976.

House, David. *Biogas Handbook*. USA: Alternative House Information, 2006.

BIOCHAR

Biochar overview
www.css.cornell.edu/faculty/lehmann/biochar/Biochar_home.htm

http://terrapreta.bioenergylists.org

Biomass gasification
http://techsci.msun.edu/cots/biomass_gasification.htm

CLIMATE CHANGE

Flannery, Tim. *The Weather Makers: How Man Is Changing the Climate and What It Means for Life on Earth*. New York: Atlantic Monthly Press, 2006.

Rising Tide (a climate justice organization)
http://risingtidenorthamerica.org

Environmental Justice Climate Change Initiative
http://www.ejcc.org

GENERAL

Heinberg, Richard. *The Party's Over: Oil, War, and the Fate of Industrial Societies*. Gabriola Island, BC: New Society Publishers, 2005.

Pfeiffer, Dale Allen. *Eating Fossil Fuels*. Gabriola Island, BC: New Society Publishers, 2006.

The Post Carbon Institute
www.postcarbon.org/

PASSIVE SOLAR

Halacy, Beth and Halacy, Dan. *Cooking With the Sun: How to Build and Use Solar Cookers*. Lafayette, CA: Morning Sun Press, 1992.

Reif, Daniel K., *Passive Solar Water Heaters*. Andover, MA: Brick House Publishing Co., 1983.

Parabolic Dishes
www.humboldt.edu/~ccat/solarcooking/parabolic/parabolic_solar_cooker_pg_3_html.htm

ROCKET STOVES

How to build a rocket stove
http://video.google.com/videoplay?docid=797446823830833401

ETHANOL

Gingery, Vincent R. *The Secrets of Building an Alcohol Producing Still*. Rogersville, MO: David J Gingery Publishing LLC, 1994.

Blume, David. *Alcohol Can Be a Gas! Fueling an Ethanol Revolution for the 21st Century*. Santa Cruz, CA: The International Institute for Ecological Agriculture, 2007.

Doxon, Lynn Ellen. *The Alcohol Fuel Handbook*. Haverford, PA: Infinity Publishing.com, 2001.

VEGGIE DIESELS

Greasecar Vegetable Fuel Systems
www.greasecar.com

Holan, Ray. *Sliding Home: A Complete Guide to Driving Your Diesel on Straight Vegetable Oil*. 7th ed. Cleveland: Ray Holan, 2006.
PlantDrive
www.plantdrive.com

icleURI=info:doi/10.1371/journal.pone.0000457.

4. For a chart of contaminants that different species of fungi are capable of degrading, see Paul Stamets, *Mycelium Running* (Berkeley, CA: Ten Speed Press, 2005).

5. Paul Stamets, "Helping the Ecosystem Through Mushroom Cultivation," Fungi Perfecti's Mycotechnology Page, www.fungiperfecti.com/mycotech/mycova.html (accessed January 2008).

6. The study was conducted by Phytotech Inc., later bought by Edenspace Systems Corporation. Information on the study is found in their Statement of Qualifications, under Magic Marker Site, Trenton, New Jersey, at www.edenspace.com/qualification.html.

7. Worcester Roots Project, Stone Soup Building, 4 King St., Worcester, MA 01610; www.worcesterroots.org.

8. Plant list compiled by the Worcester Roots Project, www.worcesterroots.org.

9. Sally Brown et al., "In Situ Soil Treatments to Reduce the Phyto- and Bioavailability of Lead, Zinc, and Cadmium," *Journal of Environmental Quality* 33 (2004): 522–531.

WIND POWER

Axial-flux windmills
www.otherpower.com
www.scoraigwind.com

Computer magnets
www.reuk.co.uk/Hard-Disk-Drive-Magnets-For-Wind-Turbines.htm

Detailed plans for constructing a turbine out of mostly recycled parts for under $150. Its blades are made from PVC pipes, and its alternator is made from a recycled permanent magnet motor. For particularly resourceful people, this design may work out to be a cheap and practical way to produce wind power in a city. Davis, Michael. "How I Home-Built an Electricity Producing Wind Turbine." 2006, www.mdpub.com/Wind_Turbine/index.html.

Hackleman, Michael A. and David W. House. *Wind and Windspinners: A Nuts and Bolts Approach to Wind-Electric Systems*. Culver City, CA: Peace Press, 1974.

Kozlowski, Jozef A. *Savonius Rotor Construction: Vertical Axis Wind Machines from Oil Drums*. Mt. Ranier, MD: Vita Publishing, 1977.

Savonius turbines and photos of ingenious windmill designs
www.southcom.com.au/~windmill/

BIOREMEDIATION

Harte, John, et al. *Toxics A to Z: A Guide to Everyday Pollution Hazards*. Berkeley: University of California Press, 1991.

Higa, Teruo. *An Earth Saving Revolution*. English edition, Vol. 2. Tokyo: Sunmark Publishing, Inc., 1998. (By the developer of Effective Microorganisms.)

Ingham, Elaine. *The Compost Tea Brewing Manual*. Corvallis, OR: Soil Foodweb, Inc., 2003. www.soilfoodweb.com/02_resources/c_tea_manual.html.

Margulis, Lynn and Dorian Sagan. *Microcosmos: Four Billion Years of Microbial Evolution*. Berkeley: University of California Press, 1997.

Raskin, Ilya and Burt D. Ensley. *Phytoremediation of Toxic Metals: Using Plants to Clean Up the Environment*. Hoboken, NJ: Wiley-Interscience, 1999.

Stamets, Paul. *Mycelium Running: How Mushrooms Can Help Save the World*. Berkeley, CA: Ten Speed Press, 2005.

US Environmental Protection Agency. *Innovative Uses of Compost: Bioremediation and Pollution Prevention*. Washington, DC: US Environmental Protection Agency, October 1997. www.epa.gov/epaoswer/non-hw/compost/bioremed.pdf.

US Environmental Protection Agency. *Citizens Guide to Bioremediation*. Washington, DC: US Environmental Protection Agency, April 1996. www.bugsatwork.com/xyclonyx/epa_guides/bio.pdf. (This version is no longer provided by the EPA.)

The Worcester Roots Project (a grassroots bioremediation organization)
http://worcesterroots.org/

ACCESS TO LAND

Branford, Sue and Jan Rocha. *Cutting the Wire: The Story of the Landless Movement in Brazil*. London: Latin American Bureau, 2002.

Wright, Angus Lindsay and Wendy Wolford. *To Inherit the Earth: The Landless Movement and the Struggle for a New Brazil*. Oakland, CA: Food First, 2003.

Tracey, David. *Guerilla Gardening: A Manualfesto*. Gabriola Island, British Columbia: New Society Publishers, 2007.

Home Sweet Home: A How-To Guide / Stories and Politics Behind Homebuying (Zine available from property.mushbanana@riseup.net)

Tempoculture—container gardening:
www.journeytoforever.org/garden_con.html

Mill Creek Farm (Philadelphia, PA)
www.millcreekurbanfarm.org

More Gardens! (New York City)
www.moregardens.org

Movimento dos Trabalhadores Rurais Sem Terra - MST
(Brazil's Landless Workers Movement)
English language website: www.mstbrazil.org

The Rhizome Collective (Austin, TX)
www.rhizomecollective.org

GLOSSARY

Adsorption: The attachment of liquids, gases, or dissolved substances to the surfaces of materials, including soil particles. Materials that are highly adsorptive help to retain nutrients in soil.

Airstone: Device that helps diffuse oxygen into water.

Aerobic Bacteria: A type of bacteria that requires oxygen in order to live.

Anaerobic Bacteria: A type of bacteria that lives in low or no-oxygen environments, including intestinal tracts and pond muck.

Anionic: A negatively charged atom or molecule.

Annual: A type of plant that lives for just one season and reproduces by creating seeds. Many annual vegetable plants require human assistance to re-seed.

Aquifer: An underground geological formation of a permeable material such as gravel or sand that stores and transmits water.

Autonomous Community: A community of people that is self-sufficient, ecologically sustainable, and socially equitable.

Bacterial Endospore: A state of dormancy that a bacterium can enter when faced with harsh conditions that can allow it to revive when conditions are more favorable.

Bacterial Remediation: The use of bacteria to degrade certain types of toxic compounds.

Bioavailability: The extent to which certain compounds are capable of being degraded by bioremediative processes; also the extent to which a chemical can be absorbed and used by organisms (including humans).

Biochar: Charcoal that has been produced from surface-grown organic matter through pyrolysis. It is used as a soil additive.

Biodiesel: A fuel made from vegetable oil that has undergone a process called transesterification which make the oil permanently less viscous.

Bioeffluents: Materials excreted by humans, including gases, bacteria, viruses, and particles, that can build up to unhealthy levels in a sealed environment.

Biofilm: A thin, slimy layer made by microorganisms as they attach to surfaces.

Biomass: The total mass of all living organisms within a specific area. Biomass also refers to agricultural and wood wastes that can be used for soil building or for producing energy.

Bioshelter: A structure similar to a greenhouse that relies on passive solar and biothermal processes for heating.

Biothermal Heating: A method of capturing the heat produced by biological organisms, such as the microbes in compost piles, or chickens or other larger animals.

Broodiness: A trait of chickens determining their likeliness to sit on a nest full of eggs and to hatch them.

Bulkhead: A two-part plastic fitting that attaches a pipe or faucet to a container while making a water-tight seal.

Carbon Load: The amount of organic matter found in wastewater.

Carbon Negative: A process that removes carbon from the atmosphere and stabilizes it, typically in soil or in biological matter, thereby reducing atmospheric carbon dioxide levels.

Carbon Neutral: A process that removes and emits equal amounts of carbon dioxide from and to the atmosphere, thereby, in theory, not contributing to global warming.

Carbon Sink: Something that sequesters carbon from the atmosphere, like a forest and the ocean.

Cationic: An atom or molecule that is positively charged.

Chicken Tractor: A bottomless cage that chickens are placed inside of, utilized to prepare a plot of land for gardening.

Cistern: Container used to store water, often used in conjunction with rainwater collection systems. Cisterns can be made of plastic, metal or concrete.

Closed Loop Carbon Cycle: A process that does not increase carbon dioxide levels in the atmosphere. For example, when plants are grown on the surface of the planet, they absorb carbon dioxide from the atmosphere. When oil is pressed from those plants and burned in an engine, that CO_2 is released back into the atmosphere, and taken up by the next generation of plants.

Compost Remediation: The process of using finished compost as a means to clean contaminated soil. The compost provides habitat for microorganisms to degrade toxic compounds and certain toxic metals form stable compounds with the organic matter in compost.

Compost Tea: A liquid culture of beneficial micro-organisms used for bioremediation, soil conditioning and fertilization, and plant disease control.

Dynamic Accumulator: Plant that has the ability to sequester specific minerals or toxic metals from the soil.

Ecotones/Edge: Transitional ecosystems, or the space where two different ecosystems meet, such as where water meets land or where forest meets field. Ecotones provide habitat to large populations that make use of aspects of both ecosystems. In designing a biological system, edge, or the amount of ecotones, should be maximized.

Endosymbiont: An organism that lives inside the body or cells of another organism, in a mutually beneficial manner.

Emergent: A type of water plant whose roots are underwater but whose stems and leaves are above the water's surface.

Energy Negative: A type of energy production whose required energy inputs exceed its outputs. Such energy sources are often subsidized financially or politically in order to remain operating.

Energy Positive: A type of energy production whose energy outputs exceed its required inputs.

Estuary: The ecosystem that exists on the borders of fresh and salt waters. Estuaries contain abundant populations and diverse species.

Eutrophication: A process that results in low oxygen levels stemming from a chain of reactions that occurs in a body of water that is too rich in nutrients.

Ex-Situ: Treatment of contaminated soil off-site, often requiring the excavation and transport of soil.

Facultative Anaerobe: A type of bacteria that is capable of surviving with or without oxygen.

Flush: A "crop" of mushrooms produced by a mushroom log.

Free Range: A method of raising animals in which they are not kept in cages.

Glazing: Glass, plastic, or other transparent material that allows sunlight to pass into a greenhouse or bioshelter.

Global North: Nations with high rates of consumption and high standards of living that typically maintain economic, political, and military control over those of the Global South.

Global South: Nations in Africa, Asia, and Latin America holding the majority of the world's population but whose resources typically flow to the Global North.

Green Manure: A nitrogen-fixing plant that is grown to be tilled into soil as a fertilizer.

Groundwater: Water found beneath the surface of the ground.

Hardware Cloth: A type of strong wire mesh with small squares, useful for chicken coops.

Hardwoods: Deciduous, or leaf-bearing trees, like maples or oaks, distinguished from softwoods, or coniferous trees like pines, spruce, etc.

Head: A measure of the pressure in a column of water resulting from the weight of the water above it.

Heavy Metals: A group of elements that can be toxic in high concentrations, including lead, mercury, chromium, and cadmium.

Hydrological Cycle: The complex process that water goes through as it moves from the ocean to the atmosphere, falling as precipitation to the Earth and then returning to the ocean once again through rivers and groundwater.

Inoculate: To deliberately introduce microorganisms into an environment.

In-Situ: Treatment of toxic soils where they are located—no excavation is required.

Microlivestock: Small domesticated animals that are appropriate to raise in an urban environment, including but are not limited to chickens, turkeys, ducks, rabbits, guinea pigs, fish, and insects.

Molecular Contaminants: Contaminants that consist of more than a single element.

Mycelia: The part of fungi's body that grows underground or through substrates, usually visible as white, ropy threads.

Net Primary Production (NPP): The total mass of all photosynthetic organisms grown in a given area over a certain period of time.

Offgassing: The process of materials releasing toxic compounds into a space.

Polycyclic Aromatic Hydrocarbons (PAHs): Carcinogenic molecules with multiple rings found in many fuels and oils; and commonly produced as a by-product of combustion.

Passive Solar Architecture: A style of architecture that utilizes the sun's direct radiance for heating interior spaces.

Passive Solar Design: A method of design that incorporates both passive solar technologies and architecture.

Passive Solar Technologies: Devices used for cooking and heating that utilize the sun's radiance with combinations of glass, insulation, and dark and reflective surfaces.

Polychlorinated biphenyl (PCBs): A persistent environmental toxin frequently found in urban environments (older circuitry, sealants, paints, etc.).

Perennial: Plant that regrows year after year from its root without requiring replanting.

Permaculture: A method of design that incorporates disciplines ranging from sciences to traditional knowledge in order to create long lasting human cultures.

Phytoremediation: A technique that uses plants to absorb toxic metals out of soils.

Plug Spawn: Small wooden dowel colonized with fungal mycelium that is inserted into a log to produce mushrooms.

Polyculture: The practice of raising any combination of plants, animals, fungi, and algae in a shared space, commonly with symbiotic relationships.

Protozoa: Single-celled organisms with organelles; more complex and larger than bacteria.

Pyrolitic Gasification: The process of heating biomass in anaerobic conditions, breaking it down into its component combustible gases, typically hydrogen, methane, and carbon monoxide.

Pyrolysis: The process by which a substance is broken down by heat in the absence of oxygen.

Rhizome: A stem that grows horizontally underground that produces leaves and shoots.

Rhizomorph: A root-like structure that grows at the base of mushrooms that can be used to propagate mushrooms.

Rhizosphere: An area of enhanced biological activity surrounding the roots of a plant.

Ricks: A structure formed by stacking mushroom logs in a crossing pattern.

Sick Building Syndrome: Ailments or symptoms suffered by people living within a building that result from combinations of poor ventilation and pollutants produced within the building.

Spawn: A material such as sawdust, grain or wood-chips that has been thoroughly colonized by fungal mycelia.

Submergent: A type of water plant that grows and lives beneath the water's surface; helpful in oxygenating water.

Substrate: A material that a fungal mycelium grows through, foe example, sawdust, woodchips, coffee grounds, and cardboard.

Succession: A natural process whereby over time one community of plants will replace another; can be observed as the grasses of an open field are slowly replaced by brush and small trees, eventually becoming a mature forest.

Straight Vegetable Oil/ Waste Vegetable Oil (SVO/WVO): Vegetable oil used as a fuel in diesel vehicles. SVO is new oil that has not be used to cook food, once it has been used it is considered WVO.

Thermal Mass: The property of materials to retain heat.

Thermophilic: Heat loving; refers to certain micro-organisms that become active at high temperatures.

Transpiration: The process where plants absorb water through their roots and release it through their leaves into the atmosphere.

Urban Heat Island Effect: The phenomenon whereby urban areas may be as much as 10 degrees warmer then surrounding areas due to the thermal mass properties of buildings and streets, combined with heat trapping smog in urban atmospheres. The urban heat island effect is often most pronounced in summer months.

Urbanite: Discarded chunks of concrete that can be used in some types of construction or in the formation of garden beds.

Veggie Diesels: Fuels such as SVO/WVO and biodiesel that are made from vegetable oils and power a diesel engine.

Viruses: A microscopic entity that is incapable of self-replicating without a host organism; many are pathogenic.

Volatile Organic Compounds (VOCs): Toxic compounds that are found in paints, solvents, and gasoline that easily volatilize, or escape into the air as vapors.

Volatilize: To convert a liquid into gas.

Wind turbine: A device that transforms the energy of winds into electrical current.

Zooplankton: Small animals or protists that float or swim in both fresh and salt water, that form an important part of the aquatic food chain.

INDEX

ILLUSTRATION AND PHOTO CREDITS

Beth Ferguson: 161

Dave Bailey: xiv, 112

John Dolley: 141

Juan Martinez: 9, 19, 34, 48, 55, 58, 61, 72, 85, 91, 96, 100, 127, 133, 148, 171, 177, 187, 190, 191, 199

Juan Martinez and Beth Ferguson: Cover, 1, 179, 200

Lisa Fithian: 205

Scott Kellogg: 7, 8 (bottom), 12, 28, 33, 36, 45, 57, 67, 78, 103, 104, 116, 117, 147, 166, 175, 202, 213

Stacy Pettigrew: 8 (top), 121, 126, 159

Starhawk: 108, 129

ABOUT THE AUTHORS

Scott Kellogg is a co-founder of the Rhizome Collective and the designer of its sustainability educational program. He is the organizer and primary teacher of the R.U.S.T: Radical Urban Sustainability Training workshop. In addition, Scott has given workshops on small-scale radical sustainability in locations ranging from the South Bronx to East Timor. Currently pursuing a Masters in environmental science from Johns Hopkins University, Scott has completed numerous permaculture and ecological design workshops, including a teachers' training. He has a BA from the New College of California. A father and activist, he currently divides his time between Austin, Texas, and upstate New York. In earlier times, Scott could be found as a puppeteer and a drumming rabbit in a nomadic circus. To find out more about Scott or to arrange for a radical sustainability workshop in your community visit www.radicalsustainability.org.

R.U.S.T.

Radical Urban Sustainability
Training

An intensive weekend seminar in urban ecological survival skills

Creating autonomous communities
with the tools of permaculture and
social activism

For class offerings and more info:

www.radicalsustainabilty.org

Stacy Pettigrew is a co-founder of the Rhizome Collective. She graduated from the University at Albany as the departmental valedictorian, receiving an honors degree in political conomy. She has served as a human rights observer in the conflict zones of Chiapas, Mexico, and trained human rights observers with the International Network for Human Rights in Quetzaltenango, Guatemala. In addition to her activities with the Rhizome Collective, Stacy is a journalist and producer with WINGS: Womens International News Gathering Service. Currently she is studying biochemistry, health, and herbal medicine. She is also a grantwriter, accounts manager, artist, gardener, and most importantly, a mom.

ABOUT SOUTH END PRESS

South End Press is an independent, collectively-run book publisher with more than 250 titles in print. Since our founding in 1977, we have met the needs of readers who are exploring, or are already committed to, the politics of radical social change. We publish books that encourage critical thinking and constructive action on the key political, cultural, social, economic, and ecological issues shaping life in the United States and in the world. We provide a forum for a wide variety of democratic social movements and an alternative to the products of corporate publishing.

From its inception, South End has organized itself as a collective with decision-making arranged to share as equally as possible the rewards and stresses of running the press. Each collective member is responsible for editorial and administrative tasks, and earns the same base salary. South End also has made a practice of inverting the pervasive racial and gender hierarchies in traditional publishing houses; our collective has been majority women since the mid-1980s, and at least 50 percent people of color since the mid-1990s.

Our author list—which includes bell hooks, Andrea Smith, Arundhati Roy, Noam Chomsky, Winona LaDuke, and Howard Zinn—reflects South End's commitment to publish on myriad issues from diverse perspectives. More at www.southendpress.org.

COMMUNITY SUPPORTED PUBLISHING

Celebrate the bounty of the harvest! Community Supported Agriculture (CSA) is helping to make independent, healthy farming sustainable. Now there is Community Supported Publishing (CSP)! By joining the South End Press CSP you ensure a steady crop of books guaranteed to change your world. As a member you receive one of the new varieties or a choice heirloom selection free each month and a 10 percent discount on everything else. Subscriptions start at $20/month.